When Giants Ruled

When Giants Ruled

THE STORY OF PARK ROW,
New York's Great Newspaper Street

Hy B. Turner

FORDHAM UNIVERSITY PRESS
New York
1999

ISBN 0-8232-1943-7 (hardcover)
ISBN 0-8232-1944-5 (paperback)
ISSN 1522-385X
Communications and Media Studies, no. 2

Library of Congress Cataloging-in-Publication Data

Turner, Hy B.
    When giants ruled : the story of Park Row, New York's great
newspaper street / Hy B. Turner.—1st ed.
        p.   cm.—(Communications and media studies ; no. 2)
    Includes bibliographical references and index.
    ISBN 0-8232-1943-7.—ISBN 0-8232-1944-5 (pbk.)
    1. American newspapers—New York (State)—New York—History.
2. Newspaper publishing—New York (State)—New York—History.
3. Journalism—New York (State)—New York—History.   4. Park Row
(New York, N.Y.)—History.   5. New York (N.Y.)—History.   I. Title.
II. Series.
PN4899.N4T87   1999
071′.3—dc21   99-19550
                                                            CIP

Printed in the United States of America
03   02   01   00   99   5   4   3   2   1
First Edition

To my wife, Helen, with deepest gratitude.
Despite her denials, this book is in your hands
because of her advice, work, and faith.

. . . a very distinguished book might be made of the more notable editors of New York daily papers. . . . The author of it ought to be a man able to delineate, characterize and color these notables, while not afraid of the devil.

John Swinton, *The Independent*
January 25, 1900

CONTENTS

ACKNOWLEDGMENTS

I became fascinated with Park Row when *The World*'s gilded dome glittered in lower Manhattan. Even before I toiled in that part of the city on such papers as the *Journal-American,* the *World-Telegram & Sun,* and the *New York Post,* I often visited the hallowed canyon that had housed so many influential newspapers and was haunted by the ghosts of great journalists. Today, only Printing House Square remains to remind us of the impact Park Row made upon New York and the nation. I regret I cannot express my gratitude to many who worked there, as well as others, who enlightened me about the vicinity but are no longer here. They include Gardiner Carroll Mulvaney of the Associated Press, who instilled in me the love of journalistic history, and Pulitzer Prize–reporter Meyer Berger, who encouraged me to write the Park Row story.

Special mention must be made of Dr. Raymond Polin, retired St. John's University professor, for his invaluable editorial assistance in revising my first version of this book. Lauren Stokes of the Palm Harbor, Florida, Library devoted a vast amount of time to procuring much-needed books, no matter how rare. Robin Leckbee of the Donnelley Library at Lake Forest College, Illinois, provided complete access to all of Joseph M. Patterson's papers. Shqipa Malousha, *Editor & Publisher*'s librarian, worked beyond the call of duty to be of assistance. I'm also indebted to the New York Public Library, particularly its Newspaper Division, for cooperation received over many years. For four years the University of South Florida Library in Tampa became a second home, and the St. Petersburg Junior College librarian grew accustomed to our faces. Thanks also go to the Library of Congress, the New-York Historical Society, *The New York Times,* and the New York *Daily News.* The *Greeley County Republican* of Kansas provided an unusual insight into Horace Greeley's popularity.

My daughter Diane L. Schrier never lost an opportunity to assist us. My stepdaughter Susan Davis did supplemental research for us at the Library of Congress and also provided us with our first computer. That made life easier in the typing of this manuscript, especially after Richard O. Mayer taught us how to use the machine and always made himself available to correct our problems. H. Paul Jeffers cheerfully answered questions night or day. Others who helped make this book possible were Maury "Tuck" Stadler, Al Tannenbaum, Milton Levenfeld, Nicholas Pileggi, Irving Paley, Ralph G. Martin, Connie Polin, Joseph Brancatelli, Jacky Philpotts, Barney Confessore, Harry Hutchinson, Jake Elwell, and Louis Boccardi. Appreciation also is due to others whose names have been omitted unintentionally but who unhesitatingly provided assistance.

This book was started long before I met my wife, Helen, but it would have been impossible to complete it in its present form without her. She manifested incredible energy in assisting me during years of research in New York City, Washington, and the Chicago area. She also spent an amazing number of hours in transcribing thousands of my notes and hers, and finally in typing the manuscript. She encouraged me by her enthusiasm and never wavered in fulfilling my dream, which became one with hers, to see this book in print.

INTRODUCTION

High technology and cybernetics have altered forever the image of newspapers. Few dailies in the United States remain the sole source of information for the majority of Americans.

For millions it is simpler to switch to the Internet or turn on television to see the morning or evening news or to watch news offered twenty-four hours a day.

Newspapers retain the tremendous advantage of presenting more news and features in greater depth than the stories offered by the most sophisticated of the other media. Circulation remains high among the dailies that have survived despite the incursion of high technology. Only in the larger cities is there more than one publication today, and where that exists cutthroat competition is even scarcer.

Once upon a time, when radio was young and television merely a dream, the cry of "Extra! Extra!" could be heard on the streets of every city where newspaper rivalry was intense. Afternoon dailies would buy their newsboys dinner and keep them from departing until late at night if a big story were about to break. Of all the newspaper thoroughfares in America, the greatest was Park Row. More publications were clustered there than anywhere else in the world. High technology has made it impossible ever to duplicate this concentration.

Park Row began to evolve as the newspaper mecca of America in the early 1830s, when New York City had grown to a metropolitan center with a population of 220,000. At this time, the city's new reservoir on 13th Street operated near the Bowery, although old-fashioned "tea-water" men continued to pump water from the middle of a large grocery store. With hogsheads mounted upon their carts, they also roamed the streets to supply customers.

Municipal gas lamps had begun to light the city only a few years before. Niblo's Garden, the center of recreation, had opened in 1823 with a patriotic gas display, and entertainment palaces were proud of their illumination. The city's population did not live too far out, and when someone suggested that 14th Street be lighted, he was met with the withering put-down, "Perhaps you will get somebody to live in it first!"

Lotteries in New York in the early nineteenth century were nearing their end. Forty-five lottery offices paid $250 each in annual license fees for a total of $11,250, with one half of the money appropriated by law to the public schools and the other to the New York Institution for the Instruction of the Deaf and Dumb. This revenue disappeared when the state banished the gambling groups.

Across the river, Brooklyn grew faster than a tree. A petition was introduced in the state legislature praying that the village would be incorporated as a city. The Senate refused to hear the prayer, although the Assembly approved, and Brooklyn was not granted a city charter until 1834.

Greenwich Village was a countryside where people went to fish or escape epidemics. In 1832 cholera terrified New York City. It had been transmitted by immigrants and was first noticed in Manhattan on June 26. By August, the city was holding a day of fast, prayer, and humiliation for the deceased thousands. No one was safe from the disease. When a law was passed requiring the Board of Health to visit quarantined persons on Staten Island, all the inspectors except an alderman died within a fortnight. A coroner's inquest into the death of a man found in the street ended with nine of the twenty witnesses and jurors dying after being stricken by cholera within a week.

Nevertheless, New York City stretched. Private residences arose on the north side of Washington Square, which had recently been made a park after serving as a potter's field. On a petition of these home owners, the name of the street was changed to Waverly Place in honor of Sir Walter Scott's Waverly novels. Nearby, the University of the City of New York (later New York University) had been granted its charter in 1831.

America was the Promised Land even in the early 1830s, and New York the city that promised most. Foreign languages, especially French and Spanish, were heard on almost every street corner, and strange cigar smoke lent an exotic fragrance to the air.

Two thousand carts rumbled along the cobblestones, shaking the streets with their din, as they delivered dry goods to the warehouses on Pearl Street and the wholesale firms on South Street. Only the Battery, facing the bay, was spared the roar of the inland trade. With its broad, flagged promenade and rows of seats extending the length of the walk, it was one of the city's showplaces.

The East River berthed the shipyards, and the North River waved hail and farewell to arriving and departing vessels. Twelve hundred sloops, painted with brilliant colors, sprinkled the Hudson River. Their sails were white, and variegated flags and streamers thrilled New York's spectators.

When Wall Street's merchants and brokers sought relaxation, they retired to the nearby Tontine Coffee-House where, sipping coffee, they damned President Andrew Jackson for his attacks on the Bank of the United States.

Park Row had originally been a stretch of American Indian path that led to the Dutch settlement of Fort Amsterdam. When it was called the Bowery Road, Native Americans had descended through it on bloody raids and destroyed the homes of the pioneer colonists. African Americans working out their freedom had been forced to jeopardize their lives by settling on the road and acting as lookouts to warn the populace when raids were being made. Travel between New York and New England moved over the trail, making it the oldest road out of the city. In the mid–seventeenth century Governor Peter Stuyvesant had ridden on it to reach his *bouwerie,* or estate.

During the Revolutionary War a courier dashed down Chatham Street, turning into Broadway and shouting the news of the Battle of Lexington. Subsequently, Gen. George Washington, coming from the Bull's Head Tavern, triumphantly led his army through the street on Evacuation Day, November 25, 1783, when the British forces sailed away. While president, Washington commenced his regular "fourteen-mile drives" in New York along this road.

By 1833, one section of Chatham Street was called Park Row because its southern end was opposite City Hall Park. It started at Ann Street and was intersected only by Beekman Street. Both streets were named for the John K. Beekmans, who owned the land. To the north, at the far end of Park Row, the Brick Presbyterian Church, once used as a prison by the British, looked out upon an open space. Other features on the Row in 1833 were the Park Theatre and Windust's café. Burned in 1820, the theater was rebuilt, but it closed permanently years later when it was struck again by fire.

John Howard Payne's opera *Clari, or the Maid of Milan,* which adapted the Sicilian air now known as "Home, Sweet Home," had opened in America in 1825 at the Park Theatre. The city went wild that year when the first performance of Italian opera in this country, *The Barber of Seville,* was given at the same theater. In the fifty years that the Park Theatre operated, it was also the nation's most prominent home of drama.

Windust's restaurant, near the theater, was the meeting place of actors, artists, musicians, and newspapermen. Over its Park Row entrance (another led to Ann Street through a narrow passage called Theatre Alley) appeared the motto "Numquam non Paratus" ("Never not Prepared"), and itinerant vendors sought to speak to Mr. Numquam or Mr. Paratus.

Windust's rooms were filled nightly between the acts and after the show.

There was a long table in the restaurant where actors ate and performed. Often, after an evening at the theater, Junius Brutus Booth, Edmund Keane, or the great but eccentric George Frederic Cooke gave performances. Cooke enacted a Shakespearean scene far more enthusiastically than he had earlier before a paying audience.

The walls of the cellar were covered with memorabilia of the theatrical world. Portraits of the great character players, quaint playbills, clippings of criticisms, and the sword with which David Garrick was said to have committed histrionic murders adorned its sides. Shakespearean quotations were commonplace, and a remark from *Macbeth* was emblazoned over the beefsteak broiler:

> If it were done, when 'tis done
> Then 'twere well 'twere done quickly.

The only papers published on the island of Manhattan were sixpenny "class" sheets, limited to four pages and issued on or near Wall Street. Long editorials espoused political or mercantile interests. Party sheets played up congressional debates, political speeches, and special messages to the legislature, while businessmen were concerned primarily with routine shipping news and current prices. There was seldom a rush to print the latest news, and aggressiveness manifested itself mainly in the publication of foreign intelligence or prominent reports of Congress. Pony expresses, sailing ships, and stagecoaches carried the news to the Wall Street editors.

Newspapers were not for the commoner. They sold for $10 a year, a price he or she could not afford. They were obtainable only over the publishing house counters, from carriers delivering them to homes, or in the coffeehouses where they were read and passed on from patron to patron. Most of the publishers would not extend themselves to gain new subscribers; that was beneath their dignity. One editor proudly claimed that his paper's circulation of two thousand was unsolicited.

This was the New York City of the early 1830s when a change occurred in newspaper publishing that led to Park Row's becoming the world's great newspaper center.

When Giants Ruled

1
Birth of *The Sun*

YOUNG HORATIO SHEPPARD arrived in New York City from New Jersey in 1830 with $1,500 to study medicine. On his daily stroll in Manhattan, he heard peddlers shouting one-cent goods to the hurrying throngs. Fruits, candy, ice cream, oysters, pocket combs, shoelaces, and other items all sold for a penny.

Print had always fascinated Sheppard, and at first he invested in various publications. But the attraction of so many products selling for so little convinced him that a small, lively paper could be published for one cent. If he could get boys to hawk it in the streets where people could see and buy, he would make money. Although the experiment had been tried elsewhere without success, no papers sold for a penny in the United States, and unlike London, no newsboys stood at street corners shouting, "Get your daily paper!"

After considering office expenses and composition and printing-paper costs, Sheppard realized he had to sell four or five thousand copies a day to clear a profit. His market would be the common masses who had no organ published in their behalf and could not afford a subscription to a class sheet.

One printing office after another told Sheppard that his plan was impractical and that it would be impossible to sell a paper for one cent. Finally, after eighteen months, he convinced printer Francis Story that a penny paper was feasible. Story wanted his close friend Horace Greeley, another printer, to join in the project. He offered Greeley an equal share in the enterprise, but Greeley insisted that the price be two cents. Despite Sheppard's plea that the words "price one cent" possessed magic, Greeley refused to join the others unless the price were raised.

Sheppard could not establish a paper alone and reluctantly agreed to sell it for two cents. By this time he had earned his medical degree but had just $50 left in cash and a promise of $200 more in paper. The total funds of the three men amounted only to about $150 when they rented a small office at 54 Liberty Street. However, Story and Greeley had friends in the printing world, and one lent them $40 worth of type. Sheppard would be the editor and Story and Greeley the printers.

January 1, 1833, was decided upon as the day of the first issue of the *Morning Post.* Unfortunately, New Year's Day proved a poor one for an experiment. It snowed all that morning, and the ground was blanketed. The newsboys on the street shivered while shrieking the name of a paper no one had heard of. The weather continued bad for several days, and not many persons searched their pockets in the biting cold air for the two cents.

Everything seemed to go wrong with the venture. Sheppard's love for the publishing business and his ardent desire to edit a paper concealed his lack of experience. Greeley was forced to take over Sheppard's editorial job and to handle that role as well as his own duties.

Despite the handicaps, several hundred copies of the *Post* were sold daily. At the end of the first week, Sheppard met all expenses, but it was urgent that the circulation rise. With his money rapidly disappearing, the doctor could not glory in his new role. At the end of the second week, he could not pay all expenses. He implored the printers to continue the paper, paying them half in cash and half in promises.

Circulation grew worse, and the hopes of the three men vanished. Sheppard told his partners he believed there was one last chance: reduce the price of the paper to one cent. A penny, he argued, is like no money at all to a potential customer. The two printers agreed with Sheppard, but the decision came too late. The *Post* collapsed entirely before the third week ended, although the last two issues were sold for a cent apiece. Sheppard's money and credit were gone, and he owed the others more than ever. New York's first penny newspaper was a complete failure.

If the *Post* had sold for a penny from the start, would it have succeeded despite the miserable weather? Was the public ready for a cheap newspaper? Greeley had wanted the daily to sell for two cents, and by winning his point, had all been lost? Was Sheppard as insane as some had thought before the birth of the *Post?*

Benjamin Henry Day did not think so. He was born in West Springfield, Massachusetts, on April 11, 1810, the son of a hatter. Day had served as an apprentice printer on the Springfield *Republican* and arrived in New York at the age of twenty-one. He drifted as a compositor among three sixpennies, the *Evening Post, Journal of Commerce,* and *Mercantile Advertiser,* before opening his own job-printing plant.

Shortly thereafter, Day became a printer for the *Free Enquirer,* a weekly run by Robert Dale Owen and Frances Wright. They were reformers who urged a national system of education, sought to abolish capital punishment and imprisonment for debt, and opposed orthodox religion. In addition,

"Fanny" Wright lectured on behalf of equal rights for women and liberal divorce laws and against slavery. She even purchased a number of slaves for an experiment in racial equality in Nashoba, Tennessee. Years later, Day's association with her came back to haunt him. The reformers gave up ownership of the *Free Enquirer* the year he joined them. Day not only continued to print the weekly but briefly became its publisher.

When an acquaintance, George Evans, assumed sole editorship of the *New York Daily Sentinel* in 1832, Day became his printer. However, the cholera plague that year and the business decline brought on by President Jackson's fight against the Bank of the United States caused his trade to suffer. The *Sentinel* was forced to discontinue the following year.

With his extra earnings from the *Sentinel* lost and a wife and an infant son to support, Day was desperate to supplement the income from his job-printing operation. Even before Sheppard's ill-fated paper was launched, he had thought of starting a penny paper, and now he was determined. Day thought of calling it *The Sun*, a name printing colleague Dave Ramsey had mentioned many times. His printer friends warned Day that a penny paper could not make money and pointed to the failures not only of the *Morning Post* but also its predecessors, the *Cent* in Philadelphia and Boston's *Bostonian*. They tried to convince him that daily newspapers were for the few and not the masses.

Day could not be dissuaded, despite ridicule and fears. He did not have much money but possessed a printing press: a single cylinder and a flatbed, the type that had been popular in Benjamin Franklin's era. Cranked by a husky worker, it could produce two hundred impressions an hour, or about three a minute. He started final planning for his paper in August 1833, a month after the *Sentinel*'s collapse. The *Sun* would be about the size of present-day commercial stationery, with three columns to a page and four pages to an issue. By contrast, the sixpenny pages measured 17½ by 24 inches. Eventually, as they grew larger, they would be described as "blanket sheets."

Although Day did not know much about publishing a newspaper and preferred printing handbills and letterheads, the *Sun* shone for the first time on September 3, 1833, at 222 William Street, a short distance from Park Row. His subscriptions were $3 a year, compared with the $10 charged by the class sheets. Unlike the sixpennies, he refused to accept subscriptions unless paid in advance. He charged the same price of $30 for yearly advertisements as the others. Ads were one inch square, ten to twelve lines, and the copy remained unchanged throughout the year, come summer or winter.

Day stayed awake the whole night before the first edition of the *Sun* was on the streets. He was his own editor, reporter, compositor, pressman, and

mailing clerk, and only a journeyman printer came in to help run off that
issue. One thousand copies were printed in four hours. Day wrote that the
paper would "lay before the public at a price within the means of everyone,
ALL THE NEWS OF THE DAY, and at the same time afford an advan-
tageous medium for advertising."[1]

The new publisher made good use of his scissors for that first number.
The local news was two or three days old, for Day took most of it out of the
sixpennies. He also gave space to a robbery of $13,000 from a mail coach
traveling between Boston and Lynn, Massachusetts. He ran anecdotes and
a short feature about an Irish captain on the front page and also published a
column of poetry. He did not think much of Mexico's internal strikes, which
received only four lines on an inside page. Advertising was also clipped out
of the class sheets. He thought this made the *Sun* seem in demand, building
the readers' interest and making people want to advertise. Most of the advertisements were about ship sailings, while some concerned situations and ser-
vants wanted.

The plunge into the new world of penny journalism proved highly successful. Thousands of New Yorkers recognized a publication designed in
their interest. Popular education was ceasing to be a fad, and people wanted
to know the news and read it for themselves, at a price they could afford.

The *Sun* did not attempt to compete with the class sheets, but in its crude,
unworldly, stumbling manner, it catered to the general public's hunger for
news better than any other American publication. Less space was devoted to
Congress and the business world. The nonpartisan tabloid was earthy enough
to be understood by the man laying gas pipes in the Bowery, by those who
handled the sloops in the North River, and by hackney coach drivers. Within
two months, the *Sun*'s circulation climbed above two thousand, and three
months later Day claimed six thousand a day.

Industrial conditions helped Day's newspaper. Improvements were made
in a paper-making machine invented in England and financed by two brothers, Henry and Sealey Fourdrinier. Not only did it produce a continuous
roll, it also reduced the price of printing paper considerably. In addition, the
crank man was on his way to oblivion when Richard March Hoe built a
steam-powered, double-cylinder press in 1832 that could strike four thousand impressions an hour. Day bought one for the *Sun* when the paper was
less than a year and a half old.

When the *Sun*'s circulation reached eight thousand, greater than that of
any other paper in the country, contemporaries criticized him for not giving
more space to politics. Day replied that the *Sun* could not be bought or

intimidated. He added that "whenever the villainous conduct of a man, or body of men (no matter to what party they may belong) may deserve exposure so sure as we hold within our hands the whip, so sure will we lash the rascals naked through the world."[2]

Day advertised for vendors of the paper in his early issues. No class publication would stoop so low as to have newsboys hawking on the streets. Day charged them sixty-seven cents for one hundred copies if they paid cash and seventy-five cents if they took them on credit. His first newsboy was ten-year-old Bernard Flaherty, who never forgot his peddling of papers. Later, after he had become famous as an international comedian known as Barney Williams, he recalled how the passersby had looked at him oddly, what with the sheet being so small and his queer, squeaking voice daring to call it a newspaper.

About a week after the *Sun* began publication, Day hired George Wisner at $4 a week to attend the 4:00 A.M. police-court sessions, write up items, and, later in the day, set type. In addition, Wisner became Day's editor. The circulation grew, as the paper highlighted racy, sensational, and human-interest stories. It was a technique first employed by the London *Morning Herald* and by Sunday newspapers in the British capital.

The masses enjoyed reading about humorous or morbid court cases, as well as murders, suicides, and other crimes. Stories of the city's unimportant people and incidents that the class papers ignored were played up, as were those involving animals and unusual families. A visit by Whig statesman Henry Clay to New York did not excite Day, but when Jackson delivered an address to Congress that first December, three of the *Sun*'s four pages were devoted to it.

The *Sun* occasionally printed sports stories that appealed to its readers. In one, it reported how two prizefighters, Phelan and McGregor, departed by steamboat with their friends from the foot of Warren Street to Bloomingdale:

> The combatants fought fifty-two rounds, which lasted nearly two hours—at the end of which Phelan was worsted. But the fact of McGregor's biting Phelan's finger nearly off, at the fifth round, entitles the latter to the money. McGregor is an Irishman and Phelan (who has a hand in almost everything of the kind which occurs here) claims to be American born. The stakes were $200 a side.[3]

Despite the *Sun*'s success, Day would not raise Wisner's salary. Instead, he gave his associate a half-interest in the *Sun*, although Wisner displeased him by slipping in a paragraph or poem on the horrors of slavery at every opportunity. The publisher did not care for antislavery crusading even though he had worked on the *Free Enquirer*. Finally, in the spring of 1835, when Day could no longer stand Wisner's "damned little Abolitionist articles," he paid the writer $5,000 in cash for his share of the paper.

The aristocratic sheets ignored Day and his paper at first, when they were not mocking him. However, as the *Sun* grew, they took time from quarreling among themselves to aim more powerful shots at the penny upstart. Its circulation increase angered the mighty, hot-headed Col. James Watson Webb of the *Courier and Enquirer*. When Day launched his paper, the *Courier*, as Webb's journal was often called, claimed a daily circulation of 4,500, the largest in the city. Webb sneered at the *Sun* as penny trash. Day asserted that it was better than the ten-dollar trash imposed upon the public by the class sheets. He pointed out that, since the *Courier* increased its size a few days before, it was now large enough for a blanket and two pairs of pillowcases. That, he said, was an insult to a civilized community.

Webb was one of the few aggressive sixpenny editors in New York who bragged of his newspaper's circulation. That aroused Day, who offered to bet Webb $1,000, with the money to go to the Washington Monument Association, that the *Sun* had a circulation twice as large as that of the class sheet. Webb would not take the wager.

As the *Sun* increased its profits, imitators cropped up. One of the first penny newspapers was *The Man*, published by Day's friend Evans. It championed labor unions and women's rights. That was in 1834, and labor was stirring. But *The Man* discontinued after little more than a year, unable to compete with the *Sun* and other penny journals that retained readers by sandwiching in labor news with various types of stories.

Another imitator of the *Sun* was the *New York Transcript*. It was published by three printers, with humorist Asa Greene as the editor. The *Transcript* followed the *Sun* in size, makeup, and contents and emphasized sports events, including prizefights, horse races, and footraces. English-born William H. Attree, a police-court reporter at $3 a week, wrote of illicit sexual relations and filled his columns with coarse humor. The *Transcript* was even more sensational than the *Sun* and for a while threatened the existence of Day's paper.

The *Transcript* also eschewed politics and published objectionable patent-medicine advertisements. When a sixpenny journal attacked the cheaper papers for running such ads, the *Transcript* struck back:

> The *Commercial Advertiser*, in its eagerness to accuse the penny papers of being
> "enamored of quackery," seems entirely to have forgotten its own share in the

encouragement of quacks. Only two or three weeks since, it published a very long article, approving and recommending the treatment of a certain Homeopathic doctor, in the cure of cholera.[4]

The *Transcript* claimed a circulation of more than seventeen thousand the year after starting publication. It was second only to the *Sun* and the following year boasted a circulation of almost twenty-one thousand. But the paper was doomed. The panic of 1837 dealt the *Transcript* a severe financial blow. Finally, because of friction between owners and employees, the paper succumbed two years later.

While the *Sun*'s circulation soared, Day perpetrated a deception that became the greatest in newspaper history. Until the "Moon Hoax" was published, journalistic frauds were generally unknown. The *Sun* was less than two years old when it astounded the scientific and newspaper worlds with a seven-day series of articles purportedly revealing that a great British astronomer, Sir John F. W. Herschel, had observed the moon and its inhabitants from the Cape of Good Hope. Richard Adams Locke, a descendant of the English philosopher John Locke and previously employed by the *Courier*, wrote the articles.

Herschel's discoveries, according to Locke, had been described in the Supplement to the Edinburgh *Journal of Science*, a periodical that, unbeknownst to gullible New Yorkers, had ceased publication several years before. Fake illustrations accompanied the articles. Locke wrote that the use of a telescope of unheard-of dimensions had made the amazing findings possible. The lens was twenty-four feet in diameter and weighed almost fifteen thousand pounds, with a magnifying power of about forty-two thousand times. Herschel was reported not only to have learned that the moon was habitable but also to have discovered planets in other solar systems. He was said to have obtained a distinct view of objects on the moon, seeing them as if they had been only yards away.

Day after day, Locke disclosed additional details of the moon world as "published" in the Scottish journal. There were the Vagabond Mountains, the Lake of Death, craters of extinct volcanoes 2,800 feet high, tremendous forests, and lakes as great as 266 miles long and 193 miles wide.

Then came the installment all had awaited: the description of the inhabitants. They were four feet tall, with short and reddish-brown hair covering them completely except on their yellow flesh-colored faces. Their faces resembled those of orangutans, with large mouths and lips more human than any of the simian world. The hair on their heads was darker than elsewhere and spread in two semicircles over the temples. Hairless wings with thin membranes were suspended from the tops of their shoulders to the calves of their legs.

The *Sun*'s circulation swirled upward like smoke blown by high-powered fans as New Yorkers ceased discussing mundane topics. The newspaper claimed sales of more than 19,000, *"the greatest of any daily paper in the world,* (the daily edition of the London Times being only 17,000)."[5]

When a Yale College delegation arrived to peruse the original copy of the Supplement to the Edinburgh *Journal of Science,* Day underwent a moment of perplexity, but he finally convinced the group he had the Scottish publication in an upstairs room. The men departed, apparently satisfied that the stories were authentic.

In the final article, Locke wrote that a new set of man-bats had been found. They spent their time collecting fruit, eating, flying, bathing, or merely lolling. The day after the series ended the *Sun* reported that its circulation had reached twenty thousand. At the same time, another step forward was taken in American journalism that was a complete break with the policy of the sixpennies. Day announced on the front page that all advertisements must be paid in advance.

The "respectable" papers were taken in by the fake articles, although the leader of the pack, the *Courier and Enquirer,* refrained from comment. With the hoax having run its course, the *Sun* quoted various sixpennies on the series. The *Daily Advertiser:* "No article, we believe, has appeared for years, that will command so general a perusal and publication." The *Commercial Advertiser:* "We think we can trace in it marks of transatlantic origin." The *Evening Post:* "It is quite proper that the *Sun* should be the means of shedding so much light on the *Moon."*[6]

The *Journal of Commerce* was an exception, accusing Day's paper of fabricating the articles "for the purpose of making a few pennies." The *Sun* replied that at the same time the "class" paper made the charge it also published extracts of the moon revelations and employed boys to sell it in the streets and on steamboats at six cents a copy.

The *Journal* had unmasked the hoax after deciding, in fairness to its readers who shunned the *Sun,* to reprint the revelations. Its reporter Finn was a friend of Locke. They chanced to meet at this time and were getting tipsy at a tavern when Finn mentioned the *Journal*'s plans. The story was set in type, he said, and probably would be published the following day. "Better not print it right away," Locke advised. "I wrote it myself."[7]

James Gordon Bennett, publisher of a new spicy, saucy penny paper, the

New York Herald, derided Day's publication, calling it impudent, unprincipled, and mercenary, telling untruths for money. The *Sun*, he added, "can never thrive hereafter upon the moon or any other planet."[8] A couple of days later Bennett wrote that Locke was writing a novel similar to his recent venture into astronomy and "may be said to be the inventor of an entire new species of literature which we may call the 'scientific novel.' "[9]

Three weeks before the "Moon Hoax," poet and fiction writer Edgar Allen Poe had come out with the first installment of a story dealing with a man in the moon. Called "Hans Pfall," it appeared in the *Southern Literary Messenger*, a magazine he was editing. When Poe read the articles by Locke, he destroyed his second installment, leaving his own man in space. He said he could add little to the Herschel account and that it was "the greatest hit in the way of sensation ever made by any similar fiction either in America or in Europe."[10]

The hoax paved the way for the *Sun* to become the first successful one-cent daily in the United States and one for the masses. Day had started out caring only about his job-printing operation. There was no intention of upsetting the newspaper industry, but he had unwittingly done so. Bennett felt differently. He was determined to wage a complete revolution in journalism.

2

The "Vampire Editor"

SHORTLY AFTER THE *Sun* diverted the nation with the "Moon Hoax," the religion of ALL THE NEWS was born. Its temple was the four-month-old *New York Herald*, and James Gordon Bennett its high priest. Enterprise, scurrility, and independence were its doctrines.

Bennett was born in Keith, Banffshire, Scotland, on September 1, 1795. His enemies chortled that if the saying among nurses was true—a homely baby makes a handsome man and vice versa—the infant Jemmy should have been the prettiest baby in all the Scottish land. He grew up to be squint-eyed and physically unattractive. His Roman Catholic parents wanted him to become a priest and, when he reached fifteen, sent him to an Aberdeen seminary where he studied for four years. But such a vocation was not for him, and he left. He refused to say what he did for the next five years except to admit peddling wares.

A friend in Aberdeen told him he was leaving for America, and Bennett impulsively went along. He had read the life of Benjamin Franklin and wanted to see the place where Franklin was born. Bennett sailed for the New World on April 6, 1819, and arrived in Nova Scotia.

The young immigrant taught political economy in Halifax and later in Maine and then went to Boston, where a publishing firm employed him as a proofreader. Bennett could not overcome a growing dislike of Boston and, after three years, headed for New York City. There he met Aaron Smith Willington, a South Carolina newspaper owner who hired him at $5 per week for the *Charleston Courier*. Bennett translated items from Spanish and French newspapers received from incoming ships.

While in the South, he observed slavery for the first time, from a distance that softened its harsher features. Charleston was one of the most important cities in the nation, but it did not satisfy the restless Bennett. However, he made a decision there to stick to journalism. After ten months he left the South for New York but could not find a permanent newspaper job. To keep alive, he found odd jobs as a proofreader. In drifting about, he obtained temporary work in 1824 on the *National Advocate*. It was published by Maj. Mordecai Manuel Noah who, a year later, attempted to establish a homeland for Jewish people on Grand Island in the Niagara River. Bennett became a writer for John Tryon's *Sunday Courier* and later its owner, briefly, before it went out of business. It was his first effort as a newspaper publisher.

Bennett returned to the *National Advocate* but resigned when it supported President John Quincy Adams for reelection. Bennett wrote occasionally for Noah's *New York Enquirer* and supplemented his income by penning verse, short stories, and essays for papers and magazines in New York and Philadelphia.

Washington, D.C., was a city of nineteen thousand when he went there in 1827 for the *Enquirer* and stayed for more than two years. He not only wrote straight political news but also satirized the doings of Adams's administration. These articles were the precursors of the gossip columns of more than a century later and were unique in newspaper coverage. He did not get credit for worthy articles but was made a scapegoat for criticized reports.

Bennett persuaded James Watson Webb, for whom he often wrote separate pieces, to purchase the *New York Enquirer* from Noah and merge it with his *Morning Courier*. Bennett earned $12 per week as associate editor and roving correspondent of the *Morning Courier and New York Enquirer*.

He fell into disfavor with Webb and a powerful financial group when he wrote a series of articles that defended Jackson's stand against the Bank of the United States and its manipulations in upper New York State and elsewhere. That put Bennett in the doghouse. He was assigned to cover conventions of fraternal orders and other nonpolitical events. The pro–Bank of the United States group, headed by Nicholas Biddle of Philadelphia, gained dominance over the *Courier and Enquirer*. Webb switched his allegiance from Jackson to support Senator Henry Clay of Kentucky and the Whigs. Bennett angrily quit the newspaper, and Webb lost his best journalist.

As the presidential election of 1832 approached, Bennett founded a two-cent newspaper, the *New York Globe,* to help Jackson and the Democrats. With Jackson back in office, the money-strapped *Globe* ceased publication. Bennett purchased an interest in the Philadelphia *Pennsylvanian* the following year and served as its editor until 1834, but that paper needed more money to stay afloat. Bennett asked his political cronies for $2,500, but Vice President Martin Van Buren and other Jacksonians, fearful of his independent pen and unpredictable actions, refused to aid him. The *Pennsylvanian* also foundered.

Bennett again returned to New York, incensed that his political cohorts had denied him financial assistance. He vowed that politics would no longer interfere with his newspaper ventures. The rise of the *Sun* and other penny sheets convinced Bennett that journalism's future lay in the cheap newspaper.

He applied for a job on the *Sun* but was turned down by Benjamin Day. Bennett then suggested to Horace Greeley, who was editing the weekly *New-Yorker,* that they jointly publish a one-cent newspaper. Greeley recalled his nightmare with the *Morning Post* two years before and rejected the plan. Bennett decided to publish a penny newspaper alone.

Eleven sixpenny and four cheap newspapers existed in New York City that spring of 1835. Most important of the class sheets were the *Courier and Enquirer, Journal of Commerce,* and *Evening Post* edited by poets William Cullen Bryant and William Leggett. The *Sun* and *Transcript* ruled the penny-paper field. Webb's publication had the largest circulation among the big journals, but the *Sun* claimed almost five times the sales of the *Courier and Enquirer* and more than any daily in the Union.

Bennett would not say just how much money he had at this time. Later, when he wrote about his capital, the figure varied from $350 to $550. He broached his plan for a penny newspaper to Messrs. Anderson and Smith, who printed the *Sun* and *Transcript.* They hesitated at taking on Bennett as a customer lest they offend the others, agreeing when Bennett dangled cash in front of them.

Bennett was almost forty, cynical and calloused from abuse, but he could keep his head erect. He spoke with a strong Scottish accent, was lean and rawboned, and gray lined his hair. His jaw protruded in lantern form, and his crooked nose emphasized quick, flickering eyes.

In the first issue of his new daily, he said it would be the organ of no faction or coterie and care nothing for any election or any candidate, from president down to constable. It was intended "for the great masses of the community—the merchant, mechanic, working people—the private family as well as the public hotel—the journeyman and his employer—the clerk and his principal."[1]

In that initial issue of May 6, 1835, Bennett called the newspaper the *Morning Herald* and announced it would next be published five days later. This provided him with time to organize carrier routes, create a system of distribution for the city, and permit anticipated subscribers and patrons to furnish their names and addresses. The journal became the *New York Herald* with that second issue.

Because of meager funds, Bennett was forced to use a musty cellar at 20 Wall Street for his publishing office and to light it with tallow candles. Two empty flour barrels stood about four feet apart, and a single plank resting upon them served as his desk and counter, with an inkstand on his right side. He sat on a chair near the center, busily writing and planning the newspaper's future. The left end of the board was so close to the steps of the basement that passersby could see the pile of *Herald*s placed on it for sale.

Bennett's day began at 5:00 A.M. and ended at 10:00 P.M. Among his routine duties was going to Wall Street's business center, which he knew from earlier days, and returning to write something never before attempted. This not only was the unbiased reporting of what went on in Wall Street but also the listing of stock sales as they occurred. The "money articles," as he called them, were introduced on May 11 and three days later included the sales of thirty-one stocks. They were followed by the most bitter condemnation Wall Street could hurl. The money-market reports became a regular feature a month later.

Bennett's first editions were not unusual, except for the stock-market innovation. He knew the eyes of every publisher in New York were watching him closely because of his reputation as a reporter and editor. Both the *Sun* and the *Transcript* resented the *Herald*'s association with Anderson and Smith and stopped doing business with the partners.

Before the *Herald* could become firmly established, a fire destroyed the printing plant. Type, presses, books, and papers of the three-month-old *Herald* were ruined. The blaze took almost all of Bennett's money. He feverishly raised funds to resume publication and nineteen days later was back in operation. Bennett strove to attract readers and advertisers, but with merchants content to read the older newspapers and politicians distrustful of the maverick *Herald* owner, he could not lure many of the sixpennies' readers or advertisers. The lower-income classes were already attracted to the *Sun* and the *Transcript*.

Luck intervened while the *Herald* struggled to stay alive. Benjamin Brandreth, a pill maker, was looking for a paper through which his advertising could get into many hands. William Gowans, a bookseller and a friend of Bennett, suggested the *Herald*, and a deal was made that gave Bennett enough money to survive. Brandreth's Vegetable University Pills were nothing more than bread crumbs coated with sugar, but the advertisements were enticing. The editor eulogized Brandreth and his pills when they were a financial help, but when Brandreth temporarily stopped his advertising during a quarrel with Bennett, the Scotsman attacked him vehemently. The public, he exclaimed, "is humbugged, cheated, bamboozled."[2]

Bennett knew that if he and his newspaper were talked about, it would boost the *Herald*'s circulation. He began a calculated attack on other dailies.

He singed Day's editorial skin and rattled skeletons in the closet of the class-paper publishers. Day retaliated in his columns, thereby spreading word of Bennett and the *Herald* to readers of the *Sun* who had never heard of or had taken little notice of them.

Stung by Bennett's constant taunts and Wall Street reports, editors of the aristocratic newspapers fumed. An irate Dr. Peter Townsend, Noah's associate at the *Evening Star,* encountered Bennett on Wall Street and struck him on the cheek. This was one of the many whippings that would make Bennett the most assaulted editor New York would know. The feisty Scotsman turned the attack to his advantage by reporting it in the *Herald* the next day. New Yorkers were astonished. They were used to editors horsewhipping one another before the penny press came into existence, but those affairs had rarely been mentioned in print.

Day was delighted by the assault upon Bennett: "A certain lean, lizard looking animal, who squints prodigiously, edits a penny paper, and pours the poison of low and unprovoked abuse on almost every cotemporary [*sic*], to induce them to notice him, received on Wednesday evening in Wall street, a decent personal chastisement for his impudence."[3]

Day's snickering rankled Bennett, never one to ignore criticism:

> The blockhead of the Sun would give a thousand pounds for such a squint as I have got. . . . But *n'importe*—if I squint as the Sun alleges and as I admit, there are some other things I do not do. I do not advertise in my paper to receive contributions for a distressed family of females *and then pocket the money myself.* Neither did I publish the *ingenious jeu d'esprit* of Richard Adams Locke and pocket all the fruits of the publication, thus defrauding the poor and highly ingenious author his well earned gains.[4]

Bennett challenged Townsend to a duel, and they faced each other with pistols in Hoboken, New Jersey. The matter was more than a mere disagreement between two men; it had become a showdown between Wall Street newspapers and the one-cent sheets. The *Herald* gave minute details the next day, listed the names of sixpenny editors who sided with Townsend, and added: "The penny editors, forgetting their private quarrels, backed Bennett and the *Herald* against the field."[5] Webb dropped a white handkerchief and counted to five. Townsend and Bennett, ten paces apart, wheeled, raised their weapons, and fired. They both missed.

The *Herald*'s circulation rose with that issue. Bennett discovered that while his personal life was his own, people paid to read about it. Now he had to convince the public that his newspaper was more than chitchat and that it contained all the news it wanted. The opportunity came two months later with the worst fire in the city's history.

Snow lay on the ground the evening of December 16, and the temperature dropped below zero. The blaze started on Merchant Street, and flames quickly destroyed wooden and brick buildings. Even new stores equipped with iron shutters and doors, slate or copper roofs, and copper gutters disappeared. When the copper melted, the steaming liquid ran off in explosive rivers that only served to spread the all-consuming fire.

That night explosions followed in rapid succession for thirty minutes. They came from a store where huge quantities of saltpeter had been stored. Tar, turpentine, and flying timbers swirled on the East River until they reached Brooklyn, enflaming homes and naval storehouses. The cry went out to blow up an area of buildings to create a firebreak. A barge was dispatched from the navy yard in Brooklyn to the magazine at Red Hook for gunpowder. A cellar was mined, and heavy timbers were placed on the powder kegs and against floor beams. Despite the deliberate explosions, the fire was uncontrollable. Citizens relieved the water-pumping fire fighters, whose clothes, frozen to their bodies, had to be cut off.

The Great Fire dislodged one thousand firms. Damage in almost twenty blocks of buildings was estimated at up to $20 million. Fourteen of the twenty-six fire-insurance companies that operated in New York were ruined completely, while the others suffered financial losses. Six newspapers were made inoperable. The others devoted considerable space to the disaster, despite their four-page limitation.

Bennett surveyed the ongoing fire and listed the number of businesses consumed. "Great God!" he wrote after calculating the damage, "in one night we have lost the whole amount for which the nation is ready to go to war with France! Gracious Heaven! is it a punishment for our madness? Forgive us our sins as we forgive those that sin against us."[6]

The *Herald* reported that 538 buildings had been destroyed, but the *Evening Post* declared the number to be 647. The *Sun* agreed with the latter at first but revised its figure when it became convinced the *Herald* had been more accurate. Bennett's paper was the first to list the names, streets, and numbers of the establishments swept away in the Great Fire.

The *Sun* claimed it published an extra edition of thirty thousand copies the following day. Day announced that the presses had run for almost twenty-four hours without a stop. Not to be outdone, Bennett announced that fifty thousand copies were being run off in one day—which, if not exaggerated, would have made it the largest number of any single edition in journalistic history. The ingenuity of the *Herald* surpassed that of other papers. While his competitors printed an old map of the burned-out district, Bennett not only did the same but also introduced a woodcut that pictured flames engulfing the Merchants' Exchange Building on Wall Street. For the first time, an illustration was as timely and informative as words.

Bennett had shown New York that his newspaper not only could provide the news better than any other penny sheet but also could set the pace for the class journals at far less cost to the reader.

A few days after the fire Bennett wrote that the post office had moved from "preposterous" quarters on Pine Street to the rotunda halfway between Broadway and Chatham Street. He predicted that its departure from the Wall Street area would revolutionize newspapers: "No event has taken place for years that will more tend to make New York a second Paris, in the quick, rapid and cheap distribution of intelligence by the miniature daily press, than the removal of the Post Office to the Rotunda."[7]

No Audit Bureau of Circulation existed in those days to check circulation claims. The *Sun* maintained that its twenty-two thousand sales surpassed those of the rest of the country, and even the *Transcript* boasted it was ahead of the *Herald.* But on New Year's Day the uninhibited Bennett asserted that his paper had reached a circulation "among business men, the intelligent public, and families of all classes, *four times as large* as any small paper ever did in the same period."[8]

When Day announced plans two days later to improve his paper typographically, Bennett retorted that the *Sun* was "the same lowbred, vulgar, licentious sheet of infidelity it was when it was called the *Free Enquirer.*"[9] He charged that Day had purchased the publication for $400 and still owed the entire amount. The *Sun* denied Bennett's accusations, and Bennett replied that when Day succeeded Fanny Wright as editor, he pursued the same course "not so much like a flagitious hypocrite as he is now—but equally for the destruction of all religion and morality."[10]

To boost readership, Bennett aimed his editorials at a former boss: "It is with heartfelt grief that we are compelled to publish the following awful disclosure of defalcations of our former associate, Col. Webb, of the Courier and Enquirer, in his Wall street operations. To-morrow we shall give our commentary."[11]

A letter followed from Henry Lynch, a Webb associate in stock manipulations, and Bennett expressed his opinions about Webb the following day. That was more than the tempestuous colonel could tolerate; he had warned the Scotsman six months before not to step on his toes. Webb encountered

Bennett on Wall Street, knocked him down, and thrashed him with a walking stick. The *Herald*'s circulation increased the next day when Bennett described the beating:

> THE ASSASSIN WEBB, by coming up behind me, cut a slash in my head, of about one and a half inch in length, and through the integuments of the skull. The fellow, no doubt, wanted to let out the never-failing supply of good humor and wit which has created such a reputation for the HERALD, and, perhaps, appropriate the contents to supply the emptiness of his own thick skull.[12]

Day gloated at the whipping. It gave him an opportunity to put down both publishers:

> Low as he had fallen both in the public estimation and his own, we were astonished to learn, last evening, that Col. Webb had stooped so far beneath any thing of which we had ever conceived it possible for him to be guilty . . . to descend to a public personal chastisement of that villainous libel on humanity of all kinds, the notorious vagabond Bennett.[13]

The struggle to capture the public imagination continued among the one-cent journals. Bennett resolved to kick up a small revolution by changing entirely the disposition of the reading matter and advertisements of his "saucy" *Herald*. This was displaying the latest news on the front page on a regular basis, a system used widely in Paris. However, New Yorkers were not ready to buy that change, and Bennett returned to the traditional use of the first page for advertisements, travel stories, and fiction. Page 2 was again reserved for the most important news. But the *Herald* continued to prosper, and Bennett enlarged the size of his newspaper by more than a third.

It was not long before Bennett made an art of sensational journalism. Dorcas Dorrance was a beautiful, twenty-three-year-old prostitute who went under the name of Ellen Jewett. She was murdered with a hatchet in a brothel at 41 Thomas Street on April 9, a Saturday night. The accused killer was Richard P. Robinson, nineteen years of age and well-connected.

Bennett considered this the newsbreak to increase the *Herald*'s circulation—a titillating mystery thriller. His first headline of the slaying read, "MOST ATROCIOUS MURDER." The story was filled with lurid details: the infliction of three blows, the setting fire to the beauty's bed, the raising of the alarm by Rosina Townsend, madam of the bawdy house, and Robinson's honorable employment as a clerk and bookkeeper for a merchant on Maiden Lane. These were the elements of a successful news story.

He visited the murder scene, recorded his observations, and sold more newspapers to eager, morbid readers. A *Herald*-hater said that Bennett returned to the brothel "like a vampire to a newly found graveyard—like the carrion bird to the rotten carcass—like any vile thing, to its congenial element."[14]

Readers were spellbound by his description of the victim's loveliness:

> It was the most remarkable sight I ever beheld. . . . I can scarcely conceive that form to be a corpse. Not a vein was to be seen. . . . The perfect figure—the exquisite limbs—the fine face—the beautiful bust—all—all surpassed in every respect the Venus de Medici according to the casts generally given of her.[15]

Presses could go only so fast and broke down because of the steam engine attached to them. Bennett explained that the "constant call for the Herald was beyond anything that ever was seen in New York. . . . We could have sold thirty thousand copies yesterday, if we could have got them worked."[16]

Investigative reporting of crime stories in America was born with Bennett's pursuit of the Jewett case. A change came over him after he visited the murder scene a second time. At first, he was convinced of Robinson's guilt, but he began an independent investigation of the killing and seemed to change his mind about the circumstances implicating the suspect:

> Can they not be shown to be naturally growing out of other persons' guilt—of a deep laid conspiracy of female rivals—of the vengeance of female wickedness—of the burnings of female revenge? The cloak—the hatchet—the twine—the whitewash on his pantaloons—the traces of blood—all the circumstances accumulating to cover the youth with guilt—may yet be explained on the trial.[17]

More and more Bennett wondered publicly about Robinson's guilt. The mystery spread throughout the East Coast. New York's other major penny journals, the *Sun* and *Transcript,* joined with the *Herald* in playing up the thriller, and copies of all three papers sold quickly in neighboring cities. During a visit to the brothel, Bennett discovered a large painting that revealed an attractive woman "in disorder and on her knees, before two savages, one of them lifting a tomahawk to give her a blow on the head. . . . If a rival in the same line of life wanted to make away with such a troublesome competitor, would not that picture, perpetually hanging there—visible at all hours—suggest to female vengeance or female design the very act that was perpetrated?"[18]

As the *Herald*'s circulation soared, Bennett introduced the interview to American journalism. It was a question-and-answer session with Rosina

Townsend, madam of the murder house. He wrote that he had been accompanied by another gentleman and that both would swear the report was authentic.

Rosina, Bennett asserted, had stated that on the night of the murder she had opened the door for Robinson, whom she knew as Frank Rivers, and that he passed her by with his face muffled in his cloak. She also said she later brought a bottle of champagne to Ellen's bedroom upstairs. When she opened the door, she found Robinson lying on the bed.

> Question.—What was he doing?
> Answer.—He was lying on his left side, with his head resting on his arm in the bed.

The madam added that, sometime after she had let him in, she smelled smoke, went to Ellen's room, and upon doing so, the smoke rushed out. She raised the alarm of fire and a watchman was called, and they found the victim lying on her burning bed.

> Q.—Had you ever seen Frank previous to the night after you let him in?
> A.—Yes, once. . . .
> Q.—How did you know that the person you let in was Frank?
> A.—He gave his name.
> Q.—Did you see his face?
> A.—No—his cloak was held up over his face, I saw nothing but his eyes as he passed me. . . .
> Q.—Who gave the information where Frank resided?
> A.—I did; I knew his right name to be Robinson and that he boarded in Dey street; the officer went and arrested him there, as they said, in bed.

Bennett pointed out that Rosina had given the whole story to the police, that she alone saw Robinson in bed, that she alone first entered the girl's chamber and alone told the officers who had committed the murder and gave them the Dey Street address. "Is it not extraordinary," Bennett asked, "that she should know a man so easily without seeing his face—as it was covered in his cloak? . . . She is the author and finisher of the mystery."[19]

Bennett now professed his belief in Robinson's innocence. Other New York publishers denounced him for it, and the *Sun* was particularly hostile. When Bennett published a letter purporting to come from the real murderer, the *Sun* lashed out at him: "We know it to be a fact, that this wretch actually received a bribe of $50 from the friends of the murderer Robinson, to create, by this infamous means, a public rumor of his innocence."[20]

Bennett claimed the "ridiculous" allegation was made because of the *Her-*

ald's ballooning circulation. The *Sun* also reported that the conversation between Rosina and Bennett had never occurred. It quoted Rosina as saying
she had never in her life "exchanged a word with its depraved inventor."[21]
Bennett insisted he had actually conducted the interview and hammered
away at the madam. He believed that she either was the killer or knew
someone other than Robinson who had committed the crime. Bennett demanded to know her private history and the stains on her life. He wrote a
bawdy verse of four stanzas about her that began:

> Rosina's parts for all mankind,
> Were open, rare and unconfined,
>   Like some free port of trade;
> Merchants unloaded here their freights,
> And agents from each foreign state,
>   Here first their entry made.[22]

Robinson's trial opened in June, and day after day Bennett maintained
that Robinson deserved acquittal. Witnesses swore that it was impossible for
Robinson to have been at the brothel on the murder night. Rosina Townsend
gave conflicting replies that Bennett had noted during the interview. The
evidence, he wrote, favored Robinson, except for her testimony, and he
added that everything incriminating Robinson was only by implication. The
defendant was acquitted and fled the city, as did the madam. No one else
was brought to trial for the crime.

A murder case with unprecedented sensational coverage had captured the
American public's interest. The penny newspapers were the instigators in
arousing strong public excitement. The *Herald* led the pack, and its rise in
sales infuriated the irascible Webb. Again he assaulted Bennett, and again it
was described in the *Herald:*

> My damage is a scratch about three quarters of an inch length, on the third
> finger of the left hand, which I received from the iron railing I was forced
> against and three buttons torn from my vest, which any tailor will reinstate for
> a sixpence. His loss is a rent from top to bottom of a very beautiful black coat,
> which cost the ruffian $40, and a blow in the face, which may have knocked
> down his throat some of his infernal teeth, for any thing I know: Balance in
> my favor, $39.94. . . . I am positive Webb is insane.[23]

Bennett hurled another threat to the Wall Street newspapers the next day
that he would put them out of business: "The days of Webb and his impotent
paper are numbered. . . . I have begun a revolution in the newspaper press
that nothing can prevent from being carried triumphantly into effect. I shall

now show from this day forward what a mighty engine the penny press is capable of becoming."[24] Bennett had proven by his reportorial skill at the Great Fire, his resourcefulness in gathering news, and the suspenseful treatment of the Jewett case that he had no peer as a journalist. He railed once more at the larger sheets and denied their charges that the small dailies were immoral and destroying the character of the Wall Street press:

> They have no character to destroy. The greatest curse to this country is the manner in which the large sixpenny press has been conducted—and the infamous, profligate, and immoral lives of many of its conductors, backers and supporters. . . . Until every sixpenny paper be put out of existence, we cannot expect a return to sound morals, good manners and general integrity.[25]

Criticism from both penny sheets and class papers could not force Bennett to modify his ways:

> No man or party can buy me.
> Neither man or devil—thousands of them—can intimidate the editor of the Herald.
> Get out of my way, ye drivelling editors and drivelling politicians—I am the voice of One crying in the wilderness, prepare ye the way of the Lord and make his path straight.[26]

With the demand increasing for his paper, Bennett turned to a cash-basis policy, similar to the system introduced by the *Sun*. Under the plan, while the class papers held overdue bills from advertisers who in some cases never paid, the penny papers lost no such money. But as time went on, Bennett went beyond Day.

Bennett raised the *Herald*'s price to two cents that summer. Realizing that many readers would resent the increase, he explained:

> I want to feel how stiff, saucy, and perpendicular as a poker $35,000 or $45,000 a year will make me. . . . With this sum I shall be enabled to carry into effect prodigious improvements, and to make the Herald the greatest, best and most profitable paper that ever appeared in this country.[27]

Bennett was confident of his ability: "Shakespeare is the great genius of the drama—Scott of the novel—Milton and Byron of the poem—and I mean to be the genius of the daily newspaper press."[28]

While Bennett preoccupied himself with the Jewett mystery and strove to create a revolution in the press, an old acquaintance was actively staging his own revolt.

Samuel Houston had known Bennett when he was a correspondent in

Washington. He appeared in New York later and tried to persuade Bennett to go with him to Texas. Houston told the Scotsman that his fortune would be made there and that he would run the government newspaper. The man whose name would resound throughout the land with "Remember the Alamo!" also said he planned to go to Mexico. Business commitments forced Bennett to decline Houston's invitation.

Despite his growing financial strength, Bennett's funds were still too limited for him to cover the war for Texan independence when it was in full force. On April 21, while the Jewett murder entranced New Yorkers, Houston scored a brilliant victory at the Battle of San Jacinto Creek, and Santa Anna was captured. Weeks later, the news was reported. Bennett was delighted and declared, "As sure as the sun is in Heaven, Samuel Houston will be President of the United States."[29] When Dr. Anson Jones, the last president of the Republic of Texas, visited the *Herald* offices years later, the incident was mentioned to him. "Ah!" said the smiling Jones, "Texas was the place for Houston, and New York for Bennett; Texas would have been too small for Bennett."[30]

President Jackson caused a furor that summer of 1836 with his "specie circular" order. It directed the government to accept only gold and silver or Virginia scrip in payment for public lands. The paper structure of America's banks began to crumple. Bennett, reporting on Wall Street activities, had warned a few months before, "The national exchequer is gorged—indigestion is the disease—and unless Congress immediately take medicine, and throw up all the surplus revenue again into circulation, we shall see terrible times."[31]

Inflation was strong during the winter. Van Buren succeeded Jackson in the White House in March and faced the onslaught of disaster. Eight hundred banks were suspended in May. The populace generally agreed with Jackson and Van Buren that the blame rested with the Bank of the United States. Wall Street was staggered by the panic and its press shaken in its advertising revenue, but Bennett emerged stronger. "I will cause a greater revolution by the means of the daily paper," he wrote, "than did Voltaire and all the Cyclopediests in France, during the last century in Europe."[32]

The sixpenny papers seized every chance to blacken the *Herald*'s impudent eye. One opportunity came when Bennett audaciously published a list of three hundred insolvents caught in the bank collapse. No other publisher would have thought of doing so, but in Bennett's eagerness to release their names, he had slipped. A few who had not failed were included. One of them, John Hagerty, no Bennett admirer, sued for libel, even though the editor corrected the mistake the next day. The *Journal of Commerce* echoed the feelings of the class papers. It denounced the *Herald* as a "dirty little paper" for daring to publish the list of failures and said that Bennett, if he got his deserts, would be horsewhipped every day. Bennett was fined $500. A group of sympathizing subscribers collected that amount and refunded to him the fine he had paid.

Much-needed advertising now flowed to the *Herald*, and while some of its claims were outrageous, news remained strictly accurate and ahead of the competition. More woodcuts were run. Bennett published one of the earliest political cartoons, which reflected the controversy between Jackson and Van Buren on the one hand and Nicholas Biddle and the Bank of the United States on the other. Another was the first war map known to have been published in a newspaper, printed during the Canadian Rebellion of 1837–38.

With money to spend, Bennett expanded his interests. He published an evening edition, the *Evening Chronicle*, but found it more profitable to call it the *Evening Herald*. A *Weekly Herald* for country subscribers was also issued.

During the summer of 1837 Bennett again trumpeted his horn: "While every newspaper about me is going to the devil and getting into debt, I am daily increasing, enlarging and perfecting the beautiful system which I had the sagacity and good fortune to adopt two years ago."[33] He reported that he had made arrangements to hire three correspondents in Washington, out-stripping anything before attempted by the press in the country. Bennett was on his determined course of revolution. He attributed the paper's increase in profits to his cash system and predicted, prematurely, that it would destroy every paper in Wall Street in less than two years:

> I may say without vanity that I am the Napoleon of the press. . . .
> This great revolution in the newspaper press I began for the public good. Its success will forever destroy the corrupt political *cliques* that heretofore have governed the press.[34]

Bennett's greatest success that year was what he viewed as the breaking up of the Wall Street press monopoly. Until the *Herald* showed a profit, it had been unable to compete with the class papers in their most vaunted area: the race for news from incoming ships. News schooners of the *Journal of Commerce* and *Courier and Enquirer* vied with each other years before the *Herald* appeared. These boats would sail fifty to one hundred miles out into the Atlantic to meet ships arriving with the latest commercial and financial intelligence from the British Isles, continental Europe, and elsewhere.

Almost in this activity alone had the sixpennies shown much enterprise in the days before the coming of the penny press. Bennett charged that the Wall Street news establishment concealed the foreign news for hours or days to foster stock speculation. His increased revenue enabled him to purchase two schooners and a smaller craft. These vessels routinely ventured farther out to sea and received news before their rivals. During one fifty-day period, *Herald* readers obtained news from seventy vessels a full day ahead of the readers of other journals.

The Long Island Railroad, incorporated in 1832, was an important link in transmitting this news. After the *Herald* ships procured the intelligence from incoming ships, they delivered it to the railroad's Long Island terminal at Montauk. It was then rushed by locomotive and ferry to New York.

The first steamship to cross the Atlantic, the British side-wheeler *Sirius,* came into New York Port on the morning of April 23, 1838. Another steamship, the *Great Western,* arrived a few hours later. These two vessels, reaching the harbor the same day, created a tumult. Bennett again asserted prematurely that the Wall Street press would be destroyed in less than two years because of the advent of the transoceanic steamship: "The only advantage the Wall street prints have had over the cash papers was their news boat establishments supported at an expense of $10,000 per annum. The smallest paper can have the latest news as soon as the largest."[35]

The *Sirius* was also the first steamship to sail for Europe from America. It left New York eight days later with Bennett one of its forty-seven passengers. He was on his way to his native Scotland for the first time in almost twenty years. During his absence, a group of young men, including his assistant and future managing editor Frederic Hudson, would run the paper. In his canny manner, Bennett had sold most of his personal possessions before sailing, in case disaster befell him on the voyage.

Bennett interviewed persons throughout England and, after visiting his family in Keith, Scotland, traveled to Glasgow, Dublin, and Paris. Once more, Bennett created something new in American journalism: the foreign correspondent. Prominent Americans overseas had occasionally sent letters to newspapers, but no regular organization of professional writers existed to report the European scene to the American press. Bennett hired six men from London, Paris, Berlin, Glasgow, Rome, and Brussels to form a corps of foreign correspondents for the *Herald.*

During his stay in Europe, Bennett sent many letters to the *Herald.* One described Queen Victoria at her coronation:

I had a very fine view of her beautiful little feet and neatly turned ankles. . . . Her bust is most exquisite—her smile quite amiable—her cheeks very fair—exceedingly so—her mouth small and delicate—her lips rosy, like a May morning—her face slightly oval—and the color of her hair—it is almost impossible to give it a name—but I should say it was something between auburn and chestnut; perhaps a *light chestnut.*[36]

After his return to the United States that October, he made arrangements for correspondents in Mexico, Texas, and Canada. The *Herald* published advance news notices that were sent free by express mail to small inland newspapers one mailing ahead of their appearance in the *Herald.* The newspapers acknowledged the contributions and spread the *Herald*'s name. These news reports were forerunners of those released by the press associations in later years.

The *Herald* more than kept pace with its rivals in the gathering and transmission of the news as the years went by. Additional means of communication were used as they became available: carrier pigeon, pony express, and telegraphy. At times, the paper did so independently or in joint enterprises.

Substantial coverage of annual religious conventions and synods was unknown until the *Herald* realized its value during the spring of 1840. Years afterward, this would be warmly welcomed, but churchmen at first resented the paper's reporters. The *Herald* was condemned from pulpit, rostrum, and editorial desk. A sixpenny paper ridiculed Bennett for his religious coverage, and the *Herald* answered, "King of the American, declines publishing an article giving an account of the Rev. Robert Newton, because he 'does not hold the pulpit to be within the sphere of newspaper criticism.' What an ass King is! Pray, what is the use of newspapers, but to publish the daily events of life, social, religious, political or financial?"[37]

Never had one publisher done so much with one newspaper. The class sheets and the cheap papers were determined to stop Bennett. They wanted to halt the personal blasts he inflicted on them and to eliminate a competitor who cost them readership and advertising income. But they were not alone in their distaste of Bennett. The clergy of all religions loathed him with the same spirit.

Bennett opposed the close association of clerics and politicians. "I am," he wrote, "a believer in religion—in lofty pure religion as taught by the founders of Christianity—but I am a rank and inconvertible infidel in dirty politics and dirtier forms of government."[38]

Religion was one of Bennett's favorite topics, and he employed satire, ridicule, and denunciation in discussing it. He fanned the intense antagonism existing between Protestants and Catholics in some quarters. Clergymen of all denominations despised him, but in their readiness to read of tirades or sex scandals involving the others, they bought the *Herald.* "A more corrupt, infidel, and rotten race of clergy than the clergy of the present age," he wrote, "has not existed since the time of Caiphas and Ananias, the high priests and high scoundrels of Judea, in the time of Augustus Caesar."[39]

Bennett enjoyed refurbishing biblical history. He professed that one reason he had accomplished so much in three years was a "constant feeling of adoration, love and enthusiasm toward the Blessed Virgin and her whole sex."[40]

Bennett delighted in discoursing on the ways of Moses: "I don't think much of Moses. A man who would take forty years to get a party of young women through a desert is only a loafer."[41]

Turning his sights on Presbyterians, he offered a $500 reward "to any handsome woman, either lovely widow or single sempstress, who will set a trap for a Presbyterian parson, and catch one of them flagrante delicto."[42]

Although he had studied for the priesthood, he assailed the Catholic Church: "She has seen her best day . . . and aught henceforth to be preserved in Museums, or venerated as an old Gothic edifice, or Grecian temple, but no more."[43] Bennett called the city's Catholic Bishop Dubois "old, weak, pompous and somewhat tremulous in his voice. It is full time that he were in Abraham's bosom or rather Abigail's bosom, as a warmer and more downy place of rest."[44]

He lumped together all the groups he felt were not living up to ethical and moral standards: "The educated, refined, wealthy, and higher orders are the most corrupt, rotten, disgraced, demoralised race on the face of the earth. The statesmen, politicians, clergy, legal, judicial, of these classes are the veriest scoundrels that ever yet were marshalled to hell. . . ."[45]

Bennett could be as lustful as any man. Sex was used to stimulate the *Herald*'s circulation growth, although it was looked upon by many as a lewd and obscene sheet. "I don't mind lasciviousness," Bennett was quoted as telling his reporter William Attree, "be as lascivious as ever you like, but dam it, don't be vulgar."[46]

Parents forbade their youngsters to read the paper, but the offspring surreptitiously smirked and giggled as they shared Bennett's latest, indecent witticisms. The *Sun* and *Transcript* attempted sensationalism, but the sensually oriented *Herald* reigned supreme in shock treatment to attract readers. He could inject prurience or irreverence into criminal, religious, and political matters. "Men and women after twenty-five or thirty," he wrote, "may be permitted to cheat each other as much as they can. It is merely diamond cutting diamond—six of one and half a dozen of the other."[47]

Bennett made a special appeal to feminine readers. He jested in print with them and spoke often of his squint. Women wrote to him, and he published their remarks and poems. Some were dedicated to the editor; others were written about him. Some were clever, some salacious, and some letters written by the editor himself appalled the moral-minded. Toward the end of the nineteenth century, Elizabeth Meriweather Gilmer, writing under the name of Dorothy Dix, achieved fame as a dispenser of advice to the lovelorn. Her tradition was carried on in columns such as "Ann Landers" and "Dear Abby," written by twin sisters. However, sixty years before Dorothy Dix established her reputation, Bennett became the first person in American journalism to ease the woes of the forlorn woman.

The column began under the heading "Female Correspondence," when Bennett wrote that he had received letters from five women. One plea for assistance came from Catharine of Troy, New York. Her search for solace and his answer produced much talk among the lovebirds of the day. She wrote:

> One short year ago I was gay and thoughtless, and the happiest of all my young companions. . . . About this time there came to this place an itinerant singing master, who succeeded in establishing a school, which in an unlucky moment I consented to attend. . . . his insinuating address and pleasing manner so blinded my eyes that in a few months I gave ear to his vows of everlasting fidelity and love. . . . I have now been married about three months, and am the most wretched creature in existence. My husband proves to be a worthless character. . . . He has not yet entirely deserted me, but absents himself from his home days and nights in succession. . . . as a last resort I appeal to you. Now do tell me, dear Mr. Bennett, (for I have heard you are such a good creature) what I shall do.

Bennett regretted her plight, but his reply came as a warning to other women:

> Alas! poor Catharine! You are not the only victim of these vagabonds, who, under various professions, wander the country seeking only whom they may devour. . . . There is no remedy for poor Catharine but to weep and be miserable. When a woman once makes a false step she is gone forever. How careful, therefore, ought young ladies guard the avenues of their hearts, and fly from the slightest approach of evil![48]

Social events were relatively unexplored until Bennett cast his sights on them. He explained he wanted to give New York high society an originality that would outstrip the worn-out races of Europe. He did not publish the names of socialites, merely identifying them by the first and last letters of their names, with dashes in between. The city's oldest and richest families did not appreciate his reports, but they feared his devastating pen.

The *Herald*'s first big splash in the society field came when aristocrat Henry Brevoort permitted the paper to cover an elegant costume ball in his new mansion on Fifth Avenue and 9th Street. Attree turned up as a knight in armor. The *Herald* devoted four columns on the front page to the affair, and illustrations showed rooms in the Brevoort home.

The opposition was unable to halt the progress of the *Herald*. Weakly, it watched Bennett's accomplishments as he attacked any paper and in any matter. His hatred turned fiercely against the *Sun*, which continued to claim the largest circulation in the world. Bennett sneeringly called it the "nigger penny paper." He printed figures that mocked the readership and sales claims of the *Sun* and wrote:

> The circulation of the nigger penny paper, called the *Sun*, is rapidly diminishing . . .

Circulation among the abolitionists,	1,000
" " genteel niggers,	500
" " low "	400
" " mulatoes,	200
" " boot blacks, &c.,	100
Given to the boys,	1,000
Aggregate,	3,200[49]

Bennett also fired some of his most powerful shots at Webb's newspaper: "From that atrocious concern has emanated the *mob spirit*, which is worse than cholera, panic, war, famine, or pestilence. The Courier & Enquirer is, we believe, the first newspaper ever owned and controlled by the Devil—by the Evil One—by Satan and his whole legion!"[50]

Bennett unleashed his venom toward another former employer, Mordecai Manuel Noah: "A Jew—an impudent Jew—an unconverted Jew. . . . There never was a Jew, either king or banker, that did not break and go to the devil sometime or other."[51]

When the *Journal of Commerce* decided to adopt the cash system for advertising at half price, together with the cash system for subscriptions at a reduced price, Bennett again wrote of his revolution.

As 1840 arrived, Bennett stated that the paper's circulation had quadrupled in a year so that it was now more than twenty thousand. He was certain a full-fledged revolution was under way and announced that he was printing a daily advertisement of the Walnut Street Theater in Philadelphia. It was the first time a daily newspaper in one city advertised the theaters of another city so far away.

When the *New York Daily Whig* closed its doors a month later, Bennett termed it a warning to the Wall Street newspapers of the destiny that the revolution would bring upon them. Shortly after, two more sixpennies ceased publication.

As spring bloomed, the time had come for a final showdown between the *Herald*'s owner and the class papers. Twice before, efforts to boycott the *Herald* had failed. These movements had been unorganized, and both times the paper's circulation had profited. Bennett's political and financial articles, as well as his bad taste, vigorous attacks, and arrogance, had brought on the earlier endeavors to stifle the *Herald*. However, his news sense and cash policy in advertising not only had turned the paper into a success but had dealt a damaging blow to the aristocratic dailies.

This time, there was nothing slipshod about the boycott to drive Bennett out of journalism. All of the groups that despised him participated: politicians, bankers, brokers, clergymen, businessmen, and society notables.

The assault was carefully organized. The sixpenny sheets, *Evening Signal, Courier and Enquirer,* and *Evening Star,* plotted the *Herald*'s destruction. The *American* joined with them, as did the *Journal of Commerce* and the *Express.* The *Sun* and other cheap papers, the *News* and *Mercury,* also allied themselves with his foes.

Poet Park Benjamin, a former literary editor for Greeley's weekly *New-Yorker,* had founded the *Evening Signal* some months earlier. More than five years before he had become upset when the *Herald* accused him of plagiarizing a song from the *Transcript* to the degree that even the last line of every verse was similar. Benjamin had remained silent, had waited for revenge, and then launched the move to destroy Bennett.

His enemies called the crusade the Moral War. Bennett termed it the War of the Holy Allies. The pretext for the onslaught came when a dispute erupted between Bennett and a James P. Phillips over the authorship of *Natalie,* a play by Noah. Benjamin fired the first shot on May 27 when he sided with Phillips. He denounced Bennett for his "daily habits of blasphemy, obscenity and falsehood . . . the levity and profane familiarity of all his allusions to the Deity . . . his personal lampoons upon private and public institutions." Benjamin called Bennett a venomous reptile and added that he was a "notorious scoffer, liar and poltroon, trodden on and spit upon in the open street, times without number."[52]

Noah raged against Bennett in his *Evening Star*. He charged that Bennett used his paper "as the highwayman does his pistol, *'your money or your life.'* " Noah wrote that Bennett's "hush money, commonly called *Black Mail*, is his great and despicable source of revenue. . . . Let him be indicted for every act of profanity and indecency; let fine after fine strip him of his ill-acquired wealth, and a short sojourn in the Penitentiary bring him to a full sense of his disgraceful career."[53]

Webb was equally critical. He accused Bennett of waging a vendetta against him because his *Courier and Enquirer* refused to notice the *Herald* when it made its debut: "From the day that the *Herald* was first published, it has been characterized by the most barefaced and infamous slanders; by the lowest species of scurrility; by a degree of disgusting obscenity which could not fail to call a blush in the cheek of the most degraded courtizan [*sic*]."[54]

Webb threatened to publish daily the names of everyone advertising in the *Herald*. He warned that he would not renew contracts with operators of public amusement places if they continued to advertise in Bennett's sheet. Thomas S. Hamblin of the Bowery Theatre, an old Bennett enemy, withdrew his advertising from the *Herald*. The editor claimed the withdrawal was due to the *Courier and Enquirer*'s owning a large amount of Hamblin's theatrical stock. Other advertisers refused to be coerced and continued doing business with Bennett.

Having exchanged blows with the *Herald* for five years, the *Sun* eagerly joined the action of the sixpennies. In one vicious attack it accused the *Herald* of publishing as truth that the president of the United States visited houses of prostitution when in New York City.

Hostility to the *Herald* found support wherever its sales were considerable, including Boston, Philadelphia, and Albany. Newspapers everywhere across America editorialized for or against the *Herald*. The struggle even stirred England as epithets rolled out of the mouths of the presses.

The assault did not faze Bennett. He scoffed at his attackers as penny mosquitoes and referred to Benjamin as a "half Jew, half infidel with a touch of the monster." He derided the crippled Benjamin's physical handicap and referred to him as Hervio Nano, a dwarf then prominent on the English stage: "What does it prove, Hervio, to see a poor wretch whose vices have brought the curse of God on his legs so that he cant [*sic*] use them at all!"[55]

When Noah's paper denounced him, Bennett retorted: "Suits, assaults,

3

The Reformer

IN THE YEAR AFTER THE ATTEMPT to ruin Bennett, the cheap newspapers reached a point at which their position was unshakable, but they lacked the respectability associated with the larger, more costly dailies. Horace Greeley was ready to take the plunge into penny-paper publishing. In the eight years since he had helped launch the *Morning Post,* he had become a familiar figure in the Park Row area, with his gaunt body swinging unevenly, yellow locks hidden by a battered hat perched on the back of his head, and a white coat that clung endearingly to him.

Greeley was certain that he could produce for the masses a decent product that avoided sordid news and sensationalism and commanded the patronage of businessmen and politicians. He scoffed at the *Sun,* believing it suppressed the truth by calling itself neutral while not giving both sides of party issues. As for the *Herald,* Greeley considered it a sewer-sheet and Bennett a scoundrel who catered to gullible readers while describing them as "the codfish aristocracy."

Greeley was born on February 3, 1811, near Amherst, New Hampshire, on a fifty-acre farm that forced his father into debt. His mother taught Horace, the third of seven children, to read, and he acquired the knack of reading upside down. This skill proved helpful later when he became a printer.

Just before Horace was three, he was sent to his grandfather's home in Londonderry, where he went to school for three years. He lived with his parental family after that, going to school in Amherst and nearby Bedford. His formal schooling ended at thirteen, when his teacher admitted that the youngster knew more than he did and that there was no point in his further attendance.

Print fascinated the boy. At eleven years of age Horace tried to get a job as a printer's apprentice but was rejected as too young. At fifteen he was hired as an apprentice at the *Northern Spectator* in East Poultney, Vermont, and later became a journeyman in western Pennsylvania and upper New York State. It was during this period that statistics and party movements and leaders caught his attention. They influenced his judgment of important issues throughout his career.

Greeley traveled to New York City by foot and canal boat when twenty. His extra clothes were bundled in a stick carried over his gangling back, and ten dollars padded his pocket. He looked like a bumpkin, and one job after another was refused him. David Hale, an owner of the *Journal of Commerce,* eyed his ragged clothes and called him a runaway apprentice who had better go home to his master.

Returning home was not for Greeley, but trying to find employment proved difficult. When his money was almost gone, he was hired by West's printing firm on Park Row to set type on a Bible for six dollars a week. He labored all hours, his "case" lighted at night by a candle stuck in a bottle. Only his excellent work saved Greeley from being fired when owner John T. West returned to his plant to discover the new outlandish-looking hireling.

More notice soon was taken of Greeley's work than his dress and manner, and jobs came more easily. Before long, he and his friend Francis Story set up a printing firm. Greeley was worth about $1,500 when they published their own weekly newspaper, the *New-Yorker,* little more than a year after the *Morning Post*'s failure. The publication consisted of literary matters, news, poetry, and editorials by Greeley. In that first issue he published a story taken from the *London Monthly.* It was called "Delicate Attentions" and was written by an obscure British writer using the name of "Boz." That was the introduction of Charles Dickens to American readers.

Greeley did not make much money out of the *New-Yorker.* The publication had been started with a dozen subscribers and increased to nine thousand. It was sent to them on credit. A large number never paid up, and the cost of collecting from others consumed the proceeds. After two years, the partnership was dissolved. Greeley took over the *New-Yorker,* and Jonas Winchester, whose brother-in-law Story had drowned, became partner and assumed the more profitable job-printing business. Greeley struggled financially during the seven and a half years the weekly was published, and at its end subscribers owed him $10,000.

Greeley married Mary Youngs Cheney, a petite schoolteacher from Connecticut, in 1836. They had met while both were at Dr. Sylvester Graham's vegetarian boardinghouse. The explosive, neurotic "Molly," as she was called, proved as eccentric as Greeley himself and difficult as a mate, mother, and mistress of household. There were periods of ardent devotion, of neglect, and of indifference. They were probably both more of a burden than a help to each other and to the four of their nine children who survived infancy.

The Whig Party Central Committee of New York State decided to issue a party sheet in 1838. Thurlow Weed, editor of the *Albany Evening Journal* and a leading party man, looked over the field for someone to run the projected paper. He liked the *New-Yorker's* pro-Whig editorials and conferred with Greeley in Manhattan. Greeley agreed that for $1,000 a year he would edit a small weekly, the *Jeffersonian,* to be published in Albany.

Greeley solved the problem of editing weeklies in both Albany and New York by catching the Albany night boat on Saturday, making up the *Jeffersonian* on Sunday and Monday, and taking the boat back to New York on Tuesday. During spare moments in the capital he condensed the assembly's debate reports for Weed's *Journal* and wrote some of its editorials.

A friendship formed among Weed, Greeley, and Governor William Henry Seward. When William Henry Harrison was nominated for the presidency in 1840, the New York party leadership felt that only Greeley could properly edit its campaign paper, the *Log-Cabin.* Because of its popularity, the publication was continued after the election. But Greeley's expenses were high, and as with the *New-Yorker,* the touch of Midas was lacking. It was then his thoughts turned to starting his own penny paper in New York.

No Whig paper for the multitudes was published in the city that spring. The *Herald* and *Sun,* the most popular cheap journals, claimed political independence while inclining toward the Democrats. Most of the sixpennies favored the Whigs, while only the *Journal of Commerce* and *Evening Post* inclined toward the Democrats. If a successful Whig paper could be sold cheaply enough to combat the penny and two-cent sheets, the Whig Party would make strides among the laboring classes.

Greeley had his own ideas for his daily. Party papers generally praised their own men and damned the others, but he was determined not to be servilely partisan to the Whigs, as the class journals were. He planned to advocate the principles and praise the measures of the Whigs but would dissent from their course and even denounce the party's candidates if they lacked ability or integrity.

Greeley appreciated the competition he faced from the *Sun* and the *Herald.* Moses Yale Beach had purchased the *Sun* from his brother-in-law Benjamin Day three years before for $40,000. The panic of 1837 had hurt Day financially, and he sold out. He said later that the silliest thing he ever did in his life was to part with the paper.

Greeley knew his main opposition would come from Bennett, who he thought would disgrace a pigsty. The *Sun* might have a larger circulation, as it claimed, but the *Herald* was the most talked-of daily. Its readers were more influential than the *Sun*'s, even though some of the *Herald*'s readers sneered at Bennett. Greeley felt that if his newspaper, the *New-York Tribune,* were to prove a worthy rival to the *Herald,* he would have to challenge Bennett by providing subscribers with all the news they wanted. That was something no respectable newspaper seemed to do.

Greeley based some of his hopes for the *Tribune*'s success on Bennett's foibles. The *Herald* still heard derisive blasts from the respectable elements. Although Bennett had ceased some of his more despicable practices, his less frequently used vituperative lash had lost none of its sting. Greeley hoped to make his publication the essence of purity. Police news, which he thought immoral and degrading, would be omitted. He would disdain advertisements with absurd claims such as curing cancer with sarsaparilla. There would be no space for theater news or theater advertising because he considered its whole atmosphere unwholesome.

Twenty men were employed in the publication of the *Tribune.* Greeley boasted in particular of two worthy editorial assistants. George Snow, a friend, handled the Wall Street news, and Henry Jarvis Raymond was his all-around aide.

New York City's population had grown to more than three hundred thousand when the thirty-year-old Greeley launched his daily on April 10, 1841, at 30 Ann Street, across the cobblestoned way from the *Herald.* He was worth about $2,000 when the paper appeared, most of it being in type. A personal friend and Whig political associate, James Coggeshall, had lent him $1,000 to get the project rolling. Also, warm friends such as Coggeshall and Noah Cook had collected about five hundred subscribers for the first number. After the paper was run off, five thousand copies were distributed—but there was difficulty in even giving some away.

Greeley never had known, and never would know, anything about balancing books. None of his other ventures had been too successful financially, and the *Tribune* seemed destined to follow that pattern. That first week his expenses ran to $525, but the receipts were only $92.10. The circulation reached eleven thousand by the end of the seventh week, but his money continued to disappear despite the rise in subscriptions.

Greeley wrote a protégé, Rufus Wilmot Griswold, in July: "I am poor as a Church mouse and not half so saucy. I have had losses this week, and am very perplexed and afflicted. I feel limber as a rag. But better luck must come. I am fishing for a partner."[1]

Thomas McElrath, a lawyer and former bookseller, proposed a deal that Greeley accepted. He supplied $2,000 in cash for a half-interest and equal partnership in the newspaper. He also handled the business and management ends of the paper, and Greeley never again lost a hair worrying about paying off the next day's notes. His future pecuniary headaches—and he had many—would not be caused by the newspaper but by making bad investments and giving money to friends.

Crime and theater news eventually found space in the *Tribune*, and McElrath lowered the bars of advertising a bit. Meanwhile, Greeley's quill pen scribbled away, often illegibly, at provocative editorials and articles.

On the first day of the daily issue, Greeley made known his feelings about the *Sun* and the *Herald*. He accused the *Sun* of hostility, and he decried Bennett's paper: "It would be impossible for a journal so notoriously unprincipled and reckless to do us more harm than the *Herald* does, unless by coming out in our favor."[2]

The opposition wasted no time in harrying Greeley. With the *Herald* now a two-cent paper, the *Sun* considered itself foremost in the penny field. Domestics, the indigent, and the unemployed were among its chief purchasers. The *Tribune* aimed its appeal at a higher class, yet Beach resented the new paper and its editor. The *Tribune* provided twice the reading matter for the same price, its news was always the latest, and Greeley's editorials were impressive.

Some readers of the *Sun* switched to the *Tribune*, and it seemed in danger of being outcirculated by the new daily. Beach could not tolerate this and set out to destroy the *Tribune*. An attempt was made to bribe *Tribune* carriers to give up their routes, newsdealers were threatened with being deprived of the *Sun* if they were caught selling Greeley's paper, and Beach had boys in his office whip those found selling the *Tribune*. The public enjoyed the quarrel; it bought more *Tribune*s and boosted its circulation.

The feelings of Greeley and Bennett toward each other were those of hostility from the day the *Tribune* was founded. It was never more evident than in Greeley's reply, when he received a letter from a reader complaining about Bennett's newspaper: " 'H.B.' who has recently been slandered in the Herald, writes us to advise him whether to cowhide the Editor or not. We say, Refrain by all means. You cannot make him into a gentleman—it has been tried a hundred times—but you may make yourself a blackguard."[3]

When the *Tribune* criticized the appearance of women in a procession in the city, Bennett jumped upon Greeley. He described him as "a poor, miserable, dried vegetable, who takes more pride in the society of swarthy negroes [*sic*] at his breakfast table, than virtuous ladies of his own color."[4]

The *Tribune* raised its price to two cents on its first anniversary, and Gree-

ley moved the plant to Nassau and Spruce Streets. The paper faced an open
space at the end of Park Row and remained there for more than eighty years.

Greeley vied endlessly with Bennett in the coverage of news, but when a
big story erupted, neither the *Tribune* nor any other paper could match the
Herald. Charles Dickens's arrival in New York in 1842 was an event of
public excitement. Bennett played up his appearance by describing every
move to make his stay memorable. According to the *Herald,* when a person
exclaimed, "The Dickens has come!" the answer would be, "The Dickens
you say!" The *Tribune* did not give as much space to the author of the
Pickwick Papers as did the *Herald,* but the visit gave Greeley an opportunity
to plead for an international copyright law so that authors would not be
deprived of royalties.

The great statesman Daniel Webster spoke in Boston that September. For
days the *Herald* had boasted it would publish the address first and probably
print as many as fifty thousand extras. Bennett dispatched "a corps of reporters" to ensure that the *Herald* would receive the best coverage. The *Tribune*
sent only Raymond, and other New York sheets were also represented.

After Webster's oration, reporters caught the night boat back to New
York. They amused themselves, whiling away the time in laughter and drink
until they arrived at their destination. Raymond sat quietly in a back cabin,
writing speedily. One of the others wondered what the *Tribune* newspaperman was doing and investigated. He discovered that a fully equipped, small
printing office had been placed on board. As Raymond finished a page, a
compositor immediately set it in type. The boat arrived in New York waters
at 5:00 A.M., with Raymond's report, eight columns long, completely set in
type.

The opposition was stunned. Bennett raved, bested at his specialty of
providing the news first. He felt there was only one thing he could do: prove
the *Tribune*'s story false. Excerpts recorded by his reporters and by Raymond
were published in parallel columns to try to prove his point, but to no avail.
The youthful Raymond had succeeded Bennett himself as the city's outstanding reporter. The swiftest writer in New York, Raymond had devised
his own shorthand system.

Greeley became the talk of the town when James Fenimore Cooper, a
Democrat, filed a libel suit against the *Tribune*'s editor. The suit was one of
many the novelist filed after his return to the United States from a seven-
year stay in Europe. He excluded the people of Cooperstown, New York,
from enjoying a promontory that ran from his grounds into Lake Otsego.
The village's Whig newspaper supported the residents, and Cooper sued its

editor for libel and won. Later, when the author attacked American ways and manners in his book *Home As Found*, Whig editors throughout the state, including Colonel Webb and Weed, criticized the work. Cooper responded with more libel suits and won most of them.

When the Weed trial came up, the Whig editor-politician lost by default. Weed wrote his friend Greeley about the trial, and the letter was printed anonymously in the *Tribune* and included mention of the $400 awarded Cooper. The letter added: "The value of Mr. Cooper's character, therefore, has been ascertained. *It is worth exactly four hundred dollars.*"[5]

Cooper sued the *Tribune* for that comment, and Greeley conducted his own defense. The novelist won and was awarded $200. Greeley wrote an eleven-column report about the trial under the title "Cooperage of the *Tribune*" and later called it "the best single's day work I ever did."[6] New York laughed with Greeley, and more than two hundred papers in the state wrote favorably about his ludicrous account. Cooper was embarrassed, and again he sued Greeley, this time for $3,000. But there was more than mere humor in Greeley's lengthy article. He criticized the actions of some judges in libel cases as endangering the freedom of the press. Seward, now a former governor, defended Greeley in the second suit. Legal tactics delayed the case, and it never came to trial.

The *Tribune* was prospering when tragedy struck in February 1845. A blaze destroyed its offices, necessitating a return to the old second-floor and attic offices at 30 Ann Street. Not a paper in the editorial rooms was saved. All of Greeley's manuscripts and correspondence and his collection of valuable books were lost, and only mail lists were rescued. Damage was estimated at $18,000, with $10,000 of that insured. Proprietors of seven other papers, including the *Herald* and *Sun*, came to the *Tribune*'s aid. Greeley praised their assistance, writing that they had placed their offices at his disposal. All employees worked arduously the next day to issue an edition, and it appeared at the usual hour. Greeley described the disaster:

> Aside from all pecuniary loss, how great is the suffering produced by a fire! A hundred little articles of no use to any one save the owner, things that people would look at day after day, and see nothing in, that we ourselves have contemplated with cool indifference, now that they are irrevocably destroyed, come up in the shape of reminiscences, and seem as if they had been worth their weight in gold.[7]

Before the end of May, Greeley was operating in his new offices.

At that time, overland horse expresses remained important in conveying news, despite the magnetic telegraph invention of Samuel F. B. Morse. Congress had approved $30,000 for construction of an experimental line between Washington and Baltimore, and the first message—"WHAT HATH GOD WROUGHT?"—was flashed successfully between the two cities on May 24, 1844. It was not too long before the horse express and the telegraph proved that they could work together.

Greeley opposed the entry of the United States into a war against Mexico. When Congress authorized President James K. Polk to call for fifty thousand volunteers and approved $10 million for the fighting, Greeley called the chief executive the "Father of Lies" and said the House of Representatives had virtually declared war on Mexico:

> It means that, so far as our Government can effect it, the laws of Heaven are suspended and those of Hell established in their stead. It means that the Commandments are to be read and obeyed by our People thus—Thou *shalt* kill Mexicans; Thou *shalt* steal from them, hate them, burn their houses, ravage their fields, and fire red-hot cannon balls into towns swarming with their wives and children.[8]

Stung by Greeley's feelings, Polk denounced those who opposed the war as unpatriotic. A war meeting was held at City Hall Park at which there was talk of mobbing the *Tribune* offices across the way, but nothing occurred.

With the war in full force, collaboration between horse express and telegraph became essential. Senator Clay delivered an important speech in Lexington, Kentucky, in support of the conflict. Despite ill feelings among their owners, the *Tribune, Herald,* and *Courier and Enquirer* joined in bringing the address to readers. A horse express raced the eighty-four miles in five hours to Cincinnati, where the reporter's notes were transmitted by telegraph to New York City, and the speech published two days after delivery.

Bennett's news sense prevailed again when the *Herald,* on February 22, 1848, was first in the nation with a summary of the Treaty of Guadalupe-Hidalgo that ended the war with Mexico, three days later printing the treaty in full. The war increased the size of the United States, but it drained the country financially.

However, an event had occurred in newly acquired California in the month before the treaty that changed the picture: the discovery of gold at Sutter's Mill near Sacramento. The precious metal was not reported found until March, when it was mentioned by the *Californian,* a San Francisco paper transplanted from Monterey. The new governor of the territory, Col. Richard Barnes Mason, visited California in August and then went to Washington with $3,900 worth of gold packed in a tea caddy. He arrived just before Polk delivered his annual message to Congress on December 5.

When the president mentioned the discovery, the world changed. Greeley wrote: "We look for an addition within the next four years equal to at least One Thousand Million of Dollars to the general aggregate of gold in circulation." He followed that with: "The perilous stuff lies loose upon the surface of the ground, or only slightly adheres to rocks and sand. The only machinery necessary in the new Gold mines of California is a stout pair of arms, a shovel and a tin pan."[9]

Tens of thousands of "Argonauts" began a mad dash to California. With the arrival of the new year, the prospectors became known as "forty-niners." The *Tribune, Herald,* and *Evening Post* each sent out about ten thousand copies a month of special California editions. Steamers sailed around Cape Horn to San Francisco with the papers, and although the news was stale, the miners eagerly bought them for at least a dollar apiece. The peak year was 1852, when $81 million worth of gold was found. Within a quarter of a century, the total panned reached almost $1 billion.

The need to match Bennett in the procurement of news was urgent and costly. The sixpennies and the cheap dailies were expending too much money. The class sheets refused to recognize Bennett as an equal until David Hale of the *Journal of Commerce* entered the *Herald*'s office during the Mexican War. Hale disliked Bennett as much as the other Wall Street editors, but he realized that a pooling of reporters was vital. He proposed that their papers join forces to cover major stories.

A year passed before others followed in Hale's footsteps. In May 1848 representatives of six of the most important New York newspapers—the *Tribune, Herald, Courier and Enquirer, Journal of Commerce, Sun,* and *Express*—met in Beach's quarters. The result was the establishment of the first really cooperative news-gathering organization, the Associated Press.

The *Herald* and *Tribune* clashed over their circulations, notwithstanding their cooperation on some news stories. The *Herald* asserted for almost a year that its circulation was forty thousand, and once it claimed fifty thousand. Greeley ridiculed the figures and challenged Bennett to an audit. The *Herald* and *Tribune* agreed that the loser should pay $100 to each of the city's two orphan asylums. Impartial judges were selected. Their report in February 1849 showed that each paper had a circulation of more than 28,000 but that the *Herald* led by 750. For the first time, their circulations had been verified. The public now could gauge the assertions of Bennett and Greeley by the nonpartisans' study, but not until 1914 would there be an Audit Bureau of Circulation to validate claims.

The *Tribune* paid the money but protested that the *Herald* should not have included a presidential edition published only once. Before long, the circulation battle flared anew. Bennett charged that the *Tribune*'s sales had dropped to eleven thousand: "Since the *Tribune* became the organ of social-ism—which is only another title for irreligion, atheism, robbery, and swin-dling, under the name of philosophy and philanthropy—the daily circulation of that paper among the practical and intelligent people of this country has diminished very materially."[10]

False, cried Greeley:

Our receipts of all sorts for the last year have been materially heavier than ever before. . . . We say and publish just what we think right and urgent, being nobody's "organ" and accountable to no one. . . .

The Herald has doubtless increased its daily circulation of late—but how? By unmeasured servility to Slavery it wins patronage at the South, where ours is limited; by wholesale pandering to licentiousness and vice, it has made itself the recognized oracle of the gaming-house, the brothel and every place of infamous resort throughout the land.[11]

Bennett responded sarcastically the next day: "We shall not reply in the same strain. We shall treat him as a sober, sensible being, who occasionally wears a new hat, sometimes puts on a pair of pantaloons, and, at remote intervals, has his boots blacked, like a man and a Christian."[12]

The *Herald* and *Tribune* were America's leading newspapers during the late forties. Greeley never could see a newspaper through Bennett's eyes, but the *Tribune* had proved it could compete with and even, on occasion, surpass the *Herald* in supplying news to the public. Yet if it had relied solely upon challenging the *Herald*'s specialty, prompt coverage of the news, the *Tribune* would not have survived, just as many another journal had fallen by the *Herald*'s wayside.

National magazines were almost unknown in the first decade of the *Trib-une*'s existence. Laborers and farmers in New England and the West, where communication remained in a backward stage, relied upon the weekly news-paper. In the *Weekly Tribune*, launched five months after the daily, Greeley's editorials on the issues of the day were respected among the plain, simple people who would discuss his views. Greeley wanted to improve their lot, and they sensed his honesty. When differences arose within the family or among neighbors over a public question, they turned to him. Ralph Waldo

Emerson wrote Thomas Carlyle that Greeley "does all their thinking and theory for them, for two dollars a year."[13]

The influence of the *Tribune*'s editorials was unsurpassed in the nation. Although some of Greeley's ideas were quixotic, he also had his practical, progressive side. He urged farmers to adopt scientific methods in their labors, and he constantly told men seeking his advice to take to farming. His foes, ever ready to make him a laughingstock, accused the *Tribune* of being agrarian. His supporters called him "The Farmer's Friend." He advised young readers who did not know what to do to turn their faces to the West, for he maintained that great opportunities existed there.

Greeley believed that farmers and wage-earners could best be served if the federal government were to impose a protective tariff. He felt that both segments were injured by cheaply manufactured products from England. Greeley remained adamantly opposed to free trade throughout his life.

Most readers of the "Try-bune," as some called it, were familiar with his controversial views. He opposed more liberal divorce laws but declared himself for women's rights and reported on their suffrage conventions and meetings. He denounced his enemies when they unfairly accused him of believing in free love. Greeley advocated vegetarianism, deplored the use of alcohol, and urged temperance.

The forties saw the uprooting of European political institutions. In America, the *Tribune* became the voice of social conscience. Greeley was deeply distressed by economic conditions that adversely affected the working classes. All his life, he had seen the struggle of the poor for enough money to feed and clothe themselves. Their suffering in the winter of 1838 had horrified him. Many had starved, frozen to death, or died from disease. Begging was rampant, and pride disappeared. Greeley had asked himself why such things existed and if they were inevitable. He did not know what to do to eliminate the suffering, but he knew something must be done.

Albert Brisbane of Batavia, New York, supplied an answer. He had met François Fourier in Paris and become imbued with the Frenchman's theories on ridding the world of its social ills. After his return to the states, Brisbane wrote a book on "Association" as propounded by Fourier and showed it to Greeley. The *Tribune*'s editor was convinced that the plan would alleviate the suffering of the lower classes.

Articles on the subject of Fourieristic Association began appearing in the *Tribune* on March 1, 1842. It called for every man to have the right to work, with labor, skill, and capital being rewarded in proportion to contributions.

The basic form of organization would be the phalanx, which was to be an essentially agrarian cooperative community.

Fourierism attracted people who had their own ideas of a utopian world. Among them were some transcendentalists, including the Reverend George Ripley, Nathaniel Hawthorne, and Charles Anderson Dana. Conservatives, however, denounced Greeley's preachments on Fourierism. In addition, Webb resented Greeley's encroachment upon his position as the foremost Whig editor in the city. When Greeley proposed reducing post office rates for newspapers, Webb tried to boot him out of the party with ridicule:

> The Editor of the *Tribune* is an abolitionist; we precisely the reverse. He is a *Philosopher*; we are a *Christian*. He is a pupil of Graham, and would have all the world live upon bran bread and sawdust. . . . He is the advocate of Fourierism, Socialism, and all fooleries which have given birth to the debasing and disgusting spectacles of vice and immorality.[14]

Greeley overreached himself in his quarrel with Webb. To his discomfort, he found himself in a dispute with his former chief assistant, Raymond, who had gone over to the *Courier and Enquirer*. When the controversy over social reform arose again in 1846 between the *Tribune* and the class paper, Greeley challenged Webb to a public discussion of Fourierism. Webb accepted, and Raymond, a moderate conservative, was chosen to do written battle with Greeley. Each antagonist wrote twelve articles on social reform over a six-month period, and when the debate ended, the *Tribune* no longer championed Fourieristic socialism. No winner was announced, but years later Greeley admitted that his advocacy of views on social reform resulted in failure.

The *Tribune*'s stand on Fourierism alienated many conservative readers, although it attracted liberal writers, including Dana, Ripley, Margaret Fuller, and Bayard Taylor. When Dana went to Europe in 1848, he met philosopher Karl Marx. Dana liked his theories, which were based partly on Fourieristic principles, and convinced Greeley of the European's ability. For years, in the 1850s and until the outbreak of the Civil War in 1861, Marx contributed weekly letters to the *Tribune*, explaining his social beliefs at $5 an article.

Accusing the *Tribune* of exploiting its employees, Greeley's enemies taunted him. They challenged the editor to show his sincerity by turning the paper into an association. The challenge was accepted, and on January 1, 1849, Greeley and his partner, Thomas McElrath, set up the *Tribune* Association, the first American newspaper to be placed under corporate control.

The *Tribune*'s value was estimated at $100,000, and it was turned into a joint-stock company with the issuance of one hundred shares at par value of $1,000 each. Greeley was given 31 and ½ shares, McElrath 50 and ½ shares, and nine employees bought the rest. Greeley and McElrath controlled the paper, although some of the employees enjoyed part ownership. The stock plan proved a failure for the unbusinesslike Greeley, because the number of shares he possessed eventually dwindled to only six.

Just one year later, Greeley showed his concern for labor unions by becoming the first president of the New York Printers' Union, later Typographical Union No. 6. That organization burgeoned into one of the strongest craft unions in the world, and printers erected a statue of him.

Politics charmed the "White-Coated Philosopher," a name Bennett had bestowed on Greeley. By now, Weed, Seward, and the *Tribune*'s editor dominated the Whig Party in New York State. With Weed's behind-the-scenes skill, Seward's influence, and Greeley's editorial pen, the trio also made an impact on national elections.

Greeley himself served three months as an interim congressman from New York during the winter of 1848–49 and kicked up a big fuss. He believed a legislator should serve the people. Before he left Washington, he introduced the first homestead bill to make small tracts of federal land directly available to settlers. That gave the little man a better chance to own some land. Although Greeley did not succeed with his proposal, a homestead measure was finally enacted in the sixties.

Greeley also supported a measure to eliminate fraud in mileage allowances to congressmen. It not only embarrassed many but also incurred their wrath when he exposed the abuses in the *Tribune*. One of those who had overcharged the federal government by $676.80 was a representative from Illinois, Abraham Lincoln. The bill was defeated in committee.

Congressman Greeley also attempted to offer a resolution to change the name of the nation to "Columbia," but a floor fight interfered. In addition, he was unsuccessful in efforts to end flogging in the Navy and the serving of grog to sailors and marines. He also failed to end the House practice of giving extra pay to subordinates of congressional members at the end of sessions.

Greeley had succeeded, however, in shaping the *Tribune*'s daily and weekly editions into a style that frequently would make the American newspaper perform as an advocate of reform. Great issues were plaguing the nation. One of them was slavery, and Greeley's opposition to it was unmistakable. When the *Evening Post* accused him of willingness to divide newly acquired territories with slaveholders on equitable terms, Greeley hissed in an editorial, "You lie, villain! wilfully [sic], wickedly, basely lie."[15] As the controversy over slavery mounted, Greeley's voice would be among the loudest in the nation. He could not foresee that his greatest—and most troublesome—years lay ahead.

4

The "Little Villain"

As THE 1850s got under way, New Yorkers thronged Broadway, heading for Barnum's American Museum. When they were not speaking of Gen. Tom Thumb, they were admiring Jennie Lind, the Swedish Nightingale. More than half a million people lived in New York City, almost a one-third increase in five years. The population growth and the Industrial Revolution had a profound impact on the way news was gathered and put into print.

New York's outstanding reporter, Henry Jarvis Raymond, sailed to Europe in May 1851 for a rest. He knew that when he returned to America he would plunge into the biggest undertaking of his life—the launching of his own penny newspaper.

Raymond was born of French extraction in Lima, New York, on January 24, 1820. The son of a farmer, he could read at three and write at five. He graduated from the University of Vermont in 1840 at the age of twenty. While a student he had submitted articles to the *New-Yorker* without pay, but following a visit to Greeley in New York after graduation, he became a poorly paid assistant to Greeley. Barely able to survive on his small salary, he applied and was approved for a teaching position at a North Carolina school. Greeley offered to match the pay if he would remain. Raymond accepted and became Greeley's right-hand man at the *New-Yorker* and then at the *Tribune* upon its founding the next year.

At first, Greeley thought he had erred in asking Raymond to stay, but the employee amazed the editor with his tireless efforts and his steadily improving skills. "Abler and stronger men I may have met; a clever, readier, more generally efficient journalist I never saw," Greeley later admitted.[1]

Raymond's newspaper days with Greeley and the *Tribune* ended in 1843, when he joined the *Courier and Enquirer* at $25 a week, $5 more than he had been receiving. He was elected to the New York State Assembly in 1849 and rose to become speaker in 1851. His refusal to exert his influence on behalf of Colonel Webb's candidacy for the U.S. Senate was bitterly resented by the latter. Their association ended that year, after Webb unfairly accused his aide of conducting the newspaper as an antislavery journal when he had assumed its temporary editorship.

Raymond was no longer a member of the *Courier*'s staff when he made his trip to Europe. The loss of the job did not disturb him, as he and Albany banker George Jones had considered starting their own paper in New York City. The idea had originated during the recent winter, when they were walking across the icy Hudson River near the state capital. Jones surprised Raymond when he mentioned that Greeley's *Tribune* had netted $60,000 the year before.

Raymond suggested they start their own newspaper in New York. Jones and another Albany banker, Edward B. Wesley, decided to form a company with Raymond that would publish a quality daily in New York City.

A void existed in New York journalism that Raymond believed the prospective paper could fill. The class sheets lacked the aggressiveness of the cheaper publications and did not supply their readers with as much news. Although the *Herald* led in that area, conservative New Yorkers continued to ban the paper from their homes because of Bennett's cynical, shocking ways. They also shunned the *Sun,* feeling it was fit only for the lowest type of reader. Moses Yale Beach had retired, and his sons, Moses Sperry and Alfred Ely, managed the *Sun.*

As for the *Tribune,* conservative readers considered it a highly moral, uplifting journal, since Greeley believed in a protective tariff and supported the right party. But his ardor for Fourierism and the rights of the working class alienated them. That was another paper they would not bring home.

Raymond was determined that his publication should give readers as much news as the *Herald* but without Bennett's scurrility. He would offer editorials as vigorous as those in the *Tribune* but without Greeley's radical stances. As a clincher, the one-cent price of the planned journal, the *New-York Daily Times,* would make it competitive with its rivals.

The days of launching a daily on $500 or $1,000 were gone. Richard March Hoe's rotary-web, revolving-surface "lightning presses" had been invented in 1847 and cost more than $20,000 each. Telegraphic and mechanical expenses added heavily. The three partners formed Raymond, Jones & Co., with stock capitalized at $100,000, and were joined by five others who participated in the ownership. Jones and Wesley received twenty-five shares apiece. Raymond received twenty, a gift from the others who appreciated his ability.

When Raymond announced his intention of publishing the *Times,* he had no trouble hiring experienced journalists. These men recognized his talents and were eager to be associated with him. The assistant foremen of the *Tribune*'s composing and press rooms, as well as a dozen printers and three of Greeley's editors, quit the *Tribune* to work for Raymond. News of his plan and the announced price of one cent worried the cheap papers. They feared his ability, and their strategy was to discredit Raymond before the unborn *Times* could get started. During the summer he was called an abolitionist, a radical, and a lawbreaker who did not believe in the Constitution. He was nothing like their distorted pictures; he was a moderate conservative who believed in doing the fair thing and taking a cool view of situations without becoming too alarmed.

When Greeley had launched the *Tribune,* Moses Yale Beach had sent newsboys to attack his hawkers, but the attacks served only to help promote sales for Greeley and set back the *Sun.* As the *Times*'s publication date neared, Greeley forgot the rough time Beach had given him. Now the *Tribune* warned its own newsboys that if they carried the forthcoming paper, they would risk losing their *Tribune* routes. But the threat proved futile, as carriers ignored the warning. The move against the *Times* gave it valuable free publicity that supplemented its own methods of spreading its name. The *Times* employed every legal advertising means, even the unusual move of buying space in those papers eager to crush it.

A publication prospectus was printed on handbills that blanketed the city, and it was also published in the advertising columns of hostile newspapers, including the *Tribune.* It declared that the *Times* was not being established to advance party, sect, or person. Raymond also stated that it would zealously maintain those principles essential to the public good held by the Whig Party, but that its columns would be free from bigoted devotion to narrow interests.

The "public good" cited as a reason for publishing the *Times* was a far cry from the original mission of the sixpenny organs that did not cater to the masses and scorned the use of newsboys to peddle their papers on the street. It was now standard policy for a successful newspaper to seek all the news and to print more of it, instead of merely publishing information to please vested interests.

The railroad, telegraph, ocean steamer, foreign correspondents, and press associations had all advanced the progress of dailies in providing more independent journalism. A successful journal need not depend upon a political party for subsistence. It could openly support or criticize a party, and only the management of a publication could dictate its policies. Newspapers that continued to bow to political or economic bosses were wobbling on their last circulation legs.

The first number of the *Times* rolled off the presses on September 18,

1851, in an unfinished brownstone at 113 Nassau Street, a block east of
Park Row. Workmen had labored furiously to complete the building by the
publication date, but some of the paper's employees had to perform their
tasks temporarily across the street.

Raymond challenged Bennett's news domain in that issue. He promised
that the *Times* would present all the news of the day from all parts of the
world, and that he intended to make it as good a newspaper as the best of
those issued in the city. He assured readers that the *Times* would speak for
itself on all topics, political, social, moral, and religious, and urged that it be
judged accordingly.

Raymond also wrote that the *Times* would be conservative but not to the
exclusion of advocating radical reform when necessary: "We do not believe
that everything in Society is either exactly right, or exactly wrong;—what is
good we desire to preserve and improve;—what is evil, to exterminate, or
reform."[2] He added that the paper would be temperate and not written as if
it were in a passion, unless that really were the case.

The middle-class reader supported the *Times* almost from its beginning,
but Raymond was not overconfident. When the first number appeared, he
commented, "I must work hard for five years to put this bantling on a solid
footing."[3] As sales exceeded fifteen thousand within seven weeks, Raymond
wrote that the *Times* had reached a circulation never before commanded by
any paper at the end of three years.

When his paper was less than three months old, Raymond saw an opportunity to boost its circulation with the impending appearance of Hungarian
freedom-fighter Louis Kossuth. He had struggled without success to liberate
his compatriots from the bonds of Austrian despotism. Kossuth was coming
to the United States to seek financial, material, and political aid for his cause.
Most papers in New York were effusive in praising Kossuth, but Raymond
shone as his chief protagonist. Raymond believed in the Magyar's cause, but
he wanted to impress the public with his coverage of the Hungarian's stay.

Six days after Kossuth's arrival in New York Harbor on December 5,
1851, a municipal banquet was held for him at the Irving House in Manhattan. In addressing the audience, Raymond praised the Hungarian as an
illustrious champion of history who had begun his career as a member of the
press, explaining that it was through the press that he had struck the first
blows at the despotism of Austria.

A few days later the press gave a dinner in Kossuth's honor at the Astor
House. It was the first time New York newspapermen had so assembled, and
the affair led to the city's first press club. Bennett was not present because

its organizers had refused to offer tickets to the *Herald*. Before Kossuth had landed in the United States, Bennett had opposed the Hungarian's desire for fleets, armies, and money to be sent overseas to make good the recognition of Hungary. He had also warned that this action would embroil the United States in a war on the European continent for the extinguishment of despotism. However, always concerned with printing the news, Bennett devoted the whole front page to the dinner.

Ever ready to follow public favor, Bennett at first exulted over Kossuth's arrival. However, as the flush of the patriot's presence faded, he frowned at the Magyar's struggle for independence and sniped at him at every opportunity. Opposed to antislavery advocates, Bennett lamented that Kossuth was permitting American abolitionists to identify themselves with the Hungarian and his aims. He accused Kossuth and his party of looking forward to the repeal of the Fugitive Slave Law and added, "We have had enough of humbug."[4] Bennett continued his slurs on Kossuth, and Raymond bristled. "The *Herald*," he snapped, "is the recognized organ of quack doctors, prostitutes and the Common Council."[5]

When Kossuth sailed from these shores in July, seven months after his arrival, he had failed in his chief objective: to obtain the government's aid for his fight against Austria. A week after his departure, the *Herald* intimated that he had left the United States secretly to escape lawsuits contemplated by his creditors in New York: "He entered the city with all the pomp, and ceremony, and enthusiasm, which of old attended the victorious general in a Roman triumph, and has left it secretly and in disguise without a solitary huzza to bid him God-speed."[6] During his stay in America, Kossuth raised only about $90,000 from private sources.

Condemnation of Bennett had been commonplace for many years, but not until the fall of 1852, after the *Herald*'s paper bullets had spattered Kossuth's name and cause, did the tactics against him turn almost deadly. Approximately three months after Kossuth's departure, a cylindrical package about six inches long, addressed to Bennett, was delivered to the *Herald*'s office. Written on the outside of the parcel was "Native silver and copper ore from the Cuba Mountains with letter inside the box." Unable to open the lid, Bennett handed the package to managing editor Hudson. He tried to remove the cover with his penknife, and as he did so, black powder seeped from the package and fell onto his desk. Some of the powder was thrown into the grate and exploded. Police were called, and upon examination, a makeshift bomb of pine wood, matches, and rifle powder was discovered.

Three weeks passed before news of the thwarted bombing appeared in the

Herald. Said Bennett of the incident: "We would not have taken any notice of this diabolical attempt were it not that we think it is, under the circumstances, our duty to society to do so. We only regard it with scorn and contempt." He added that he would not be swerved even if "there was a whole manufactory of torpedoes in full operation for our special benefit."[7] Raymond was unsympathetic about the assassination attempt and noted that Bennett had left town just four days after the incident. Bennett and Hudson claimed later that they knew the identity of the culprits and that only insufficient proof had prevented arrests. Nothing more was done about it.

By the time of the attempted bombing, Raymond felt as bitterly toward Bennett as did Greeley. Not only had Bennett's vitriolic attacks against Kossuth undermined his efforts to enlist aid for his cause, but they had also hurt Raymond's efforts to promote his paper with his championship of Kossuth.

In addition, Bennett had made charges against the *Times* that angered Raymond. Two months before, when the *Times* ended its first year, Raymond wrote that his paper had been more successful than any new daily of a similar character ever published in the United States. But despite its impressive circulation, the *Times* was losing money. Nowhere had a newspaper incurred such high expenses in its first year. Two major changes were made: the number of pages was doubled to eight, and the price rose to two cents. The move gave the paper more room for both news and advertising and delighted Bennett. He wrote that the price increase had resulted in a drop in the *Times*'s circulation and that Whig leader Thurlow Weed had advanced the *Times* $10,000. Raymond immediately responded:

> The *Herald* may rest assured that, whether it makes, or loses, $50,000, The *Times* will not only be published every morning, but that . . . it will not find it necessary to resort to such balderdash as that of which the *Herald*'s readers are getting sick, in the shape of Editorials . . . and that long before the end of its second year, it will have more subscribers than the *Herald* ever had.[8]

The *Times*'s circulation did decline, and managerial personnel changed with the passing months. Raymond, however, continued as editor, and slowly his policies paid off.

The Whig national convention was held at Baltimore that year. Raymond became a prominent political figure and enhanced the prestige of the *Times.* Southern Whigs hoped to choose a presidential candidate friendly to their interests. Northern delegates permitted them wide latitude in writing the platform, in return, they hoped, for Gen. Winfield Scott's nomination. Raymond, who first attended as a *Times* correspondent, wrote his paper, "If Scott is not nominated, they will charge breach of faith on the South."[9]

A distorted report was wired to Webb at the convention by the *Courier*, and he informed the Southern leaders. They demanded Raymond's ejection from the meeting hall on the final day of balloting, but by this time, through political maneuvering, he had become a delegate. When Congressman Edward Cabell of Florida called Raymond an abolitionist, the editor charged that some Southerners were bullying Northern representatives in Congress and in national conventions. Not for years had a Northerner dared say anything so audacious to them. From then on Raymond was established as a foremost Whig.

Weed and Senator Seward, omnipotent in New York Whig affairs, were delighted by the turn of events at the convention. They had earlier singled out Raymond as a newspaper editor with whom they wanted to work in New York City. Greeley's "isms" were too much for them to stomach, and he had embarrassed them during his brief congressional stay. Weed and Seward had been forced to tolerate Greeley as long as no other cheap Whig paper wielded influence in New York. Their confidence in Raymond soared.

Greeley raged when the Democratic Party candidate, Franklin Pierce of New Hampshire, was elected president in November. "Gen. Scott is overwhelmingly defeated," he wrote, "and the Whig party is not merely discomfited, it is annihilated. We have no prophetic ken and make no pretense to reading the future, but we do not see how the Whig party as such can be rallied again."[10]

Raymond immediately took advantage of Greeley's dismal forecast. He declared that the *Tribune*'s editor was no longer a Whig and denied the party was finished: "All the Whigs have to do now is to carefully preserve their organization, to watch the tendency of public affairs, and *to wait until they are wanted*."[11]

The *Times* benefited from Raymond's political friends. A new state law required all New York City banks to publish weekly financial statements at regular advertising rates in one newspaper, and this daily was to send proof sheets to other journals, which would not receive remuneration. The *Times* was selected as the paper to be reimbursed. Once, when it was late in sending its complete set of proofs to the *Tribune*, Greeley's temper flared. He accused Daniel B. St. John, superintendent of the state banking department and a former *Times* stockholder, of having the measure passed expressly to favor the *Times* at the expense of its rivals. The state official denied the charge.

Greeley replied to St. John that he had received a "most insolent and scoundrelly" letter from Raymond, who offered to send the proofs at Greeley's convenience if he would credit them to the *Times* instead of to the banking department. "All this insolence of this little villain," the *Tribune*'s editor continued, "is founded on your injustice."[12]

The "Little Villain" tag clung to Raymond for the rest of his life. Greeley termed Bennett and his paper the "Satanic Press." The Scotsman retaliated by calling Greeley "Mephistopheles." The appellations stuck to their targets, and none was ever allowed to forget the damning epithets hurled in the heat of journalistic rivalry.

Greeley's fury mounted the following year when Weed refused to support him for governor but approved Raymond's candidacy for lieutenant governor. The *Times*'s editor was elected over his Democratic and Native American (Know-Nothing) opposition. Raymond's new political position was the last straw for Greeley. He dissolved the informal political partnership of Weed, Seward, and himself by sending Seward a letter of separation. The contents remained undisclosed for six years until 1860, when Greeley obtained his revenge.

Bennett had no strong aspirations for public office. He was aware that his reputation was too odious for him to be considered a serious candidate. He was satisfied to retain his independence and domination in reporting the news. Now and again, however, the *Times*'s ambitious staff beat his paper in covering an event and was not above using unethical means.

The steamship *Arctic*, bound for New York, sank in the North Atlantic in September 1854, after a collision with the French ship *Vesta* while returning from Liverpool. Hundreds were on board, and their kin were frantic when the vessel did not sail into the harbor on time. Early one morning the night editor of the *Times* overheard talk on a horse car in Park Row that the *Herald* had the story of a survivor from the *Arctic*.

He rushed back to the *Times* building and ordered the presses stopped. He offered fifty dollars to a pressman, who had once worked for Bennett, to procure the first copy of the *Herald*. The employee succeeded, despite heavy secrecy in the *Herald*'s pressroom. The article was copied almost completely and ran on the *Times*'s first page. When the *Herald* finally reached the street, the *Times* had already been distributed for an hour. Bennett was furious. Two days after the theft of the story, an editorial in the *Times* appeared to be aimed at him. It fired away in Bennett-like language at what it termed the "slashing writer":

> How he rejoices in skunks, polecats and carrion! . . . In his creed, no one can be mistaken; he is a liar outright, a child of the Devil. . . .
>
> The slasher . . . can afford to be braver than the bravest. The very virtue

of society, that gives him immunity from a barbarous custom, is a license for daily outrages. Neither private worth nor public merit, neither the purity of home nor the sanctity of the grave, is safe from his unhallowed intrusion.[13]

Greeley spent time during the 1850s in Washington, working as a correspondent and writing his trademark editorials from there, while Charles Anderson Dana directed the *Tribune* at home. He often published stories that embarrassed Greeley and dared to omit articles written by him. The *Tribune's* founder pleaded with his assistant to write softly of many situations, since the blame fell upon him as the paper's chief spokesman. He even wrote Dana that he would have to quit the capital unless he stopped attacking people without consulting him.

Greeley's stay in Washington resulted in another headache for him. He strongly believed that the West should be developed and that one way to do it was for the federal government to approve railroad land grants to states and private companies. During a congressional investigating committee hearing on the conduct of more than twenty members in 1857, the charge was made that Greeley, while a Washington correspondent the year before, had received a draft for $1,000 to help pass the Des Moines Navigation and Railroad Bill. In his naive fashion, he had accepted the money from a friend, who asked him to take it to New York and keep it there until drawn a few weeks later.

Raymond had been antagonistic at times toward the *Tribune's* editor, but he refused to believe his former employer had been dishonorable. Greeley publicly explained the situation in a letter that the *Times* printed. The explanation appeared with a statement by Raymond in which he said that he wholly approved Greeley's version of the facts and that he was the innocent dupe of a payoff in aid of the bill.

The *Times* outgrew its building at Beekman and Nassau Streets as it continued to prosper in 1857. The paper sought to buy the property of its former neighbor, the Old Brick Presbyterian Church. The plan irritated Bennett, and he accused the *Times* of stock-gambling. Raymond struck back and charged the *Herald* with "puffing" various concerns that ruined investors by issuing stock for an amount out of proportion to its actual value. An article signed by Bennett stated that he never had had any connection with any stockjobbing company of any kind, nor did any other person have any control or authority over the columns of the *Herald.*

The clash between the papers continued. Wesley, a founder of the *Times,* had set up a syndicate to buy the church. A private sale failed to materialize, and an auction was scheduled. When Bennett heard of it, he wrote:

The Wall street stockjobbers of the *Daily Times* announce in their own journal that they will sell at auction, some time next week . . . the old Brick Church, including, we suppose, the remains of the dead, consisting of old human bones and human ashes which still cling about the foundations of that building. Nothing escapes these inveterate speculators. They deal in shinplaster banks, dirty hotels, small theatres, broken down railways, fancy stocks. . . . Wesley and Co. beat Shakspeare [*sic*]—they buy and sell human skulls at auction, and make them a profitable article of merchandise on Wall street. How Satan will enjoy that auction! It will be entirely to his taste.[14]

The *Herald* printed a list of fifteen railroads that it said the *Times*'s proprietors were engaged in either buying or selling, as well as the ventures mentioned earlier. The *Times* struck back by giving extracts of the *Herald*'s alleged puffing of different companies from January through December 1853, and added that future years would also be explored. Raymond said that if the proprietors of the *Times* were engaged in everything claimed by Bennett, they must be the most remarkable men of the day because they seemed to control everything.

When the Old Brick Presbyterian Church property was auctioned a week later, the *Times* bought it for $100,000.

The fastest means of conveying information from Europe was by steamboat. Cyrus W. Field, a businessman who had amassed a fortune in the paper business, labored with others to finance and lay a successful transatlantic cable. His dream was called "the rat hole" until he gained the support of Peter Cooper, president of the Atlantic Telegraph Company. British and U.S. ships cooperated in laying and completing a cable on August 5, 1858, from Valentia, Ireland, to Trinity Bay, Newfoundland. By connecting with land wires, the first transatlantic telegraphic communication link was extended down the American coast to New York.

Eleven days later, President James Buchanan received part of a message from Queen Victoria: "Her Majesty desires to congratulate the President upon the successful completion of this great international work, in which the Queen has taken the deepest interest."[15]

Buchanan immediately acknowledged the queen's cable. The next day, after slight repairs to the cable, the president received the rest of the British ruler's message. Less than two weeks later, the first news dispatch was delayed a day by Nova Scotians who refused to let anything interfere with their sleep.

Great municipal festivities were held to celebrate the cable's success. More than one million people flocked into the city on September 1 to watch a parade of ten thousand from the Battery to the Crystal Palace site, now Bryant Park. While the cheering went on, the last message for some time was being sent that day. Faulty insulation caused the cable to collapse completely on September 4. Not until after the Civil War would a permanent cable be laid.

Years of editing had not quenched Raymond's love for reporting. If the cable had not failed, he could have reported overnight the news of the war in Italy between the French and Italians on one side and the Austrians on the other. When the Austro-Sardinian War erupted in April 1859, he covered some of the battles himself, assisted by his Paris correspondent, Dr. William Johnston, whose pen name was Malakoff. With the cable unavailable, steamers were again the fastest conveyers of news across the Atlantic.

Exclusive reports of the fighting were the prizes sought by American, English, and French journalists. The *Times* of London, called the "Thunderer," was rated the first newspaper of the world. To beat the mighty British daily was considered as valuable as a battlefield victory. Three Americans— Raymond, Malakoff, and Judge James Forsyth of Troy, New York, a longtime friend of Raymond—were in the same party observing the Battle of Solferino.

That night, the trio found a small tavern near the scene of action. They grouped around a table, with candlelight to guide them, as Raymond wrote of the fighting. He finished his story at 4:00 A.M. Malakoff, using their horses and carriage, placed the dispatch on the Emperor's Express bound for Paris. Mrs. Raymond was in the French capital. She received the report with instructions to ship it on the first and fastest steamer leaving France or England for New York, regardless of expense. Within thirty hours the news was aboard a vessel departing Liverpool for America. The *Times* of London received the news by the same express, but it could not make the ship in time. Raymond had accomplished the impossible. His story was published ten days before the "Thunderer" arrived in New York.

Publication of the report increased Raymond's prestige, but the *Times* became an object of ridicule just four days later. While Raymond covered the battlefront, William Henry Hurlbert supervised the paper's editorial page. He and some friends, after much revelry, accompanied an acquaintance to a steamer leaving for Europe. The farewell over, Hurlbert returned to the *Times* building, thinking of four different subjects on which he would write. Feeling the effects of the drinks, he wrote of them all without changing paper. The completed editorial, "The Defensive Square of Austrian Italy," was a botched effort. Part of it read:

> Austria has neglected nothing that might assure her dominion over the waters of the Danube. She has done all in her power to favor the development of Europe, which is the pacific development of England . . . and if we follow the windings of the Mincio, we shall find countless elbows formed in the elbows of the regular army. . . . If we follow up the course of the Mincio, we shall find innumerable elbows formed by the sympathy of youth.
>
> Notwithstanding the toil spent by Austria on the spot, we should have learned that we are protected by a foreign fleet suddenly coming up on our question of citizenship. A canal cuts Mantua in two; but we may rely on the most cordial Cabinet Minister of the new power in England.[16]

The *Times* apologized for the blunder and published the editorial as it should have been written. A "confusion of manuscripts sent up at a late hour" was blamed for the hodgepodge. Hurlbert's stay with the *Times* was limited after that, but his muddled article was not forgotten. Two years later, the *Herald* wrote that Hurlbert glorified himself "on never sitting down to write his press articles until after dinner, a fact that will account for the singularly devious and unsteady character of the famous disquisition on the elbows of the Mincio, which set the town in a roar."[17] Even as late as 1871 the *Sun* poked fun at the editorial.

A group of men seeking an ideal newspaper were disappointed that Raymond had followed Greeley's path in realizing news could not be ignored merely to maintain purity. They wanted a religious daily, with "living Christianity" asserting itself more positively than had yet been done. These men wanted no crime reports, slanders, or divorce suits in print and no details of murders to divert their readers. They were confident their type of paper would appeal to the masses if sold for one cent.

With Alexander Cummings of Philadelphia as its founder, the *World* was born on June 14, 1860. About $200,000 was spent trying to guide it along as a highly moral journal, but the paper failed to meet expenses. Some of the *World*'s financial supporters became dismayed at the losses, and the daily changed hands. It came into the possession of Democratic financiers and politicians, including August Belmont, Augustus Schell, and New York City Mayor Fernando Wood. Its religious aspect was dropped, and the *World* became a general newspaper, with Manton Marble taking editorial control.

In November the price of the paper was raised to two cents, and on July 1, 1861, the *World* merged with the *Courier and Enquirer*. The absorption ended Webb's newspaper career, and his sixpenny paper wound up as one of the low-priced publications that he had despised and fought. The revolution that Bennett had waged for more than twenty-five years against the Wall Street press was finally over, but it had necessitated the contributions of Greeley and Raymond. Political cliques no longer dictated to newspapers, and the cash basis of advertising, so vital to newspapers today, had destroyed the credit system.

Gone was the hold that the sixpenny papers had maintained on readers who scoffed at the cheaper sheets for their excessive emotionalism and lack of objectivity. The lower-priced publications had proven they could produce a better, more profitable product than the older, more expensive dailies.

The *World*'s quarters were at 35 Park Row, close to those of the *Times*, which had become the first daily bearing a Park Row address. The *Times* had laid the cornerstone of its building on the former grounds of the Old Brick Presbyterian Church in May 1857, and construction was completed the following year. The *Times* covered the northern apex of the triangle formed by Park Row and Beekman and Nassau Streets, having as its address 41 Park Row.

Geographically, the dailies had moved northward since the day when most of them were located on or near Wall Street. The new *Times* building was diagonally across the street from the *Tribune*. An open space in front of the *Times* building and opposite City Hall Park had no name until the *Times* opened its new offices in 1858. It became known as Printing House Square, after the location of the *Times* of London, but not until 1940 did the city officially recognize the title. Not only dailies, but also Sunday papers, weekly journals, foreign publications, paper warehouses, and job-printing houses were represented in the Park Row area. Eventually, Park Row would become the number one newspaper address in the world. .

As the 1850s ended, rumblings could be heard everywhere of the coming storm of sectional antagonism and civil war that would ripen and tear apart the nation. Newspapers in other cities spoke with strong voices, but the *Herald, Tribune, Times,* and other dailies in New York would thrust their opinions more forcefully than ever upon the country. Their circulations would rise to unprecedented levels, as the hatreds and rivalry that seethed among Bennett, Greeley, and Raymond would blaze as never before. Through these editors, and others, Park Row would play a dominant role during the critical times about to follow—a role of influence surpassed by that of only one other address: the White House on Pennsylvania Avenue in Washington.

5

Lincoln and the Giants

GREELEY's *Weekly Tribune* possessed the largest newspaper circulation in the nation, and he tolerated no compromise with the institution of slavery. Raymond had no love for bondage, but he believed that slaveholders and politics, rather than slavery itself, produced the greatest conflict. Bennett steered the *Herald* in slavery's favor. His was not the only paper in the city extolling the blessings of the South's way of life, but its prestige was immense below the Mason-Dixon line, where it was the most popular Northern daily. He praised any congressional bill permitting slavery to operate, as long as Southerners bought his paper.

Bitter contention broke out in 1854 between the two sections of the country, as slavery became an issue within the newly organized Kansas and Nebraska Territories. Illinois Senator Stephen A. Douglas introduced a measure that would permit slavery in Kansas and Nebraska if the settlers there so desired.

The *Tribune* daily filled its pages with articles on the dispute. Greeley warned that approval of the legislation would lead to fighting. When the measure carried in May, Southern extremists fired a cannon to celebrate their victory. Bennett later wrote that his *Herald* was about the only Northern paper that had the moral courage to come out boldly in favor of the Kansas-Nebraska Bill when it was brought forward.

The *Tribune, Times,* and *Post* urged Free-Soilers to defend the new districts. Money to buy weapons poured into the *Tribune*'s offices, and one-dollar subscriptions amounted to $22,000. The Reverend Henry Ward Beecher's congregation at the Plymouth Church in Brooklyn added its own funds to purchase arms. Rifles could not be sent openly, so they were forwarded in boxes and dubbed "Beecher's Bibles" as they flowed into Kansas. Greeley and other New Yorkers contributed a six-pound cannon, which vanished en route. The South blamed Greeley for the bloodshed in Kansas. Virginia condemned him as unfit for society, and pro-slavery Northerners agreed he was a devil.

Tensions between North and South resulted in Greeley's being physically assaulted for the first time in his life. In February 1856, while he was writing news stories and editorials from Washington, Congressman Albert Rust of Arkansas accosted him on the street, struck him in the face, and soon after attacked him with a cane that broke over his arm. The Arkansas Democrat was incensed over *Tribune* articles that favored an antislavery candidate, Nathaniel P. Banks of Massachusetts, for Speaker of the House.

Another reason was that the Republican Party had entered the national political scene. Greeley became a shining light of the organization, after the name "Republican" first appeared in the *Tribune* on June 16, 1854. So did Raymond, who was one of its founders, and the views he expressed were those of moderate Northerners. They wanted to fight Southern interests in the territories and endorsed armed resistance of the Kansas Free Staters.

The Republicans replaced the Whigs as the leading opposition to the Democrats. James Buchanan became the Democratic candidate for president, and the Republicans nominated John Charles Fremont, whose expeditions in the Far West had brought him fame. While Greeley and Raymond supported Fremont, Bennett was in a quandary over whom to back. He hated the abolitionists but was not sure of Republican strength, and reluctantly he threw his pages in favor of Fremont. After Buchanan's nomination, Bennett called him cold, timid, and noncommittal. However, once Buchanan won the election, Bennett switched his allegiance to the president-elect.

The Kansas riots presented a preview of the battle between North and South. Chief Justice Roger B. Taney and a majority of the Supreme Court declared in an 1857 decision against a slave named Dred Scott that Congress could not exclude slavery from the territories. Greeley and the Free-Soilers assailed the court and its decision, but Bennett defended the ruling.

Abolitionist John Brown of Osawatomie, Kansas, felt that the greatest service a man could render to God was to free the slaves and believed that he must incite a rebellion for that purpose. Accompanied by a band of twenty-one, including five Blacks, Brown raided the federal arsenal at Harpers Ferry, Virginia, on October 16, 1859. The band seized wagon loads of rifles and killed seven people. Seven of Brown's men, including two of his sons, died in the attack, which was quelled by government troops, under the leadership of Col. Robert E. Lee, thirty-six hours later.

The *Herald*'s coverage of the insurrection was unrivaled. When congressmen interviewed Brown at the armory, a *Herald* reporter was the only newspaperman present, providing Bennett's paper with an exclusive story. Alongside the *Herald*'s first report of the raid was William Henry Seward's "irrepressible conflict" speech in Rochester, New York, a year before. The senator had warned that the United States must become either a slave-holding nation entirely or a free-labor country entirely. The juxtaposition of the articles led the reader to believe that the assault on the arsenal was the result of the address. "It opened in treason, robbery and murder," wrote Bennett, "and has appropriately closed in the blood of the misguided fanatics who lent themselves to the doctrine of the 'irrepressible conflict.' "[1]

Because Greeley had supported Brown in his Kansan activities, efforts were made to associate the *Tribune*'s editor with the raid. The South blamed Greeley for the assault, although he had been unaware of Brown's plans and had even written that the whole affair seemed the work of a madman. Bennett rejoiced when the court found Brown guilty of murder, treason against the Commonwealth of Virginia, and inciting the slaves to insurrection. He called the death sentence against Brown just and pleaded in vain with the government to try others, including Seward, for the raid.

Presidential contender Abraham Lincoln had obtained a wide reputation by debating Douglas and taking an antislavery stand. He challenged the South to come up with evidence that even one Republican had been involved in the Harpers Ferry assault. The challenge was issued during his first visit to New York City on February 27, 1860, when he spoke in Cooper Union Institute at a meeting over which Bryant of the *Evening Post* presided.

The audience greeted Lincoln's speech with applause and cheers, but newspaper opinions varied. Bennett considered the "rail-splitter" merely another Republican speaker and emphasized his awkwardness. The ardently pro-Seward *Times* referred to Lincoln as a noted political exhorter and prairie orator. Greeley, delighted by the address, wrote that no man ever had made such an impression on his first appeal to a New York audience.

Republicans gathered in Chicago that May for their national convention. Seward was the man of the hour. He was too much of a radical to many, but it seemed inevitable that he would be nominated. Greeley could not forgive his erstwhile political partner for slighting him in favor of Raymond. He had waited a long time for his revenge, and he meant to get it by preventing Seward's nomination. Weed controlled the New York delegation, of which Raymond was a member, and Greeley attended as a delegate from distant Oregon. His candidate was former congressman Edward Bates, a slaveholder from Missouri who, Greeley rationalized, held fast to the doctrine that slavery was an evil to be restricted.

Seward's forces seemed too strong to Greeley to let anyone else be nominated. But the *Tribune*'s editor, an object of curiosity and worship at the convention, strayed from delegation to delegation, predicting defeat for the New York candidate. Seward's stronghold was broken on the third ballot.

Some of Bates's ballots were switched to Lincoln, and votes poured in for the man from Illinois.

Greeley did not care about Lincoln's nomination, but he relished that Seward had lost. Raymond angrily charged that the failure of Seward, while governor, to secure political offices for Greeley had led him to campaign for his downfall. He mentioned Greeley's 1854 letter to Seward that had dissolved the partnership of Weed, Seward, and Greeley and charged that the *Tribune* editor's main purpose at the convention was to defeat Seward. Greeley denied the accusation.

It almost broke Bennett's heart to see Lincoln elected. "Greeley wants the Postmastership and ought to get it," lamented Bennett, for "he and his associates have done more to build up the republican party and place it in power by the election of Lincoln than Seward, Thurlow Weed and all their confraternity have ever done."[2] By "associates," he alluded to Raymond and Bryant, and he later wrote that "without New York journalism, there would have been no republican party."[3] While the *Tribune, Times, Evening Post,* and *World* rejoiced at the Republican victory, the *Journal of Commerce, Express,* and lesser papers hated to see Lincoln triumph.

Confronting the country was the threat of secession because of Lincoln's election. South Carolina voted to withdraw from the Union on December 20. Outgoing President Buchanan refused to take action, and the president-elect remained silent. Bennett warned that, if the current policy continued in Washington, the Southern states would be drawn into the vortex with South Carolina and an attempt would be made to prevent Lincoln's inauguration.

Lincoln's continued silence raised Bennett's temperature: "Honest Old Abe Lincoln, whose achievements as a rail-splitter now form part of the history of the country, has latterly been engaged in a new line of business, a rather high branch of wordwork, to wit—the manufacturing of Cabinets."[4]

Bennett insisted that Lincoln announce his plans and promise concessions to the South. He charged that pro-Unionists were in favor of no compromise and rigid coercion, even to civil war, and declared that peaceable recognition was the only escape from a general and ruinous war.

The *Times* and *Evening Post* stood adamantly against compromise. They remained firm in their positions that if the states seceded, they must be returned to the United States by coercion. Greeley shuddered at the thought of military action. Just weeks after Lincoln had won the election, he wrote: "If the Cotton States unitedly and earnestly wish to withdraw peacefully from the Union, we think they should and would be allowed to do so. Any attempt to compel them by force would be contrary to the principles enunciated in the immortal Declaration of Independence—contrary to the fundamental ideas on which Human Liberty is based."[5]

As Mississippi, Florida, Alabama, Georgia, Louisiana, and Texas followed South Carolina with acts of secession, Greeley changed his attitude. The *Tribune* boldly announced: "NO MORE COMPROMISE! NO CONCESSIONS TO TRAITORS! The Constitution As It Is!"[6]

Lincoln declared at his inauguration that he was opposed to interference with slavery where it existed but was determined to maintain the Union unbroken. Raymond approved of the message. It was too mild to please Greeley, but he was confident that the president would become more vigorous. Bennett thought Lincoln should have contented himself with telling the audience a funny story and letting it go at that.

No immediate action seemed forthcoming. The country waited uneasily. The *Times* and *Tribune* grew impatient. On April 3 Raymond wrote, "Wanted—A Policy." That same day Greeley pleaded, "Come to the Point!"

"Honest Old Abe," Bennett snickered almost daily, and claimed the government was really in the hands of three or four leading Republican journalists in New York City. He called Lincoln "incompetent, ignorant and desperate."[7] "It is becoming too evident," Bennett warned, "that so far as a vicious, imbecilic, demoralized administration possesses power, the hideous horrors of civil war are about to be forced upon the country."[8]

On April 12, when Confederate forces set off the Civil War by the bombardment of Fort Sumter at Charleston Harbor, South Carolina, the *Times* published some of the epithets hurled at Lincoln by fire-eating newspapers:

> "ourang-outang," . . . "demon," . . . "incarnate devil"; . . . "Western Abolition bloodhound," and an "Illinois baboon," and that his Christian name is "Old Ape."
>
> We learn, also, from the same well-informed and genteel sources, that Vice President Hamlin is a "negro [*sic*]," a "nigger," a "mulatto," a "half-breed," and "octoroon," and a "filthy Maine negro,"—that he is "illegitimate," "idiotic," and a general monster of such beastly depravity and crazy imbecility, that our Christian quill refuses to write the words in which he is depicted.[9]

Papers published extras on the night that news of the Fort Sumter attack was received in New York City. Park Row overflowed with ghostlike spectators silently reading the bulletins on the newspaper-building façades. The next day Raymond wrote that people expected Lincoln to meet the worst emergency in the government's history with courage and swift action proportionate to the crisis. Party clamor, he added, is drowned by the roar of cannon aimed at the heart of the American Republic.

The city's masses suddenly discovered they were loyal to the Union. Pro-slavery persons and institutions became objects of hate. An excited mob surged toward the *Herald* building on April 15, the day after Bennett's paper set the world's circulation mark of 135,000 copies. His employees barricaded windows and doors. Outside, the crowd demanded that Bennett display an American flag, while debating the destruction of his offices. No flag was in the building, and an office boy was dispatched hastily to a bunting store to obtain the Stars and Stripes. The fury of the mob abated at the display of Bennett's patriotism.

The *Herald*'s owner took precautions against future outbursts from crowds: a small arsenal of ammunition and rifles was purchased and secreted. However, Bennett never forgave Greeley for *Tribune* articles that reported on the near riot. But Greeley was not alone in his criticism of Bennett. On the day of the threatened mobbing Raymond wrote, "Is there no limit to the *Herald*'s open advocacy of treason and rebellion? That print has done every-thing in its power to encourage and stimulate the secession movement. It has vilified the Government, belled the people of the Northern States . . . and done everything in its power to incite the South to the open war unto which they have at last plunged the country."[10]

Southern forces were advancing in late June, when a bulletin-type notice appeared at the head of the *Tribune*'s editorial page:

THE NATION'S WAR-CRY
Forward to Richmond! Forward to Richmond!
The Rebel Congress must not be allowed to meet there on the 20th of July. By that date the place must be held by the National Army.[11]

As the declaration appeared day after day, other papers picked up the battle slogan: "Forward to Richmond." Congress met in a special session on July 4. The Union was not ready for battle, but the public knew only how won-derful it would be to capture the rebel capital. When the Northern forces were defeated at Bull Run on July 21, the public forgot it had encouraged the *Tribune* and only remembered the paper's agitation.

Greeley was blamed for the disaster. The *Tribune* was damned, circulation fell, and advertisements were withdrawn. "Forward to Richmond" had not been Greeley's idea. Washington correspondent Fitz Henry Warren had written that phrase while Greeley was in the West, and Charles Anderson Dana had assigned it to its position atop the editorial page and kept it there.

To readers, Greeley was the *Tribune,* and they believed that he wrote everything published in the newspaper. They did not know how often Dana had
ignored his advice to tone down an article.

The opposition screamed for Greeley's scalp. Bennett called him a deplor-
able failure as a military leader. Raymond claimed that Greeley's thirst for
public office was responsible for his dictating to the government. Frenzied
by the thunderous denunciations hurled at him, Greeley replied in a signed
editorial titled "JUST ONCE." He said he was not seeking to be relieved
of any responsibility for urging the advance of the Union Army into Virginia,
although the precise phrase "Forward to Richmond!" was not his. However,
he added, he was prepared to be a scapegoat for all the military blunders of
the past month. "Henceforth," he wrote, "I bar all criticism in these columns
on army movements, past and future. . . . Correspondents and reporters may
state facts, but must forbear comments."[12]

The tragic defeat inflicted upon the North at Bull Run drove Greeley
frantic, and he felt it was the *Tribune*'s fault. In a letter to Lincoln he said:

> This is my seventh sleepless night—yours too, doubtless—yet I think I shall
> not die, because I have no right to die. . . . You are not considered a great
> man, and I am a hopelessly broken one. You are now undergoing a terrible
> ordeal, and God has thrown the gravest responsibilities upon you. Do not fear
> to meet them. . . .
>
> If the Union is irrevocably gone, an Armistice for thirty, ninety, 120 days—
> better still for a year—ought at once to be proposed with a view to a peaceful
> adjustment.[13]

When Lincoln saw the letter, he realized Greeley's mental condition. They
had corresponded previously, and it was unlike anything Greeley had written. The president ignored his panic-stricken advice.

Union forces saw mainly defeat that first year. Lincoln's call for seventy-
five thousand recruits heightened public anxiety. The government acted to
muster support and curb opposition by the New York press. In August a
federal grand jury handed up an indictment against pro-slavery newspapers,
and they were deprived of mailing privileges temporarily. The daily *Day
Book* was suppressed and later reappeared as a weekly for a few years.

No attempt was made to crack down on the *Herald.* Bennett's ability to
shift with the winds of public opinion once again stood him in good stead.
The mob threat against him had produced a change in his editorial stance
toward the government. He resented the competition's enjoying a field day
at his expense, and he launched his own, undeclared war upon other papers

in the city. Bennett's chief targets were the *Tribune, Times,* and *Evening Post.* These were pro-government papers, favoring all the views he detested. He described them endlessly as the "niggerhead" press; lesser foes—the *World, News,* and *Express*—represented the "copperhead" press. He referred to the *World, Tribune,* and *Times* as "the *World,* the flesh and the devil."

Bennett charged that the "Abolition Incendiaries," as he called Greeley and Raymond, were conspiring to overthrow the Union. He called upon the federal government to suppress their newspapers and the others for being incendiary. He claimed that the pro-administration papers planned a conspiracy against the president. Bennett spoke of cowardly journalism and charged that Lincoln's chief troubles were caused by the Republican papers that had elected him, the *Tribune* and *Times.*

As the war progressed, it was important for Washington's relations with England to be of the best. However, the *Herald* attacked the British government. When *Macmillan's Magazine* criticized his journal as a "notoriously southern paper" restraining its sympathies only because it feared mobbing, Bennett denied the charge. He said the *Herald* had always advocated the Union cause and that, even before the fall of Fort Sumter, it had protested that secession was revolution and had called on Buchanan to put it down by force.

If Gen. George Brinton McClellan had had his way, Raymond's *Times* would have been suppressed on charges of treason. The paper on December 4 devoted half of its front page to a map of the forts in the Washington area and the divisions defending them. "Little Mac" irately wrote Secretary of War Simon Cameron that there was treasonable intent on the part of the daily. Cameron sent Raymond a letter, enclosing a copy of the general's complaint. Raymond replied that the map was from a lithographed copy published in Washington and sold openly at all bookstores and in the lobby of the Willard Hotel without objection from McClellan or anyone else. He also said the names of the forts were collected from McClellan's own general orders of September 3 and furnished from his office for publication in newspapers.[14]

Shortly after the conflict had erupted, Charles Craske, a New York engraver, developed a curved stereotype plate for a rotary press. The process, first employed by the *Tribune,* enabled papers to set up the printing of entire pages, a valuable addition at a time when circulations were high and speedy runs urgent. Bennett boasted of the *Herald*'s huge circulation. He maintained that his paper sold more than one hundred thousand copies daily, the greatest in the country, while the *Times* and *Tribune* each distributed only about twenty-five thousand.

Raymond could tolerate Bennett's insults no longer. He challenged the *Herald*'s editor to wagers on different circulation figures, for an amount totaling $25,000, with all the money going to the families of war volunteers. Bennett overlooked the circulation wager he had made with Greeley in the late forties and refused to bet, saying it was against his religion.

The climax in the Raymond-Bennett battle arose unexpectedly. The usually cool-headed Raymond resorted to an undignified tactic. On the front page the paper ran two caricatures of Bennett dressed in Scottish festival apparel and with horns cropping out of his head. Quotations from the *Herald* as well as the *Times*'s betting offers accompanied the illustrations. The caption under the first caricature read, "Brother Bennett (Profanely Styled "the Satanic,") Inflating his Well-Known First-Class, A No. 1 Wind-Bag, *Herald.*"

Printed under the second caricature showing a deflated Bennett: "DISASTROUS RESULT! Brother Bennett Resorts to the Consolations of Religion."[15]

Readers were shocked by Raymond's act and complained about the dramatic lapse from his usually high moral level. He regretted his reckless decision. His paper did not benefit from the attack, and the *Herald* was not hurt. Bennett returned to claiming that both the *Times* and *Tribune* had circulations of 25,000–30,000.

The Union troops rolled back the Confederates with the advent of 1862, and Greeley split with Dana that year over *Tribune* policy. Dana was all for war, horrifying pacifist Greeley. Dana resigned and became assistant secretary of war under Edwin M. Stanton. Greeley, eager to get back into the saddle of editorial management, again ran the *Tribune* as he wished.

Gone was Greeley's despondency of the year before. He asked Speaker of the House Schuyler Colfax how he should support Lincoln's efforts toward emancipation of the slaves. The president answered him directly, thanked him for his proposed aid, and suggested that, as the North was ready for the measure, it should be urged persuasively and not menacingly upon the South. Lincoln said he would prefer to have the border states move first, but if this could not be done in a reasonable time, he would like legislation to possess three main features: compensation, gradualness, and the vote of the people.

The Union lost its first struggle of the year in the Seven Days Battles of June 26–July 2 at Richmond, and Lincoln issued a call for three hundred thousand men. Greeley supported him, and James Sloan Gibbons, the *Eve-*

ning Post's financial editor, encouraged the move with a front-page song, "We Are Coming, Father Abraham." It began:

> We are coming, Father Abraham, three hundred thousand more,
> From Mississippi's winding stream, and from New England's shore,
> We leave our ploughs and workshops, our wives and children dear,
> With hearts too full for utterance, with but a silent tear,
> We dare not look behind us, but steadfastly before,
> We are coming, Father Abraham, three hundred thousand more.[16]

With the defeat fresh in mind, neither Congress nor any border state would approve of the compensation clause for emancipation. Lincoln read his draft of the Emancipation Proclamation to the Cabinet on July 22, and Secretary of State Seward suggested that the document be withheld until the Union Army regained ground. When the president agreed and shelved the proclamation, Greeley was infuriated. He wanted Lincoln to move at once and, in an open letter, "The Prayer of Twenty Millions," pleaded with the president to carry out the new Confiscation Act and urged freedom to slaves who had fled to the North.

Lincoln replied to Greeley in a message released through the press. He had used the *Tribune* editor's appeal to gauge public reaction, and it provided the president with the opportunity to state his position on slavery: "My paramount object in this struggle is to save the Union, and is not either to save or destroy Slavery. . . . What I do about Slavery and the colored race, I do because I believe it helps to save this Union."

In a letter below Lincoln's, Greeley wrote that he had not intended to impeach the sincerity of the president's devotion in the saving of the Union: "I never doubted . . . that you desire, before and above all else, to re-establish the now derided authority and vindicate the territorial integrity of the Republic. . . . *Do you propose to do this by recognizing, obeying, and enforcing the laws, or by ignoring, disregarding, and in effect defying them?*"[17]

Lincoln had learned what he wanted to know. After the victory of Antietam, he announced on September 11 that, unless the seceded states returned to the Union by New Year's Day, he would free all slaves in the states still in rebellion. The editors of the *Times, Post,* and *Tribune* were exuberant. The elated Greeley made clear how he felt: "It is the beginning of the end of the rebellion; the beginning of the new life of the nation. GOD BLESS ABRAHAM LINCOLN."[18]

The Union forces swept to victory in one battle after another early in 1863 while losing only two. Although Lincoln had called for three hundred

thousand volunteers in June 1862, only eighty thousand enlisted by the fol-
lowing March, and Congress authorized the Union's first draft measure.
One provision allowed anyone who wanted to escape conscription to pay
$300 for a substitute. The first drawing of draftees was scheduled to start in
New York City on Saturday, July 11, 1863.

Rumors spread that riots might occur on that day, to be incited by a secret
political and pro-secessionist organization called the Knights of the Golden
Circle, but all was quiet. On Sunday, grumbling groups gathered on street
corners. They accepted the act calmly, but resentment grew as they read the
Sunday papers and saw how they could be drafted because they could not
raise the money.

Only the Metropolitan Police were available when the riots began the next
day, with the throwing of stones into the windows of the provost marshal's
offices. Men, women, and children participated, most of them Irish immigrants. As the rioting gained momentum, the class of enraged persons
changed. These were described by the *Times* as ruffians ready to pillage and
plunder, criminals from the city's hoodlum quarters skilled in the habits of a
tribe of savages.

Organized agitators with Southern leanings stirred the rioters into frenzy.
Armed with bricks, clubs, and a few rifles, they burned the Second Avenue
Armory, set fire to the residences of prominent men, ransacked the home of
Mayor George Opdyke, killed anyone who dared impede their actions, and
smashed the heads of policemen. The harrying mob struck African-Ameri-
can pedestrians with iron clubs before hanging them on the nearest tree or
lamppost. They attacked the Colored Orphan Asylum on Fifth Avenue,
between 43rd and 44th Streets, reportedly killed a little Black girl found
hiding under a bed, and set fires throughout the building.

Gangs ransacked a boardinghouse where Greeley was believed to eat.
Then they rushed to the *Tribune* building facing Printing House Square,
singing:

> We'll hang old Greeley to a sour apple tree,
> We'll hang old Greeley to a sour apple tree,
> We'll hang old Greeley to a sour apple tree,
> And send him straight to Hell!

Greeley could not be found in the *Tribune* building. The *World* spread a
rumor that he had spent the day at Windust's café on Park Row and left it
in disguise. The *Herald* wrote that Greeley escaped from the mob with the
aid of a policeman and a friend. The *Tribune* denied the stories. It said he

had worked from 9:00 A.M. until dinnertime and walked through the crowd to the restaurant; after that, Greeley and two friends took a carriage to his lodging, with no sort of concealment or disguise.

It was nighttime, and Greeley had already left the area when the mob surged into the *Tribune* building. Furniture was destroyed, counters were wrecked, doors and windows battered, and fires started. Only the arrival of the Metropolitan Police dispersed the rioters. The fires were swiftly quelled, and the *Tribune* did not skip an edition. The next day Raymond wrote that the *Times* had not always agreed with the *Tribune* but that it was regrettable that Greeley's building had been attacked. Raymond added that the *Tribune* had the aid of some of his employees in protecting Greeley's property.

The loyalist papers took no chances after that assault. The *Times* and *Tribune*, on opposite corners, were fortified in military fashion. Raymond ordered the entire *Times* building lighted, making the plant the most illuminated place in the city. Two newly invented Gatling machine guns were set in position on the first floor. Raymond took charge of one, and the other was manned by Leonard Walter Jerome, grandfather of Britain's World War II prime minister, Winston Churchill.

Bennett was jubilant when the rioting erupted. He had waited two years to see Greeley squirm when faced with the wrath of the mob, as he had been after the firing on Fort Sumter. Bennett called the outburst the rage of the people, and the *World* identified the crowd as laboring men of the city.

Raymond denounced those descriptions of the rioters: "These are libels that ought to have paralyzed the fingers that penned them. . . . The people of New-York and the laboring men of New-York are not incendiaries, nor robbers, nor assassins. They do not hunt down men whose only offence is the color God gave them; they do not chase, and insult, and beat women; they do not pillage an asylum for orphan children."[19]

The *Times* maintained it was resistance to the draft that had sparked the riots. The *Tribune*'s view differed, saying it was absurd to blame the outburst on anything but sympathy with the rebels. The *Tribune* maintained that at the bottom of all the arson, devastation, robbery, and murder was the fear that slavery and the Rebellion must suffer.

Political, economic, and social discontent that had been festering for years also contributed to the uprising. Two thousand people were reported killed in the most shameful outburst the nation had known, but later studies indicated the actual number of fatalities may have been fewer than 150.

Greeley, disenchanted with Lincoln's moderate antislavery and reconstruction stands, opposed his renomination in 1864. In addition, much to

Greeley's disgust, Raymond was appointed to draft the platform when the Republican convention opened in Baltimore in June.

Neither Greeley nor Bennett cared to see Lincoln reelected, but the president realized the necessity of having their papers on his side. He let it be known that he proposed to nominate Bennett as minister to France. Bennett had no interest in holding public office, but the message was enough, and the *Herald* switched its allegiance to Lincoln. Soon after the second inauguration, the president offered him the post to France, but it was declined. "If I wanted to go to Europe," said Bennett, "I would take fifty thousand dollars, and go at my leisure."[20]

Greeley was more difficult to convince. Before the election Lincoln wrote him to ask for a meeting. When Greeley did not reply, George Hoskins, later speaker of the State Assembly and congressman from New York, informed him that Lincoln planned to make Greeley postmaster general if he won reelection. Greeley did not believe the president, but Hoskins said he would stake his life on Lincoln's word. The next day the *Tribune* announced that, henceforth, it would fly the banner of Abraham Lincoln for the next president.

After Lincoln's triumph, Greeley waited impatiently for his appointment, but none came. On April 14, 1865, Greeley told Hoskins he had heard nothing from Lincoln. His friend replied he would go to Washington that night to see why the president had been silent. As Hoskins stepped off the train in the capital the next morning, newsboys were shouting the news of the president's assassination.

The art of journalism reached a pinnacle during the war years. Newspapers in Chicago, Philadelphia, St. Louis, Boston, Baltimore, Toledo, New Orleans, and Cincinnati all strove to compete with those of the great city and distinguished themselves, but none surpassed the New York papers.

Greeley and Raymond spared no expense in providing their readers with the best coverage possible. The *Tribune* bowed to the magnitude of the war when, once the fighting was well under way, it took advertising off its front page for the first time and replaced it with news stories.

Greeley and Raymond, as always, were forced to recognize the superiority of their most hated adversary. Almost sixty-six years of age when the war began, Bennett saw the *Herald* develop news reporting to a greater extent than journalism had known—an accomplishment made necessary by a crisis as important as a large-scale war. "It would be worth my while," said Raymond, "to give a million dollars, if the devil would come and tell me every evening, as he does Bennett, what the people of New York would like to read about next morning."[21]

The war correspondent was a type of reporter completely foreign to the American public. About five hundred of them covered battles for the North alone. Their one goal was to get the story, and to do that, they risked their lives and shared the hardships of soldiers. They became known as the "Bohemian Brigade." The *Herald* alone boasted more than fifty "specials," the largest staff of battle reporters in the country. The time had come when Bennett possessed enough money to treat an event as he wished, and the *Herald* spent an unheard-of half a million dollars in covering the war. Whatever he might say editorially, he insisted that news stories contain no bias, and he emphasized accuracy.

The *Tribune* and *Times* each had about twenty correspondents, and they were as capable as the *Herald*'s. Despite their efforts, newspapers did not always get the story right. An erroneous report had the Union forces winning the first Battle of Bull Run; a false story told of the capture of Mobile, and a bogus Lincoln proclamation in May 1864 called for a draft of four hundred thousand men and a day of fasting and prayer.

Before the war began, Bennett called his staff together to discuss its possibilities, and the way the paper should be handled in case it did break out. When Fort Sumter was bombarded, six *Herald* reporters were below the Mason-Dixon line, ready to report the attack. A Southern department was established in the *Herald*'s offices to collect all information that came from the rebel states. The friendliness that Bennett had shown the South for years paid dividends in sources of information.

Less than four months after the shooting erupted, the *Herald* published a list of military forces in different camps of the Southern states. Names and grades of general officers were included. Confederate Secretary of War LeRoy Walker said he could not have been furnished a more correct roster if he had required one. The South believed that someone in authority in Richmond must have provided the information.

Herald correspondents let no means escape for getting the news back to New York. A soldier once entered the *Herald* building, after being released from Libby Prison in Richmond where Bennett's men were confined. He snipped off a hollow button from his uniform and told an editor that a letter was in it. The message was written on tissue paper and described activities in the rebel capital.

In the *Herald*'s office, artists illustrated maps showing topography, routes, troop movements, and men in command. A quarter-page, a half-page, and a full-page map were all used extensively, and no other paper in the country could compete with Bennett's. The war enabled him to add to his list of journalistic "firsts." Casualty lists were published in the *Herald* before anyone else thought of them. Circulation rose as families rushed to read the names, addresses, and regiments of the dead, wounded, and missing. Rosters of the South's military forces appeared in incomplete form until a day in June 1862, when the *Herald* published a full rundown.

The disclosure astounded everyone except *Herald* insiders. Washington was incredulous, and the War Department in Richmond was stunned. Clerks there were arrested and accused of passing the information. The *Tribune* could not understand Bennett's accomplishment and demanded to know by what means he was repeatedly supplied with rebel newspapers inaccessible to everyone else who was loyal in the Union. The explanation was simple. Bennett's Southern department had sought out rebel newspapers, even searching ghost camps and towns, swamps, and contraband for information, and statistics had been compiled from them.

Raymond alone among the big New York publishers participated as a front-line observer. He had reported battles in Europe and was ever eager to learn for himself what was going on. After observing the first Battle of Bull Run, Raymond sent a dispatch from the field, saying that the Union forces were winning. When the tide turned a half hour later, he rode twenty-six miles to Washington to report on the change, but the government censor suppressed the telegram. Raymond pointed out that Gen. Irvin McDowell had wired the government less than two hours before about the defeat. He charged that the government had deliberately suppressed the truth and that it was unfair and unjust for it to compel the press against its will to publish falsehoods instead of facts.

Times correspondents, as did the others, kept detailed lists of expenses. Charges were made for new clothes, feed for horses, mess accounts, and exigencies. Raymond scanned the expenses, striking out those he thought unjustified. One reporter submitted his account for three months' back expenses. Raymond remarked that he had charged for a horse killed under him in battle. The writer explained that he had picked up a roving Confederate nag on the field at no expense to the office. Raymond smiled, scribbled "O.K." on the sheets, and presented him with $300 for the lost horse.

Occasionally, correspondents were arrested. Two *Tribune* reporters were among them. One was Albert Deane Richardson who, just before the first shot of the war, had worked undercover because Greeley's paper was the most hated in the South. Richardson sent letters from Memphis, New Orleans, and other cities in ordinary business forms to bankers in New York for forwarding to the *Tribune*. He and an assistant, Junius Henri Browne, were bombed out of a barge towed by a tugboat and thrown into the water while trying to run the Confederate lines to Vicksburg. They were captured and eventually sent to the Confederate penitentiary at Salisbury, North Carolina, escaping after almost twenty months of imprisonment. For twenty-seven days they dwelled in slave cabins and waded in waist-deep streams before arriving safely in Knoxville, Tennessee. Richardson wired the *Tribune:* "Out of the jaws of death; out of the mouth of hell."[22]

An outstanding correspondent was Henry Villard, whose reporting of the first Battle of Bull Run for the *Herald* and coverage of the fighting at Fredericksburg for the *Tribune* drew accolades. Villard blamed inaccurate reporting of battles on heated competition among correspondents. Following the war, he amassed a fortune in building railroads and bought the New York *Evening Post* and *The Nation.*

In May 1864 the country had heard nothing for a week about Gen. Ulysses Simpson Grant and his one hundred thousand troops fighting the Battle of the Wilderness. Grant consented to let one correspondent take out a report, and the other reporters chose the *Tribune*'s Henry E. Wing. As he departed, Grant gave him a message for Lincoln.

A disguised Wing left on horseback, crossing a river as enemy rifles fired at him. He stranded his horse in the woods and passed by his pursuers. The Confederate cavalry at Manassas Junction detained the "pedestrian" for hours. Wing fled in the night, tramping six miles along the railroad tracks to Bull Run, where he reached the Union lines.

The nearest telegraph station was twenty miles away. Only three hours remained before the *Tribune*'s offices closed. Wing offered $1,000 for a guide and a horse and, once he reached his destination, wired his friend Dana. "Where is Grant?" asked the assistant secretary of war. Wing realized Washington had heard nothing from the general and decided to bargain. He told Dana he would tell the War Department everything in return for permission to send a story to the *Tribune.* Secretary of War Stanton threatened arrest, but the president readily agreed. Wing wired his story to New York.

Washington dispatched a locomotive to pick him up. Wing arrived at the White House and was closeted immediately with Lincoln and the war chiefs. With a map in front of them, Wing described Grant's operations. When the others left the room, Wing told the president he had a personal message from Grant. Lincoln stared kindly at him. "Tell him for me," Grant said, "that, whatever happens, there will be no turning back."

Lincoln was elated. Too many generals had already turned back. Relieved, the president stooped over—and kissed Wing on the forehead.[23]

6

Death Times Three

THE END OF THE WAR saw New York City weakened in population, down 86,000 from the 1860 federal count of its high mark of 805,000. Thousands of residents had died in service, and migration from Europe had dropped sharply during the conflict. Trade was heading north beyond 14th Street along Sixth Avenue, but the publishing industry was not.

After more than twenty years at Fulton and Nassau Streets, the *Herald* moved to a white, marble-front building at Broadway and Ann Streets, at the foot of Park Row. Bennett's opportunity to publish on the nation's busiest street came when fire destroyed Barnum's American Museum three months after the war was over. He gave Barnum a check for $200,000 for the unexpired lease and $450,000 for the land. Bennett was content with the transaction until he read in the *Times* that he had paid the largest price ever in the country for a lot measuring 56 by 100 feet. He believed Barnum had inflated the value of the lease and demanded that the money be returned, but the showman insisted that a deal was a deal.

Bennett retaliated by refusing to accept any more advertisements from Barnum. The showman responded by inducing an association of theatrical and opera managers to cancel its advertising in the *Herald* until the ban was lifted. The paper criticized every play produced by the group during the boycott, which continued for two years. During that time, the *Herald* lost between $75,000 and $100,000 a year.

Park Row was entering its first stage as America's Newspaper Row, and poets sang its praises. The *Tribune, Times, World, Express,* and *Daily News* were also among the dailies on or near Park Row. All of these had been there before the Rebellion, and only one journal had been started during the war. However, before the decade ended, with a permanently successful Atlantic cable in place, almost a dozen new papers arose, many of them evening publications.

Of all the speeches Raymond delivered, the one he regretted most was given in August 1866. His old fault—or virtue—was his ability to see more than one side of a question and his desire to be fair. That led to his political downfall in Philadelphia, when Republicans and Democrats met at a National Union Convention to decide upon a course for the nation. Raymond, chairman of the Republican Party National Committee and a congressman, presented a moderate platform that counseled against vindictive treatment of the South. He defended President Andrew Johnson and declared it unjust to refuse the rebellious states representation in Congress. Raymond antagonized the radical Republicans who wanted to make the South suffer for the war. He said that every state in the land was represented at the meeting to consult on how best to perpetuate the Union.

As Raymond pointed out, Congress had reiterated that, when the war had ceased, all the states should retain their equal rights and dignity unimpaired, yet ten states were still refused representation in Congress: "In other words, a Congress in which only twenty-six States are represented, asserts the right to govern, absolutely and in its discretion, all the thirty-six States which compose the Union. . . . What is there to distinguish the power thus asserted and exercised from the most absolute and intolerable tyranny?"[1]

These were fighting words to the radicals. They became angrier when he urged support for Johnson's postwar efforts for restoration and peace. Newspapers the nation over denounced him and accused him of maneuvering "calculating trimmer" tactics. Thaddeus Stevens, the foremost House radical, had once told Raymond: "You would be worth all the world to us if you would only fight within the lines; but this plan of insisting on marking out your own line of battle is a great mistake. Don't stop there in the cold—come over to us."[2]

Republicans at the convention removed Raymond as chairman and even from the committee. Its extreme members, with Greeley in the vanguard, charged him with aiding the Democratic Party. Raymond's days as an influential politician were over. Readers objected to his championing of Johnson and canceled their subscriptions to the *Times* in droves. The reaction led to Raymond's withdrawing from further candidacy for office in government or party, and to his devoting himself completely to his newspaper.

After a trip to Europe, Raymond devoted his energies toward rebuilding the *Times*. The paper regained its popularity by fighting against easy and unsound money, seeking tariff reform, and campaigning to put the merit system into civil service. Readers liked the conservative, discerning editorials and aggressive news reports. The journal was doing so well that its owners rejected a million-dollar offer for the property at the beginning of 1869.

Shortly before summer Raymond was dead, the victim of apoplexy at the age of forty-nine. He was found lying in the hallway of his home in the early morning of June 18, 1869. John Bigelow, successor to Raymond at the paper, wrote about the death in his diary. He said he had been informed by the Reverend Henry Ward Beecher, who delivered the funeral address, that Raymond had reached his residence on West 9th Street after a visit to the apartment of actress Rose Eytinge.

Times reporter George F. Williams denounced the story as a fabrication. He said that on the night his boss died he had covered a political meeting attended by Raymond. Williams added that after Raymond sent his copy to the office by messenger, he invited Williams to join a party of friends. When it was over, the writer continued, State Senator Samuel Booth, Raymond, and he had gone to the editor's home, and the senator accompanied Raymond to the door.

Obituaries displayed softened attitudes toward Raymond. Greeley no longer thought of him as a "little villain," a trickster, a traitor to principle, devoid of honor and destitute of common honesty. The *Tribune*'s editor wrote: "Never so positive and downright in his convictions as his country-men are apt to be, he was often misjudged as a trimmer and time-server, when in fact he spoke and wrote exactly as he felt and thought. . . . There was nothing in the whole range of newspaper work that he could not do well."[3]

After Raymond's death, Bennett said to George Jones, co-founder of the *Times* and now publisher: "If he had kept out of politics, he would have made the *Times* the leading paper, and would have made hard sledding for the *Herald*."[4]

Bennett decided to give the active handling of the *Herald* to his son, James Gordon Jr., soon after New Year's Day, 1867. But the white-haired father could not entirely keep away from his paper. A telegraph wire was installed at his Fort Washington estate, in upper Manhattan near the Hudson River, so that he would be able to keep on top of news stories. Sometimes he even appeared at the office to talk with his son, who had founded the *Evening Telegram* that year. The elder Bennett occasionally offered suggestions for articles and even dictated editorials, but he now preferred tending his garden to fighting journalistic battles. He had a large collection of birds and a name for each. Henry Wilson, who later became Grant's vice president, was his robin; the woodpecker was General Butler; the goose, Sumner; the owl, Grant.

Bennett was almost seventy-seven and had amassed a fortune of more than $3 million when he died on June 1, 1872, in his Manhattan townhouse on Fifth Avenue. The *Herald* reported the next day that a "slight convulsive attack accompanied by epileptic symptoms" caused his death.

Parke Godwin, William Cullen Bryant's son-in-law and half-owner of the *Evening Post*, wrote in a hostile obituary that it was a mistake to call Bennett a great journalist. Godwin said he was merely a great news vendor and "did more to vulgarize the tone of the press in the United States than any man ever before connected with it."[5] The *World* disagreed; it said that Bennett had left his impress on every journal in the United States, and that he was "the Columbus, the Luther, and the Napoleon of modern journalism."[6]

Although Greeley could not forget his years of fierce rivalry, he was one of the pallbearers when services were held at Bennett's home. He acknowledged Bennett's contribution to the newspaper world and wrote that the Scotsman was the first journalist who went to meet the news halfway, with no other aim than to make a great and lucrative newspaper.

Greeley had little time to ponder his own future after Bennett's death. After Lincoln's assassination, some of Greeley's friends considered him the greatest man in America. Others jested that he was a self-made man who worshipped his creator. Lincoln's successor was not among his strong admirers. When Andrew Johnson was selecting his cabinet, he described the *Tribune*'s founder as "all heart and no head . . . the most vacillating man in the country . . . a sublime old child."[7]

Furor against Greeley rose again in 1867. Jefferson Davis, president of the Confederate States of America, had been imprisoned two years before when he was captured while wearing a woman's wrapper and a shawl. Seeking to avoid further bloodshed, Greeley was among twenty-one men who met at Richmond and signed a bond for $100,000 under which Davis was released. The South praised the editor, astonished to find that the man it hated was a human being and not a devil.

Most of the North was furious and attacked Greeley as if he were a traitor. Sales of his second volume on the war, *The American Conflict*, dropped sharply. In addition, thousands canceled their subscriptions to the *Weekly Tribune*. The Union League Club of New York, which Greeley had helped form during the war as a patriotic move, attempted to expel him, but the effort failed.

The *Tribune* slowly regained some of its lost circulation as the months passed, and anger toward Greeley abated. Not only was he easily identified by his shuffling walk, stooped shoulders, pouch, and white whiskers nestled under his chin, but his name always stood before the public. It forgot his bond-signing and remembered his worthy deeds and eccentricities. People recalled his advice about going West. Towns sprang up bearing his name and that of the *Tribune*. Nathan Cook Meeker, a former agricultural editor of the *Tribune*, started Greeley, Colorado, and operated it as a colony in the Fourierist fashion. Greeley Center and Greeley County, Nebraska, became dots on the map. In Kansas, communities named Tribune and Horace arose, and Greeley County was born. Years later, Kansas old-timers said that the county had named a now-extinct community after Greeley's dog.[8]

The editor still yearned for public office. He lost a bid for the Republican nomination for governor in 1868, was defeated when he ran for state controller the following year, and failed to be elected to Congress in 1870. The Republican Party was split when the Liberal Republican organization was formed to defeat Grant in his bid for a second term in 1872. The liberals sought reform and conciliation in dealing with the South and turned to Greeley as their candidate. The Democratic Party, with which he had fought all his life, also nominated Greeley for the presidency, and he accepted. He had been an ardent Republican since the party's creation and was accused of sacrificing his honor for a presidential potage.

Throughout the summer it seemed that he might defeat Grant. But commercial interests feared his radical background, and the more business became frightened, the smaller were Greeley's chances of winning. All during the campaign he worried about expenses and the *Tribune*. In July his wife returned from Europe an invalid, and she died on October 30, a week before Election Day.

Greeley was pessimistic about capturing the White House. On the eve of the election, he wrote a woman friend, "I am not dead but I wish I were. My house is desolate, my future dark, my heart is a stone. . . . Do not write again till a brighter day which, I fear, may never come."[9]

Greeley's fears proved well-founded. He won only six states, as Grant was returned to office in a landslide. The day after the defeat, Greeley was back at his desk on the second floor of the *Tribune* building. He planned to devote the rest of his life to his newspaper, and he made his intentions known in an editorial published the following day: "The undersigned resumes the Editorship of *The Tribune* which he relinquished on embarking in another line of business six months ago. Henceforth, it shall be his endeavor to make this a thoroughly independent journal, treating all parties and political movements with judicial fairness and candor, but courting the favor and deprecating the wrath of no one."

On the same page appeared another editorial, written by associate John R. G. Hassard and called "Crumbs of Comfort." The *Tribune* was described half humorously as a sort of Federal employment agency, established to get places under government for those who were indisposed to work for their living. . . . Every red-nosed politician who had cheated at the caucus and fought at the polls looked to the editor of *The Tribune* to secure his appointment as gauger, or as army chaplain, or as minister to France. . . . At last we shall keep our office clear of blatherskites and political beggars.[10]

Incensed, Greeley wrote a retraction that described Hassard's editorial as a monstrous fable, but managing editor Whitelaw Reid refused to publish it. The newspaper Greeley had made into one of the nation's most powerful was no longer his. He had given thirty-one years to the *Tribune* but now was little better than other employees. Greeley believed Reid had betrayed him, but the actual conspirator was business manager Samuel Sinclair, who had gained a controlling interest in the *Tribune*.

Once again Greeley spent sleepless nights. After displaying abnormal behavior for more than a week, he was examined by three doctors, including George S. Choate, who agreed that he suffered from acute mania. The next day Greeley was taken to Choate's private asylum for mental patients at Pleasantville, New York, near the editor's Chappaqua farm. He died at the age of sixty-one on November 29.

In little more than three years death had come to the three men who had reshaped the American newspaper and steered it toward the next century. Bennett's accomplishments were many: his gathering and disseminating of news, reporting of stock-market quotations, establishing the first corps of foreign correspondents, covering of religious conventions and synods, and publishing of newsworthy illustrations and war maps. In addition, he had introduced the newspaper interview and investigative reporting, emphasized sports events, and given wider play to crime stories.

Greeley had created a weekly newspaper that was close to being a national publication, something the young nation had not known. He had also molded the daily edition of the *Tribune*, as well as the weekly, into a voice for the people, and the paper was respected even by those who disagreed with some of his more extreme views.

Raymond entrenched himself as the third of the Giants of Park Row with his high editorial principles and objective reporting of news. He set the standards that the *Times* continued to follow for a century and a half.

Bennett, Greeley, and Raymond had brought their newspapers a long way from the days when there were only sixpenny dailies directed to certain classes of limited number. Editors the country over regretted that the day of powerful editors was dead. They feared that personal journalism was gone forever and that readers would no longer refer to newspapers as they had to "Raymond's *Times*," "Bennett's *Herald*," and "Greeley's *Tribune*." Personal journalism was being buried with the past, but one man, Charles Anderson Dana, called their lamentations "twaddle."

7

The "Assassin"

Dana, now editor of the New York *Sun*, read impatiently of the beginning of impersonal journalism and then, one week after Greeley's death, lashed out:

> A great deal of twaddle is uttered by country newspapers just now over what they call personal journalism. . . . Whenever in the newspaper profession a man rises up who is original, strong, and bold enough to make his opinions a matter of consequence to the public there will be personal journalism; and whenever newspapers are conducted only by commonplace individuals whose views are of no interest to the world and of no consequence to anybody there will be nothing but impersonal journalism.[1]

Dana was born in Hinsdale, New Hampshire, on August 8, 1819, the eldest of four children. His father, Anderson Dana, was a modest business-man, but hard times forced him to take the family to Gaines, New York, where he operated a small farm. After his wife, Ann, died of malaria, the children were divided among relatives, and Charles lived with his uncle in the Connecticut River Valley. The boy liked the rhythm of words and wrote verse when he was eight. Latin fascinated him, as did other strange sounds. All during his life he would utter them—until the day came when he could converse in at least half a dozen languages.

His family did not have much money, and at the age of twelve Charles worked in a relative's dry-goods store in Buffalo. He pursued Latin and Greek at night and later attended Harvard University. To earn expenses, he became a schoolteacher in Scituate, Massachusetts, for a year. Because his eyes had been seriously weakened in reading by candlelight, and because of a lack of funds, he left college after two years.

Transcendentalism and the Brook Farm Association in West Roxbury, Massachusetts, appealed to Dana. He was inspired by the literary power and oratorical eloquence of this intellectual community's leaders. He favored the association's aspiration for the uniting of manual labor and knowledge to improve humankind. Dana taught German and Greek at Brook Farm and at one point was the group's chairman of the council of finance. A community publication, the *Harbinger,* provided Dana with his first opportunity to write. While at Brook Farm, he met aspiring actress Eunice MacDaniel, and they were married in New York City in 1846. On their return to Brook Farm, they discovered that a fire had destroyed the central building, the Phalanastery, and doomed the experiment.

That year Dana became assistant editor of the Congregational newspaper in Boston, the *Daily Chronotype,* at $4 a week. In the meanwhile, he corresponded with Greeley, whom he had met at Brook Farm, and this led to his being hired in 1847 as the *Tribune*'s city editor at $10 a week.

Trouble splattered the Old World air, and Dana went to Europe in 1848. He arrived in Paris after King Louis Philippe had been overthrown in a revolution and a republican government established. After his return the following year, he became Greeley's first managing editor. Dana was still the idealist, seeking to improve the world and believing the path to accomplishment lay in aggressive action. Meanwhile, he prospered as his salary rose to $50 a week and he gained possession of $10,000 in *Tribune* shares that Greeley relinquished.

The more powerful Dana became on the paper, the less Greeley approved. While Greeley concerned himself primarily with writing editorials, Dana assumed the burden of management. When they clashed during the Civil War, Greeley told stockholders that he would leave the *Tribune* if Dana did not. That was the end of Dana's fifteen-year career with the paper.

Secretary of War Edwin M. Stanton gave Dana a job checking claims against the quartermaster's department at Cairo, Illinois. He later was sent to investigate stories of Grant's excessive drinking and became a special commissioner probing the pay system of the Western armies. Dana quietly reported to Stanton and accompanied Grant during the Vicksburg campaign. His reward was an appointment as assistant secretary of war, in which capacity he served from 1863 to 1865.

Shortly after the war ended, Dana became editor of the Chicago *Daily Republican,* a newly founded paper. The journal was to be capitalized at $500,000, but the money did not materialize. Dana struggled for a year, then returned to New York, determined to buy or launch his own publication in the big city.

In 1868 Moses Sperry Beach sold the *Sun,* which possessed an Associated Press franchise, to Dana and his associates for $175,000. They included U.S. Senators Roscoe Conkling and Edwin D. Morgan, former Mayor George Opdyke, William M. Evarts, Thomas Hitchcock, and Cyrus W. Field. The paper circulated mainly among mechanics and small merchants.

Earlier, Dana and his colleagues paid $220,000 for the four-story building Tammany Hall had occupied since 1811 at the corner of Nassau and Frankfort Streets. The structure overlooked Printing House Square, and its location was ideal for Dana's purposes. Park Row was convenient and contiguous to almost all places of commercial importance in New York. The area between Canal Street and the Battery and the East and North Rivers was called the counting house of the continent. Plans, furthermore, had been made to erect a new post office in the City Hall Park grounds opposite Park Row, providing newspapers with speedier facilities for distribution.

Dana moved slowly at first, contemplating many changes. His aims were disclosed on January 27, the first day the paper was issued under the new management. He said the *Sun* would have all the news, foreign, domestic, political, social, literary, scientific, and commercial. Furthermore, wrote Dana, it would use enterprise and money freely to make the best possible paper as well as the cheapest. The daily would study condensation and clearness and present the world's doings in a lively manner: "It will not take as long to read the *Sun* as to read the London Times or Webster's Dictionary, but when you have read it, you will know about all that has happened in both hemispheres."[2]

Dana added that the *Sun*'s circulation was more than fifty thousand daily and that he planned to double it soon.

A vote of confidence for the new editor came from the *Sun*'s founder, Benjamin Day: "Dana'll make a great paper of it!"[3] Dana was an iconoclast, just as Bennett the Elder had been, and he ordered his staff to "stir up the animals." But some of the *Herald* creator's ways repelled him. He forbade the spice, salaciousness, and offensiveness that had marked the old *Herald.* There were four children in the Dana family, and everything published in the *Sun,* no matter how sensational, must be fit for them to read.

Dana injected something new in his journal—something Bennett had never thought of, something Greeley had not cared about, something Raymond had been too busy to consider: a literary style. He wanted to leave the reader feeling that the writing was beautiful. Brevity was stressed in news articles and editorials. He demanded accuracy in his news and philosophy and wit in the editorials. He also sought men who could write and had imagination.

Tough, rough Amos Jay Cummings went to work for Dana some months after he had taken over the *Sun.* Cummings, a substitute printer on the *Tribune,* had been discharged from the Union Army a day before the draft riot and was one of four compositors in the building who did not flee when it was mobbed. He became editor of the paper's weekly edition and political writer for its daily. But an insubordinate reply to an order against profanity issued by John Russell Young, the *Tribune*'s managing editor, resulted in his dismissal. He showed up at the *Sun*'s office, and Dana asked why he had left the paper. "They say I swear too much," said Cummings. "Just the man for me!" replied Dana.[4]

Cummings became managing editor. He knew how to handle men, was aware of what Dana wanted, and respected his opinions. Almost overnight, the news articles had a greater sparkle. Cummings's irascible temper flared at work that did not meet his standards. Under him, the "human interest" story—the pathetic, emotional, or amusing twist of everyday existence— blossomed as never before. The *Sun* also became the people's paper, ready to stand by the working men, the trade unions, and movements for the improvement of conditions when the masses needed support.

Exposure of scandals and frauds was the *Sun*'s specialty and helped to increase the *Sun*'s sales. Dana sought out public idols whom he could hold up to his readers and destroy. President Grant was one of the targets. The editor thought Grant was the nation's greatest soldier, and during his first presidential campaign, Dana vigorously urged his election. Within days after the inauguration, however, the paper turned on the chief executive over his selections for the Cabinet. Enemies charged that Dana was disappointed in Grant's failure to appoint him collector of customs for the Port of New York. The editor hotly denied the accusation, retorting that the president had fumbled in his Cabinet choices.

Treasury Secretary George S. Boutwell offered Dana the position of appraiser in the customhouse the following month. In a letter that appeared in the *Sun,* Dana told Boutwell he did not want to abandon a superior position for one of lesser importance, and that he could do more by remaining at the paper and exposing political immorality.

The *Sun*'s stockholders resented the attack upon Grant, but Dana controlled a majority of the paper's shares. A showdown established him as ruler of the *Sun.*

Grant's installation sparked the greatest blaze of corruption and bribery the government had known. Hardly had the Washington swindlers begun operations, however, when New York City itself became the scene of a panic. Wall Street speculators Jay Gould and James Fisk Jr. had connived to become acquainted with Grant's brother-in-law, Abel Rathbone Corbin, so that they might convince the president to raise the price of gold.

The *Sun,* as did other dailies, scented the scandal before September 24,

1869, the day of infamy later known as Black Friday. "This is one of the most immoral and pernicious conspiracies ever contracted in Wall Street," Dana wrote.[5] The scheme panicked Wall Street, with hundreds of investors ruined. The excitement was halted only when Grant ordered that $4 million of the Treasury's $100 million in gold bullion be sold.

Dana at first refused to believe that Grant was implicated in the plot. As the Washington scandals increased, he changed his mind. The *Sun* published an article on the secret history of the conspiracy and the "Welchers in Wall Street," but it was pulled out of the paper after only ten thousand copies had been run. Both Bennett the Elder and Greeley had been accused of taking bribes, and now the charge was pinned on Dana. It was made by Col. James B. Mix, a *Tribune* reporter who had been captain of Lincoln's bodyguards. The accusation came in a pamphlet *The Biter Bit.* It claimed to be a narrative of Dana's blackmailing operations on the *Sun,* including the "welcher" article.

Dana criticized Greeley for having a man like Mix on his staff. He struck out at the *Tribune* for publishing "abominable falsehoods" about payoffs to current or former *Sun* employees. Dana denied he had ever received a bribe and said Greeley knew him well enough to know that no amount of money could influence him politically or affect the management of his paper.

Dana charged in a signed editorial that the pamphlet was an attempt to injure the *Sun.* He explained that "The Welchers in Wall Street" never ran its full course in the paper because he discovered that the parties whom it attacked were merely of secondary importance. He insisted that "the President of the United States was in the conspiracy, and—as any sensible man would do—I determined to go after higher game." Dana called Mix a blackmailer and said that Greeley and Young were among those involved in the publication: ". . . Mr. Greeley is a Universalist, and believes that nobody will ever go to Hell, or he could not have been tempted to stand godfather to the anonymous libel of two scoundrels and one thief."[6]

Another scandal also stirred that would fleece New York City of millions of dollars. It was the doings of the Ring, operated by "Boss" William Marcy Tweed and his Tammany gang. They swept city elections in 1868, putting in A. Oakey "Elegant" Hall as mayor. Tweed was also instrumental in electing John T. Hoffman as governor. The *Sun* joined reformer Samuel J. Tilden in an attempt to stop the Ring by blocking a proposed charter. But Tweed rammed the city charter through the state legislature early in April 1870, after which there was no holding the Ring.

A change came over Dana, and his attitude turned into one of mockery

toward the gang: "We say that Boss Tweed is the proper man for the Democracy to run for Governor next fall. . . . a great man; rich, generous, without
prejudices, spending freely the piles of money he extracts from the public
treasury, making his friends wealthy."[7]

The Ring created a board of special audit with unlimited power to approve
all claims against the city, and its members included Hall, Commissioner of
Public Works Tweed, and Controller Richard "Slippery Dick" Connally.
Although not on the board, another Ring member, Peter Barr Sweeny, was
appointed commissioner of public parks, and the *Sun* derisively described
him as Peter Brains Sweeny.

It was difficult to determine when Dana was serious. Less than a month
after the November 1870 election, the paper proposed that a statue of Tweed
be erected in Tweed Plaza and that contributions be sent to the journal. One
person sent in ten cents for the monument, adding that he had no doubt
that fifty thousand to seventy-five thousand of Tweed's admirers would also
contribute money. A few days later, however, the *Sun* wondered whether he
had any friends. It said that only four citizens had donated anything since
the daily made the appeal more than a week before.

Cohorts of Tweed, including Hall, did pick up the proposal. They formed
a "Trustees of the Tweed Monument Fund" and decided that Central Park
would be a more fitting place for the statue. The paper objected to that
locale, saying that if it had not been for the *Sun,* the idea of erecting such a
tribute would never have been realized. Tweed himself resolved the question
of the site for the monument by declining the honor. He said that he was
"aware that a newspaper of our city had brought forward the proposal, but I
considered it one of the jocose sensations for which that journal is so famous."[8] The *Sun* printed the letter on the front page with the heading "A
GREAT MAN'S MODESTY."

The Ring realized the power of the press. Whenever it was attacked by a
newspaper, city advertising flowed to that journal to keep it quiet. Between
January 1, 1869, and the end of June 1871, more than $2.7 million was paid
to papers in the city. Some evening journals received a subsidy of a thousand
dollars a month. Besides major dailies, weeklies were also silenced with
bribes, and at one time eighty-seven periodicals were paid to publish the
city's official proceedings. These papers included the *Sun, Tribune, Herald,
World, Staats-Zeitung, Democrat, Star, Express, Commercial Advertiser,* and
News.

Of all the publications in New York, only *Harper's Weekly* fought the
Tweed gang from the start. Its cartoonist Thomas Nast, creator of the Demo-

cratic donkey and the Republican elephant, relentlessly aimed his arrows at the corrupt regime. In a blast at the Boss, Nast drew the dreaded Tammany Tiger.

Times publisher George Jones did little against the Ring while James B. Taylor remained alive. Taylor was Raymond's replacement on the *Times*'s directorate and also one of Tweed's partners in the New York Printing Company. He died early in September 1870, and then, with Jones in charge and Louis Jennings as managing editor, the *Times* slowly became an ally of *Harper's Weekly.* Its attack started with "We should like to have a treatise from Mr. Tweed on the art of growing rich in as many years as can be counted on the fingers of one hand."[9]

The *Times* ceaselessly attacked Tweed or other Ring members. It criticized Hoffman's association with Tweed, chided Tilden when he seemed to take the side of the Boss or his confederates, and ripped into different newspapers as they apparently defended the gang. As the *Times* hammered at the Ring, the *Sun* charged that it was doing so because it no longer had city advertising. The *Times* replied that for six months or so after Dana had taken over the *Sun,* he made it respectable, but then "an impostor appeared upon the scene, and under the name of CHARLES ASSASSIN DANA, began abusing every respectable man in the community, from the President downward. This paid at first, but the public soon grew tired of 'blackguardism.' "

The *Times* added that the *Sun,* which it called the "Daily Scamp," was considered a disgrace in every respectable household. It said that Dana caused it to be known that he had thirty or forty paragraphs abusing *Times* staff members:

> Lies can hurt no man—but when it can be said with truth of a journalist that he has wantonly defamed private character, and turned his paper into an instrument of levying black-mail, and sacrificed every honorable friendship he possessed, and earned the distinction of telling more untruths in a more cowardly fashion than any man alive—then indeed his story points a very sad moral.[10]

Despite its daily denunciations against the Ring, the *Times* could not prove its charges. A breakthrough came when Matthew J. O'Rourke, a recently appointed county bookkeeper, and William Copeland, an employee in the city's auditing department, resigned their posts in June 1871. They were loaded with facts and figures about the Ring's corruption.

Former Sheriff James O'Brien, working with Tilden in fighting the gang, appeared at the *Sun*'s offices that month, armed with some of the transcribed documents. Dana was out of the building, and Thomas Hitchcock, a *Sun* stockholder and writer of financial articles, refused the papers. O'Brien gave his evidence to Jennings at the *Times* and two days later provided more proof of corruption. When Tweed learned that the *Times* possessed the damning data, the Ring was shaken. Connolly offered Jones $5 million to suppress the articles, but Jones replied, "I don't think the devil will ever make a higher bid for me than that."[11]

For three weeks, starting on July 8, the *Times* ran the incriminating evidence. On one occasion it published a front-page, three-column story, "The Secret Accounts." Since those were the days of primarily one-column headlines, the appearance startled readers. On the final day of the series, the *Times* issued a special, four-page supplement giving all the data that it had accumulated. Two full pages were printed in German for those who could read only in that language.

Indignation soared with each edition of the *Times* disclosing the frauds. A Committee of Seventy, with Tilden in charge, investigated the corruption. Months passed before the Ring was destroyed. Hall and Connolly deserted Tweed and cooperated with the crime fighters. Among the Ring members, only the Boss served time behind bars. After escaping from prison, Tweed was returned to New York from Spain and died in Ludlow Street Jail on April 12, 1878. The next day the *Sun* wrote, "Tweedism will long survive Tweed, and the blindness, the ignorance, and the cowardice that gave him his lease of power are even now contributing to the elevation of men as ignoble in character and base in their methods as was the man who died yesterday."[12]

The blackmail charge against Dana did not hurt the *Sun*. In addition, he claimed that his paper and not the *Times* deserved credit for ending the Ring's power. The *Times*, however, wrote almost a year later that the *Herald*, *Sun*, and *Express* "supported Tammany through thick and thin, denied and laughed at the evidence of the Tammany frauds, and were ultimately obligated to eat their own words."[13]

As time dimmed the *Times*'s feat, the *Herald* achieved a breathtaking personal success, without the assistance of its long-time managing editor, Frederic Hudson. He had retired after the younger Bennett, known as the "Commodore," took over active management in 1867. Hudson received a $20,000 annual pension on condition that he do no more newspaper work. The paper was the pride of Bennett Jr. Besides the millions his father had left him, the paper brought him a reported $750,000 a year.

The Commodore was the sole authority on the paper, and his employees had to remember that. Writers did not impress him, and he refused to pay large salaries to his editorial staff. "All the brains I want can be picked up any day at twenty-five dollars per week," he told a reporter seeking a pay increase.[14] Bennett, however, refused to fire staff members, although they could be suspended for misconduct. If the paper lost a libel suit, the writer would have his salary reduced until it equaled the amount of the judgment. One reporter resigned rather than spend the next seven years and five months paying the amount of such a judgment.

Bennett had seen the *Herald*'s tremendous success achieved by the emphasis upon news. If it meant spending thousands of dollars to get a good story, he had the money to spend. He also believed that world news coverage was vital to a paper's welfare.

One of the reporters he hired was Henry Morton Stanley. Bennett wired him in Madrid to arrange a meeting in Paris. Dr. David Livingstone, a Scottish explorer and missionary, was lost in Central Africa. The British were concerned about his fate, as was the rest of the world. Little, however, was being done to locate him. Bennett directed Stanley, "Draw a thousand pounds now, and when you have gone through that, draw another thousand, and when that is spent, draw another thousand, and when you have finished that, draw another thousand, and so on; but find LIVINGSTONE."[15]

The search started in October 1869 and ended in November 1871, when Stanley approached a man in Ujiji and asked, "Dr. Livingstone, I presume?" It took a long time for the news to get out of dark Africa. Not until July 1872 was the world made aware of Stanley's success. Bennett had achieved something almost unprecedented in journalism: the making of news rather than waiting for it to happen.

Dana attempted to crush Bennett's high spirits by publishing a lengthy letter from Lewis H. Noe of Sayville, Long Island, in which doubts were cast on Stanley's discovery. Noe and Stanley had known each other in the U.S. Navy. Noe called the correspondent a thief, forger, and blackguard. He said Stanley had beaten him on his bare back with a whip and threatened to kill him if he disclosed his infamy. Noe conceded he did not know if the reporter had found Livingstone but said Stanley had the ingenuity to fabricate a plausible story. To make matters worse, Sir Henry Rawlinson, president of the Royal Geographic Society, doubted Stanley's discovery.

The *Herald* published facsimiles of letters with Livingstone's signature that Stanley had sent Bennett, but the *Sun* refused to admit it had been in error. It said Bennett had furnished the facsimiles to Dana and that they had been compared with Stanley's letters to Noe. A front-page banner read, "IS STANLEY ANYTHING BUT A FRAUD?"[16]

Rawlinson, meanwhile, changed his mind, and his society passed a vote of thanks to Stanley. Queen Victoria received Stanley and gave him a gold snuffbox. The great, exclusive story almost immediately boosted the *Herald*'s circulation to one hundred thousand.

While the Livingstone question was at its height, Grant waged his reelection campaign in 1872. The *Sun* charged that William D. Farrand had paid Grant's brother-in-law Lewis Dent $2,500 to be appointed consul in Peru and that Grant had made the appointment.

Dana ostensibly was a staunch supporter of Greeley for president, primarily because of his detestation of the corruption and nepotism in Grant's first administration. Dana pointed out that, when Benjamin Franklin's statue was erected in Printing House Square some months before, he had proposed that a statue also stand there to honor his former employer, whom he called "our Later Franklin." A subscription was undertaken, but not enough money was collected.

Editorial-page headlines during the summer described the *Tribune*'s editor as "The Great and Good USEFUL H. GREELEY," "Office-Holders's Candidate," "Honest Horace Greeley," "Anti-Stealing Candidate," "The Candidate of Peace," and "Workingmen's Candidate." Dana also wrote of "The Doom of Grantism," but his efforts on Greeley's behalf were of no avail. When Grant won the election, a *Sun* story warned, "Four More Years of Fraud and Corruption."[17]

Scandals continued to flood the *Sun*'s pages, and Dana was Grant's most ferocious critic. The Navy Department sold business openly to contractors; tax gatherers, approved by the Treasury Department, profited out of uncollected taxes; land robbers exploited the Interior Department, and millions in excise taxes were stolen from the government. One outrage that the *Sun* exposed involved the construction of a transcontinental railroad. The Credit Mobilier company had been created to build the Union Pacific Railroad, and many members of Congress were permitted to buy shares at bargain prices. The *Sun*, under the heading "The King of Frauds," revealed that the company had bought its way through Congress.

Dana's campaigns to expose governmental fraud almost backfired on one occasion. "Boss" Alexander Shepherd of Washington, enraged by a *Sun* exposure, attempted to have Dana indicted for criminal libel in the nation's capital. A handpicked magistrate was set to try the editor without a jury, and an order for his arrest was issued. But Judge Samuel Blatchford of the U.S.

Circuit Court in New York vacated the directive. He ruled that the Supreme Court of the District of Columbia had no jurisdiction in issuing Dana a subpoena to appear before it.

With freedom of the press involved, rival newspapers in the city came to Dana's defense. He was effusive in praise of the opposition's assistance, especially that of the *Times, Tribune, Evening Post,* and *Herald,* and said that to his dying day he could never forget their support: ". . . all petty and despicable jealousies and rivalries are buried deep in the strong current of the Brotherhood of the Press—the Brotherhood Representation of the Rights of the People."[18]

Beautiful words quickly forgotten. That same day the *Sun* attacked the *Tribune* in another column for advertising itself as the "leading American newspaper."

Newspaper editors across the country began to speak of Dana as they had of the elder Bennett, Greeley, and Raymond. He had brought the *Sun's* circulation to more than one hundred thousand, and readers believed Dana wrote everything appearing in his paper. He was original, strong, and bold, although he could not provide the powerful editorials Greeley had given the nation. The *Tribune's* editor had attained his journalistic height during the Civil War, his talents discovered in much the same way that crises reveal the greatness of presidents.

The *Sun,* without an event of such magnitude, produced editorials of lesser impact. But in their concise, skillfully written fashion, they fascinated the reader, and only Dana's erratic manner of changing viewpoints prevented the paper from becoming a great force. As for his news stories, they could not compare with those that had made the *Herald's* the most enviable in the country, but Dana succeeded in his own way.

The "*Sun* story" became a common appellation among newspaper people. The old-time lead that contained flowery language but little information vanished. Writers condensed the important facts of a story, and those who padded a story merely for length's sake were unwelcome at the *Sun.* The paper contained only four pages, and the main job of keeping articles sharp and short fell to night editor Dr. John B. Wood, known on Newspaper Row as the "Great American Condenser," because of his ability to trim surplus words from copy.

When Abraham Oakey Hall was mayor of New York, he announced that he would not receive visitors as usual on New Year's Day, 1871. The *Sun,* in a merry mood, published one of the most unusual front pages in American journalism. A fanciful story—whimsical, mocking, satirical, and biting—

described a steady stream of distinguished visitors pouring into the City Hall reception room that day. Forty-three caricatures of prominent people, with descriptions, were spread across the page.

Greeley was one of the targets, and the *Sun* wrote that he had presented the mayor with a "monstrous carrot, grown on his Chappaqua farm, and a scrapbook containing his fifty-two papers entitled 'What I Know About Farming.' " Another was Commodore Bennett, "the jolly tar of the *Herald* . . . whose flipper was tipped." The paper added that the mayor, whom it called Abraham O'Hall, spotted Jay Gould sliding down the banisters. The most demeaning and undeserved description was that of Whitelaw Reid of the *Tribune*, whose propensity for fancy attire irked Dana. The *Sun* wrote that the mayor saw Reid

> in men's clothing. The Mayor recognized her at once. . . . Seeing Capt. Thorpe at the corner . . . he beckoned to him. . . . "I want you to arrest her," said Mr. O'Hall, pointing to Whitelaw. . . .
>
> "Well, well," answered the Captain; "she's a harmless little thing, but duty is duty. She's no business in men's clothing, and law is law." . . .
>
> Whitelaw was afterward released at the request of her friend Mr. Greeley.[19]

Dana made the newspaper business a profession and the *Sun* a school of journalism. He was as much an autocrat in directing his journal as Bennett with the *Herald*, and the views of the staff were Dana's. Although he did not approve of bylines, he praised a reporter whenever a good story was turned in and encouraged individuality in work. The *Sun* became the office where good writing was the common factor, and a millionaire, a socialist, a poet, and a lawyer could labor together harmoniously. Its writers acquired a reputation on Park Row as a happy family.

Dana wanted his reporters to write the facts without embellishment. "The reporter," he said, "wields the real power of the press," and when one grumbled that he was kept on police-court work, he retorted, "Young man, the greatest police-court reporter who ever lived was named Charles Dickens."[20] When another complained that his story had been cut too much, Dana replied, "The story of the crucifixion was told in six hundred words."[21]

Dana wanted his news gatherers "to tell the truth always so as to shame the devil every time."[22] He demanded the same kind of attention paid to the editing of the *Sun:* "You've got to square this paper with God Almighty and the judgment day every day you live; and that's the only way to edit a paper."[23]

Dana was always attacking someone, and the *Sun* did it with laughter, satire, and bitterness. He spiced humor with controversy as another means of building the *Sun*'s circulation.

He pitted one religion against another in such a subtle manner that there would be little offense but much discussion. But the Roman Catholic population was growing in New York, and often his paper seemed entirely pro-Catholic, to the annoyance of Protestants. Such an occasion occurred on July 12, 1871, when the Catholic Irish rioted against the Orangemen parading in New York, despite militiamen, and fifty-four persons were killed.

The Reverend Henry Ward Beecher experienced the *Sun*'s sharp editorial knife. Beecher was accused of adultery, and the paper was overjoyed. A church investigation exonerated the minister, but Dana was dissatisfied and demanded a court trial by jury. The *Sun* assailed the Brooklyn pastor without letup, and every savage attack against the minister meant a loss of several thousand sales, but the criticism continued. When Beecher was tried in court, the case ended in a jury disagreement.

The New York Post Office, called by the *Sun* "the great distributing office for the continent," opened its new building at the southern tip of City Hall Park in August 1875. It faced the newspapers that decorated Park Row and Printing House Square. Earlier that year, Park Row had been glamorized with the completion of the new *Tribune* edifice. It was ready for occupancy on the thirty-fourth anniversary of the paper's birth. Ten stories and 260 feet high, it towered above everything in the city except Trinity Church, with its 286-foot structure.

The former *Tribune* building—"the old rookery," Park Row called it—had looked decrepit compared with the impressive *Times* and *Herald* establishments. By erecting the new structure, the paper's owners had decided to dispel all rumors that the *Tribune* would soon cease publication.

The admired building became known as the "Tall Tower," and passersby used its huge clock as a beacon. On the eighth floor, where Reid kept a luxurious suite, a sign conspicuously advertised the *Tribune* as "The Leading American Newspaper," although its circulation was barely fifty thousand. In disregard of the habits of the late Greeley, a saloon operated in the basement for all of the journal's employees, but police shut it down within months. The *Times* called the impressive building a sugar refinery, and the *Sun* recommended that the *Tribune* utilize the suggestion by adding to "The Leading American Newspaper" the words "and Sugar Refinery." Dana and his crew attacked Reid almost daily in a ridiculing and satiric style. The *Sun*'s chief taunted Reid as the "young editor of the tall tower" and the "young editor with the powerful mind."

Dana resented Reid from the time he had replaced him as managing editor of the *Tribune*. Shortly after Greeley's death, Reid had obtained the majority of stock in the paper with the financial aid of Jay Gould and become its editor and publisher. Dana claimed that, although the *Tribune*'s editor possessed 51 percent of the paper's stock, Gould held the mortgage, and, therefore, Reid was only the nominal owner and a stool pigeon for the manipulator. The *Sun* accused the *Tribune* of being used to support Gould in his stock-gambling machinations: "All Wall street knows this; it is palpable to anyone who follows the course of the stock market. The young editor up in his tall tower is his silly tool."[24]

Success changed Dana. In his youth he had been idealistic, seeking to make the world better for the downtrodden classes. His years with Brook Farm, the *Tribune*, and the war had molded him so that he was concerned about people without power to speak for themselves. Even in his first years with the *Sun*, his sympathies lay in that direction. "I'm half a communist myself," he told editorial-page writer John Swinton, an ardent labor sympathizer.[25]

During those early years with the *Sun*, Dana had supported progressive education for women and women's suffrage. It pleased readers when the *Sun* condemned inequities against the masses, although Dana offered no crusading remedy. He railed against the income tax as "unequal and inquisitional," and he favored Cuba's insurgents fighting for independence from Spain. But his faith in human nature changed as the *Sun* grew more prosperous. Not only did the radicalism of his youth fade, but he now attacked coeducation, often criticized civil-service-reform bills, and hooted at women seeking to vote.

Samuel Tilden's fight against the Tweed Ring had won him Dana's respect, and with the *Sun*'s aid, he became governor of New York. In 1876 Tilden opposed Rutherford Birchard Hayes for the presidency. Marked by widespread polling irregularities, it was the only disputed presidential election in American history. Dana refused to believe that Hayes had won legitimately. When Hayes visited New York in May 1877 for the first time after the election, the *Sun* stamped the word "Fraud" across his forehead in an illustration. Readers became angry at the *Sun*'s constant references to Hayes as "The Fraudulent President," and again subscriptions were canceled. Circulation dropped from a daily average of 127,000 to 106,000 before *Sun* followers returned.

The *Sun* produced more popular slogans than any other paper in the country. Not all were written by Dana, but the public quickly took them up.

Dana was not surprised when circulation dropped as a result of some of the phrases, and he was even less surprised when readers resumed buying his paper. When "Honest" John Kelly, boss of Tammany Hall, tried in 1878 to elect Augustus Schell as mayor, the *Sun* helped defeat him with a catchphrase by William O. Bartlett, "No King, No Clown to Rule This Town."[26]

Gen. Winfield Scott Hancock might have won the presidential election of 1880 against James Abram Garfield, but a single sentence in the *Sun* helped defeat him. An editorial apparently praising Hancock's virtues referred to him as a "good man, weighing two hundred and fifty pounds."[27] The country did not know if the *Sun* had meant that as a recommendation for Hancock or whether Dana was mocking him. As the phrase spread across the land, the roar of laughter grew louder, and Garfield became the nation's twentieth president.

The *Sun* was on the upsweep, with the largest circulation in the nation. Readers appreciated Dana's independent reporting of politics and intellectual approach to journalism. The paper's future greatness seemed assured, but no one counted on Dana to assassinate another beloved figure, Grover Cleveland. And no one foresaw the presence in New York of Joseph Pulitzer. He would dethrone Dana as Park Row's overlord and upset him as no other editor had done since his purchase of the *Sun*.

8
Wonder of *The World*

NEWSPAPERS MARKED TIME, more or less, in the period that followed the Civil War, but that era ended as New York City took a major leap toward the modern age. With the arrival especially of increased numbers of Irish, German, Jewish, and Italian immigrants, the appearance and cultural character of the city began to undergo profound changes during the transitional decade of the 1880s. It was also a period when the predatory activities of corporate robber barons were little curtailed. Those who wanted to boost their personal wealth at the expense of the masses continued to manipulate Washington. In addition, the United States was becoming more internationally minded.

Fifty years after Benjamin Day launched the first successful penny paper, the name of Park Row strummed upon the heartstrings of ambitious writers. Newsmen wandering in the hinterlands could obtain a job without much difficulty by uttering the magic words "I worked for the New York *Sun.*" Poet Eugene Field, a contributor to the *Sun,* penned a laudation to its Jovian-looking editor that ended with:

> But bless ye, Mr. Dana! May you live a thousan' years,
> To sort of keep things lively in this vale of human tears;
> An' may *I* live a thousan', too,—thousan' less a day,
> For I should n't like to be on earth to hear you'd passed away.
> And when it comes your time to go you'll need no Latin chaff
> Nor biographic data put in your epitaph;
> But one straight line of English and of truth will let folks know
> The homage 'nd the gratitude 'nd reverence they owe;
> You'll need no epitaph but this: "Here sleeps the man who run
> That best 'nd brightest paper, the Noo York Sun."[1]

From Ann Street to Tryon Row, home of the greatest German-language daily in the United States, more newspapers were clustered in the Park Row sector than anywhere else on earth. Powerful and impotent journals cuddled so closely that the roar of one paper's presses could be mistaken for another's.

The *Sun*'s circulation, at 150,000, was the highest in the nation in 1883, but no paper in the nation was as financially successful as the *Herald,* and no paper published as much news. It continued to create news and publish it exclusively, stressed sailing and polo on the sports pages, and played up theatrical, social, and real-estate news more than other dailies. Europeans believed the *Herald* represented America.

Bennett had lived mainly in Europe for six years, after breaking up with his fiancée and dueling with her brother in 1877. He had homes not only in New York and Newport but also in Paris and on the Riviera, where he hosted royalty and nobility, at home and aboard his yacht.

Bryant, the Nestor of New York journalism, had died in 1878, at the age of eighty-three. For half a century he had edited the liberal *Evening Post*, which had little circulation but was respected profoundly by the intelligentsia. The new owner was multimillionaire Henry Villard, the Civil War correspondent, and its editor in chief was Irish-born Edwin Lawrence Godkin, founder of *The Nation*. His editorials proved as penetrating as any since Greeley's day. Godkin increased the paper's number of pages while reducing the size, but the circulation remained virtually static. On the day of the change, Dana wrote that the *Evening Post* would be dull in eight pages instead of four.

Other men invaded Park Row as newspaper owners. One was Albert Pulitzer, a former writer on the *Sun* and the *Herald*. He founded the *Morning Journal* in November 1882 and received a little financial aid from his brother Joseph, publisher of the *St. Louis Post-Dispatch*. The *Journal*, housed in the *Tribune* building, competed as a one-cent sheet against the *Daily News* for circulation among the tenement classes.

The *Sun's* circulation gains hurt the *World*, and owner-editor Manton Marble sold the paper to a group headed by Thomas A. Scott, president of the Pennsylvania Railroad. Jay Gould and Scott were arranging a railroad deal in 1879 when the financially ailing *World* was added to the package. Gould erected a new building at 31–32 Park Row to house his acquisition.

American journalism had seen few revolutionary changes since the days of the elder Bennett. Most of the New York papers, however, now published news articles on the front page, although most headlines were single column. Only the Commodore continued to devote the first page to advertisements. If stories were important, the headline would be followed with banks until they covered more than half a column. Illustrations and political cartoons were rare in dailies, and only when aroused would an editor as bold as Dana publish one. However, one New York newspaper, the *Daily Graphic*, differed from the others. Begun in 1873, it was the pioneer illustrated tabloid in America.

Dana had proven in fifteen years as *Sun* editor to be the heir to the men who had been towers of Park Row's personal journalism. The *Sun* shone for all and was acclaimed the country's "newspaperman's newspaper." But the situation began to change on May 10, 1883, for on that day the *World* no longer belonged to Gould but to Joseph Pulitzer, who had never known the meaning of tradition.

Pulitzer was born in Mako, Hungary, on April 10, 1847, one of four children of Philip and Louise Pulitzer. Although both parents were Jewish, Joseph never corrected the reports that his father was a Magyar Jew and his mother an Austro-German Roman Catholic. The family moved to Budapest where the father, a retired grain dealer, died when his son was seventeen. The youth yearned for military excitement, but his physique was poor and his eyesight defective. The Austrian Army, the French Foreign Legion, and the British Army rejected him. Finally, a recruiting agent for America's Union troops in the Civil War saw him in Hamburg and provided passage to the United States. He jumped overboard at Boston, swam ashore, and went on to New York.

Pulitzer enlisted in the army for a year in September 1864, joining the Lincoln Cavalry. He was six feet two, but his ailments, hooked nose, and jittery motions made him the butt of jokes. After the war ended, Pulitzer was mustered out in New York. He had earned thirteen dollars a month, and his money was almost gone. He joined the ranks of unemployed veterans who warmed themselves around the potbellied stove in the lobby of French's Hotel on Park Row. One day, however, a porter threw him out of the hotel.

Pulitzer spoke German and French fluently, but his English was poor. Someone suggested that he go to St. Louis as the best place to improve it. He managed to arrive in Missouri, but finding work was not easy. He walked the streets because he had no money to pay his landlady.

Pulitzer had two loves: books and chess. He visited a small German saloon in St. Louis where he could play chess. One opponent was Dr. Emil Preetorius who, with Carl Schurz, edited the German newspaper, the *Westliche Post*. Preetorius hired Pulitzer as a reporter at ten dollars a week. Ever ambitious, Pulitzer tried to run the whole shop. He wrote editorials and news, set type, and operated the press. St. Louis reporters were soon acquainted with the ubiquitous "Joey," and reporters for the English-language newspapers often found themselves scooped on news stories.

While covering the Missouri legislature in Jefferson City, Pulitzer observed flagrant corruption in the capital. His articles were attacking officials when Republican leaders met to select a state legislative candidate in the solidly Democratic Fifth District. It was deemed impossible for a Republican to win there. Someone laughingly suggested that Pulitzer be chosen, and they approved. He accepted and promised to clean up the courthouse gang. He was twenty-two and under age, as well as not yet being a citizen, and these factors made him ineligible for the candidacy. These technicalities were ignored as he campaigned vigorously and was elected.

Pulitzer merged his news duties with politics. When he introduced a bill to reorganize the County Court of St. Louis County, an argument ensued with lobbyist Edward Augustine, whose efforts the legislation sought to curtail. Augustine called him a liar. The new lawmaker produced a pistol and demanded a retraction, but the lobbyist refused. Pulitzer fired two shots, one of which hit Augustine in the right leg. Augustine struck Pulitzer on the head with a pistol, cutting his scalp. Representative Pulitzer was fined $100 plus costs, for a total of $400. Friends and admirers advanced the money to make the payment and before too long were repaid. Later, Pulitzer became one of the three members of the St. Louis Police Board.

The *Westliche Post*'s editors supported Greeley's presidential campaign in 1872. Pulitzer, a secretary at the Liberal Republican National Convention in Cincinnati, lectured on behalf of the *Tribune*'s editor. Disappointed in the election results, Pulitzer switched to the Democratic Party. Also, Schurz and Preetorius felt that the Greeley campaign had damaged the paper's future. Preetorius offered Pulitzer part ownership, which was accepted.

Pulitzer crusaded against gambling and corruption, and his news reports sparkled. His partners feared he might buy them out if they did not stop him. They offered him $30,000 for his interest, and he agreed. He paid a pittance for a bankrupt German-language newspaper that had an Associated Press franchise. One day later he sold the franchise for at least $20,000 to the *St. Louis Globe* and disposed of the machinery to a German group that launched a short-lived daily.

Now master of the English language, Pulitzer became a delegate to the Missouri Constitutional Convention in 1875, and the next year was admitted to the bar. He campaigned for Samuel Tilden's election as president, and when the country was in an uproar over Rutherford B. Hayes's claim of victory, Dana appointed Pulitzer as special correspondent in Washington to report on the electoral dispute. Pulitzer was impressed with the New York editor and accepted him as his model, guide, and preceptor in journalism.

Love came to Pulitzer, and he married Kate Davis, a second cousin of Jefferson Davis, on June 19, 1878. A trip to Europe followed, during which Pulitzer contributed articles to the *Sun* and decided to make journalism his permanent career. After his return, Pulitzer purchased the moribund St. Louis *Dispatch* at public auction for $2,500. It was an afternoon paper, competing with John Dillon's *Evening Post*. Dillon realized he had a strong adversary in Pulitzer and proposed a merger. Three days after the auction, the combined paper came out as the *St. Louis Post and Dispatch*, with a circulation of eight hundred.

Pulitzer warned rich tax dodgers that they could no longer get away with their manipulations. Published figures contrasted the taxes paid by the poor and the affluent. He campaigned against city evils, attacking gambling dens, brothels, and an administration that closed its eyes to wealthy citizens not paying their share of the tax burden. Dillon could not stand the pace set by Pulitzer and, in less than a year, sold his interest to his young partner for $40,000. Within three years, the *Post-Dispatch*, as it was now called, was clearing $75,000 annually.

The paper increased its circulation steadily until an incident threatened its success. Col. John Albert Cockerill was Pulitzer's managing editor when the *Post-Dispatch* opposed the election of Col. James O. Broadhead to Congress in 1882. His law partner, Alonzo W. Slayback, entered Cockerill's office about a month before election day. An argument ensued, and the editor pulled out a revolver and fatally shot Slayback. No action was taken against Cockerill because authorities concluded that the slain man had entered the office with belligerent intent. But the city was aroused, Pulitzer's enemies blamed him, and circulation tumbled. Cockerill withdrew from the *Post-Dispatch*, and the journal slowly regained readers.

Pulitzer was always physically weak, and his health had become worse during the turmoil. Physicians advised him to take a cruise on the Mediterranean. He was on his way to Europe in the spring of 1883 when he stopped in New York. He found that no strong paper there advocated the principles of the Democratic Party. The *Times* and *Tribune* were Republican, and the *Sun* and *Herald* went their independent ways.

The *World* pretended under Gould to hew to the Democratic philosophy, but the public knew he used his paper only to further his speculations. He did not want the journal, and the stench of his name kept down circulation. The *World* had no influence to speak of and was losing about $40,000 a year.

Pulitzer could not resist the temptation of owning a paper in the country's largest city. He became excited when he heard that Gould wanted to unload the *World*. The railroad wrecker named an exorbitant price of $346,000, but Pulitzer quickly agreed. He wanted a daily that would challenge Park Row's mightiest. It mattered not to Pulitzer that the purchase price included

Gould's losses, the paper's so-called "good will," and equipment, while the seller would only lease the building to him. Arrangements were made to pay Gould in installments.

Pulitzer looked like an easy mark, with his eagerness to own the paper, and Gould said, "My son George holds a block of twenty-five shares, and you do not object, of course, to his keeping those shares." "Certainly not," replied Pulitzer, "if you do not object to my carrying on the editorial page every day: 'Notwithstanding the fact that Jay Gould still owns twenty-five shares, he does not control or influence one line in this paper.' "[2] Gould sold the entire paper, and Pulitzer became the sole owner of the *World*. Pulitzer remarked later that any man could capitalize a property on earnings of 10 percent but that Gould was the only one in the world who could capitalize on a loss of 20 percent.

Pulitzer paid the first installment out of the *Post-Dispatch*'s earnings. The balance came from *World* profits, for the journal almost immediately started on the road toward becoming the greatest money-earning newspaper the country had known.

Ten was Pulitzer's lucky number. He had been born on the tenth of the month, arrived in St. Louis on the tenth, taken control of the *Dispatch* on the tenth, and took over the *World* on the tenth. Pulitzer believed that the highest mission of a newspaper was to render public service and to speak the truth fearlessly in regard to current events. To accomplish this end he proceeded to revolutionize journalism as no man had since the elder Bennett.

On the day after Pulitzer assumed full ownership of the two-cent daily, he left no doubt that he was the boss. He wrote that there was room in the city for a cheap, bright, large paper, and one that was truly democratic, "dedicated to the cause of the people rather than that of purse-potentates— devoted more to the news of the New than the Old World—that will expose all fraud and sham, fight all public evils and abuses—that will serve and battle for the people with earnest sincerity."[3]

Another Pulitzer editorial followed, in which he denounced newspapers that spoke for special interests and not for the public good. Two days later readers felt that the *World*'s new owner was a man who would fight for the masses and hated monopolies and plutocracy: "Our aristocracy is the aristocracy of labor. The man who by honest, earnest toil supports his family in respectability . . . maintaining his good name through privations and temptations, and winning from his children respect as well as love, is the proudest aristocracy in the American republic. The new *World* is his organ."[4]

That same day a *World* interview with Gould appeared on the front page, and the paper's former owner predicted Pulitzer's journal would become a great success. But, he added, "all that I'm afraid of is that it will be a little too bright, and pitch into me. . . . I'm afraid it might become dangerous."[5]

Pulitzer raided his brother's *Journal* for its best men, including managing editor Maj. E. C. Hancock. The whirlwind that was Joseph Pulitzer was too much for him, however, and Hancock was gone in less than a week. In his place came Cockerill, Pulitzer's prize editor in St. Louis.

Pulitzer published his platform within a week after buying the paper:

1. Tax luxuries.
2. Tax inheritances.
3. Tax large incomes.
4. Tax monopolies.
5. Tax the privileged corporations.
6. A tariff for revenue.
7. Reform the civil service.
8. Punish corrupt office-holders.
9. Punish vote-buying.
10. Punish employers who coerce their employees in elections.

Pulitzer recommended this platform to the politicians in place of long-winded resolutions.

As the paper rose in circulation and profits, he ordered the largest and fastest press that R. Hoe & Company could build in the quickest possible time. "How do you know you'll need it?" he was asked. "I *must* need it to succeed, and I shall succeed!" he replied.[6]

Pulitzer wanted a hard-hitting editorial page that would inspire readers, provoke them, and impel them to action. To obtain a large reading public for his editorials, he decided to have a front page that would prompt them to buy his paper.

Overnight, the *World*'s first page looked like something readers of Gould's publication had never seen. The nameplate was changed from Roman to Old English type. Twin hemispheres in the title, ordered out by Gould, were reinstated, and an old-fashioned printing press furnished a vignette setting. More readable type was used, and "ears," or boxes in circular style, were placed on either side of the paper's name on the front page within the first month—something unheard of in journalism.

Pulitzer wanted stories that would catch the reader's eye, and sensationalism provided the answer, just as it had with the elder Bennett. But unlike the Scotsman, he intended to keep his editorials on a high level, no matter how low the news might be. The first day's efforts hinted of things to come. Stories were sensational even for Park Row: a murderer's last hours in a White Plains jail; a New Jersey fire with the headline "THE DEADLY LIGHTNING—Six Lives and One Million Dollars Lost"; the report of James R. Keene's sale of pictures to his rival Gould because he was bankrupt; and a report of dynamiting activities during a Haitian rebellion.

Nothing seemed to escape Pulitzer's eyes. He handled the news and wrote editorials, gave reporters assignments of a kind they had never had before, and astonished copyeditors with his knowledge of their duties. The business office, the composing room, and the press room all came under his surveillance. Unlike Dana, who retired regularly from his work at 4:00 P.M. to spend the rest of the day with his family, Pulitzer had no personal schedule. During those first days he often worked as many as twenty-three out of twenty-four hours and scurried at midnight to nearby Hitchcock's restaurant for "biff an," the beanery's famous ten-cent plate of corned beef and baked beans.

The Brooklyn Bridge, crossing the East River, measured six thousand feet and was the world's largest suspension span. The Manhattan approach was at Park Row, opposite City Hall Park, and this meant a faster distribution of newspapers to Brooklyn. The bridge, hailed as the eighth wonder of the world, was scheduled to open on May 24, and a one-cent toll was planned for pedestrians. Although others had campaigned against evils, this provided Pulitzer with his first opportunity to crusade on behalf of the people. He urged that the fee not be collected: "The people demand a free bridge. They have had to pay for its construction, it is said, several times over. . . . The working classes of the city do not enjoy many privileges. Let them at least have free schools, free air, free daylight and a free bridge."[7] The toll was eventually eliminated, but more notably, the appeal launched Pulitzer on his road toward helping the public.

Before the formal opening, the *World* published a four-column illustration of the span under the headline "THE GREAT BRIDGE UNITING NEW YORK WITH BROOKLYN." Pulitzer assured the *Daily Graphic* it need not be alarmed "by our efforts in the illustrated line. We have no intention of attempting rivalry in that direction. The *Graphic* is the one newspaper in New York that is *sui generis* and unapproachable. We concede the field."[8] The *World,* however, did not concede the field, and Pulitzer's brand of journalism helped doom the *Graphic.*

In the early days of the penny press, denunciations were hurled at a new editor, but too many of the established papers regretfully recalled that this aided a rival's success. Dana alone noticed the new *World* at once and could not resist knocking the man who had once worked for him: "Mr. Pulitzer possesses a quick and fluent mind, with a good share of originality and brightness; but he has always seemed to us rather deficient in judgment and in staying power."[9]

Pulitzer could not tolerate that: "It may have been bad judgment on the part of Mr. Dana to employ the present editor of *The World* as a correspondent for his paper, but if the editor of *The World* has shown deficiency of judgment in journalism heretofore, it has been because he had tried not only to imitate but even to excel the *Sun* in its truthfulness, fearlessness, independence, and vigor."[10]

Day after day Pulitzer put forth the dictum that the *World* was the people's paper—and he made it a paper the people wanted to read. J. P., as he was called, did not object to his men's unscrupulous behavior in ferreting out news. His news pages were baits attracting readers to the editorial page where he bared his feelings. He compromised decency in the news columns to gain a vast reading audience for his editorials.

The staff, imbued with his spirit of conquest, upset the traditions of reporting. They intruded on rightfully shielded property, drummed upon the emotions of the unfortunate, and exploited the vices of humanity more brazenly than readers had known in decades. His stories appealed to the masses: stories of sex, money, murder, and success; stories of the powerful and the rich who dealt in corruption; and stories of the weak who were not always in the right and whom he could frown upon but champion.

The *World*'s circulation more than doubled in three months. The opposition fretted; it could not stand the *World*'s competition. Jones reduced the price of the *Times* from four cents to two in September, and Reid cut the *Tribune*'s cost from four cents to three the next day. But it was Bennett's move that pleased Pulitzer most. Years before, the Commodore had voluntarily lowered the *Herald*'s price from four to three cents as great profits rolled in. Now, he was forced to recognize Pulitzer by cutting its price to two cents. "Another victim, another victory for the *World*," Pulitzer trumpeted. "Owing to the pressure of advertising, the *World* will now enlarge its size to be at least eight columns larger than the Herald."[11]

Pulitzer increased the size of the daily edition to ten pages and the Sunday edition to twelve, eight columns larger than the *Herald*. Bennett retaliated by running a full-page advertisement in the *World* from September 27 through October 3. The only words were spread on six lines in the center of the page:

HERALD
AT
TWO CENTS.
CHEAPEST PAPER
IN
AMERICA.

Since the *World* also sold for two cents, the Commodore did not gain circulation with his price reduction. He also cut the profits of newsdealers from one-half cent per paper to one-third. The vendors complained; one newsdealer organized the others, and they refused to handle the *Herald*. Bennett was forced to establish his own routes. Much of the lost circulation went to the *World*, and only after more than a year of fighting the dealers did he settle. Bennett suffered another blow: while reducing the price of his paper, he raised his advertising rates. The *Herald*'s rates had already been the highest in town, and merchants resented the increase. They turned to Pulitzer and aided the *World*'s advertising.

Thus far, the *Sun* had been able to hold its own against the *World*. But Dana's shattering assaults backfired during the presidential campaign of 1884, and his paper's circulation plummeted. For unexplained reasons he did not want Governor Grover Cleveland nominated by the Democrats. As the race for the presidency jogged along, Dana refused to back either Cleveland or Republican James G. Blaine. He supported Gen. Benjamin F. Butler of Massachusetts, of harsh Reconstructionist fame, on the Greenback Labor ticket.

Pulitzer heartily endorsed Cleveland for president even before the Democratic National Convention was held at Chicago in July. With Dana opposing the governor, he saw a chance to elevate the *World* as the strong paper of the Democratic Party.

Dana urgently pleaded with readers to defeat Cleveland. He stressed an affair with Maria Halpin, a widow in Buffalo who had had intimacies with the governor and at least three others at the same time about a dozen years before. When a child was born out of wedlock, she claimed Cleveland was the father. The *Sun* published an affidavit signed by her stating that he had wrecked her life.

Republicans chanted as they paraded:

> Ma! Ma! Where's my pa?
> Gone to the White House,
> *Ha! Ha! Ha!*

In turn, Democrats referred to Blaine's shady dealings with their own provocative ditty:

> Blaine, Blaine, James G. Blaine,
> The continental liar from the State of Maine!

Then Dana published his most blistering editorial of the campaign. In referring to the hanging of two killers when Cleveland had been sheriff, the *Sun* wrote, "It remains to be seen in this country, whether the American people, in the person of Grover Cleveland, will elevate a common hangman to the highest office in their gift."[12]

Inflamed readers by the thousands ceased buying the *Sun*, but Dana refused to be intimidated and continued to attack Cleveland. The *World* defended the governor with forceful editorials and attacked Blaine with political cartoons. The former readers of the *Sun* flocked to Pulitzer's paper. The *World*'s circulation passed the one hundred thousand mark for the first time, an increase of seventy-five thousand in one year. Pulitzer opened the *World*'s circulation books to those who were interested. He also published a notarized statement that the number of copies sold was accurate and had one hundred guns fired in City Hall Park.

As the presidential campaign neared its end, the Protestant clergymen of New York held a meeting with Blaine as the honored guest. The Reverend Dr. Samuel Burchard, chairman of the delegation, unwittingly helped turn the tide in Cleveland's favor when he addressed the group: "We are Republicans, and we do not propose to leave our party and identify ourselves with the party whose antecedents have been . . . RUM, ROMANISM AND REBELLION!"

A cartoon of a Blaine dinner, hosted by Gould and Cyrus Field the same night, was also spread across the top of the *World*'s front page. An unusual seven-column headline described it as "THE ROYAL FEAST OF BELSHAZZAR BLAINE AND THE MONEY KINGS." Blaine was depicted surrounded by diamond-studded millionaires, including Gould, Field, William H. Vanderbilt, and Russell Sage, while a man, his wife, and their child pleaded in rags for something to eat. Not since Thomas Nast had caricatured Boss Tweed had any cartoon proved such a sensation. The *World* thundered:

> Read the list of Blaine's banqueters, who are to fill his pockets with money to corrupt the ballot-box. Are they friends of the workingman? What humbug! Are they in sympathy with labor? Fraud! Are they not mostly railroad kings, Wall Street millionaires, greedy monopolists, lobbyists, speculators, and pecu-

lators, who had grown wealthy on public grants, legislation, and special privileges? . . .

Shall Jay Gould rule this country? Shall he own the President?[13]

Newspaper Row became the city's center of attraction as ten thousand persons crowded Park Row to read the latest election returns on the bulletin boards of newspaper buildings. Election night passed without the announcement of a new president. On Wednesday, Park Row was again packed. On Thursday, the rumor spread that Cleveland had carried New York State but that Gould was tampering with telegrams to abet his speculations. Beating tin pans and holding flaming newspapers aloft, crowds proceeded down Park Row to burn his Western Union Building, but police dispersed the procession. That evening the New York press carried the word that Cleveland had been elected, a victory made possible by his slim edge of two thousand votes in New York State.

The *World* was jubilant when it was announced that Cleveland had won. Years later, Cleveland publicly wrote that he might never have been elected had it not been for Pulitzer's paper: "The contest was so close it may be said without reservation that if it had lacked the forceful and potent advocacy of Democratic principles at that time by the New York *World* the result might have been reversed."[14]

Circulation rose greatly for both the *World* and the *Sun* on the day after the voting. The *World* almost doubled its daily average with a press run of 223,000, while the *Sun* reached a sales high of 188,753. However, starting the next day, it was downhill for Dana's paper until, one week later, circulation dropped sixty-five thousand in one day.

That election of 1884 saw Pulitzer chosen as a congressman from New York's Ninth District. He resigned his seat after only four months, on his thirty-ninth birthday, because the pressures of political office interfered with his operation of the *World*.

Fate was decidedly on Pulitzer's side. Bennett had increased his advertising rates at an unpropitious moment, and Dana had crucified the wrong man. Now the *World*, under full steam, surged ahead to change completely the philosophy of newspapers everywhere.

The French had erected a 151-foot statue of Liberty Enlightening the World, which they planned to present to the United States as a symbol of friendship and democracy. Frederic-Auguste Bartholdi had created the giant figure in the seventies. An American committee had attempted for years to collect money for a pedestal on Bedloe Island, which the government had set aside for the purpose. Enough funds had been raised for a base, but $100,000 was needed for the pedestal.

Soon after Pulitzer purchased the *World*, he had tried to convince readers to contribute money for the Statue of Liberty, but the paper then lacked influence, and only $155 was raised in two weeks. With the journal now a power, the crusade resumed. A front-page story said that the committee had exhausted its treasury. An editorial said that Congress refused to appropriate the money to complete preparations and had thrown the responsibility back to the public. It pointed out that the French had commissioned a vessel, the *Isere*, specifically to take the statue to the United States:

> There is but one thing that can be done.
>
> *We must raise the money!*
>
> The *World* is the people's paper, and it now appeals to the people to come forward and raise this money. The $250,000 that the making of the Statue cost was paid in by the masses of the French people—by the workingmen, the tradesmen, the shop girls, the artisans—by all, irrespective of class or condition. Let us respond in like manner. Let us not wait for the millionaires to give this money. It is not the gift from the millionaires of France to the millionaires of America, but a gift of the whole people of France to the whole people of America.[15]

That was the opening plea. Money started coming in, with amounts as low as five cents. The paper offered prizes to those sending in the largest contributions. First prize would be two double gold eagles, or $40 in gold, and a total of $100 would be distributed. A donation accompanied the following letter: "I wonder if you will accept a little girl's mite to the Bartholdi Statue Pedestal Fund? I send you my pocket-piece—20 cents in silver—and only wish it was one of those beautiful gold double-eagles which you offer for prizes. I am a little girl, not quite eleven yet, and read *The World* almost every day, and Sunday, too."[16]

Pulitzer published the names of all contributors, some of their letters, and notices of affairs given for the fund's benefit. Children, servant girls, longshoremen, newsboys, clerks, cab drivers, and laborers took part in the crusade. Within four months, the fund was completed. More than 120,000 persons contributed the needed $100,000. The pedestal was finished the following year, with inauguration ceremonies held on October 28, 1886. Cleveland and Ferdinand de Lesseps, builder of the Suez Canal, headed the list of prominent Americans and Frenchmen participating in the festivities.

Pulitzer was honored that day. A triumphal arch stretched from the *World* building on Park Row to the post office structure across the street. Sixty feet high, the arch was the largest ever constructed in New York. Hundreds of thousands lined the streets from Canal Street to the Battery to watch a parade of twenty thousand troops. They marched from Fifth Avenue and 57th Street to the Battery, and only once did they salute—when they passed the *World* building.

During the fund-raising period for the statue, the *World* was engaged in a long fight to smash the Broadway Boodle Ring. Jacob Sharp, a reputed millionaire and owner of the Seventh Avenue Railway, wanted a streetcar franchise on Broadway. Businessmen objected to the idea of surface cars along that thoroughfare, but Sharp was determined. He bribed aldermen with hundreds of thousands of dollars to grant him a franchise. The city knew that boodling had occurred but could not prove it. The *World* campaigned against the aldermen and Sharp, and its reporters obtained the proof. A grand jury indicted almost all the members of the Board of Aldermen, as well as Sharp. Some of the aldermen fled town; others were arrested and found guilty. Sharp received a four-year prison term, after being convicted of bribing thirteen aldermen.

In the afternoon field, the leading journals were the *Evening Post, Commercial Advertiser,* and *Mail and Express.* All sold for three cents and were of a loftier tone than the one-cent *News,* which circulated among the tenement classes and had a greater circulation. Dana and his associate, William M. Laffan, launched an *Evening Sun,* with Laffan as publisher, to compete with the *News* for such readers. The new four-page journal, selling for one penny, began publication in March 1887 and became an immediate success. During the fall, its circulation surpassed one hundred thousand.

Pulitzer watched its progress, and on October 10, less than seven months after the founding of the *Evening Sun,* he issued the *Evening World.* This daily cut into the circulation of the morning edition, and for two years it lost money. It was being modeled too closely upon the conservative afternoon sheets. Recognizing the error, Pulitzer ordered his employees to stop making a three-cent newspaper for a one-cent constituency and to make it a one-cent daily. That was the impetus the paper needed, and before long its circulation passed that of the *Evening Sun.*

Assistant district attorney De Lancey Nicoll had obtained Sharp's conviction and that of three franchise boodlers. That year the Republicans nominated him for district attorney of New York County. At first, Dana had urged the Democratic Party to select Nicoll as its candidate, but then the

World cast its support for him. The *Sun*'s editor, smarting over Pulitzer's invasion of the evening field, immediately switched to another assistant district attorney, Tammany-backed Col. John R. Fellows.

Dana and his editorial staff felt that a Nicoll defeat would be a blow to Pulitzer. The *Sun* strove to beat Nicoll by ridiculing Pulitzer's religious background. As the campaign neared its end, the attacks on Pulitzer became ferocious. He became "Judas Pulitzer" to the *Sun*'s readers, while the *World* was called a "junk newspaper."

The *Sun* hammered at Pulitzer: " 'Vy? Vy? Vy?' Judas Pulitzer will shout on the day after election. . . . Will he be able to read the answer to his 'Vy?' in the returns? Who knows? Who cares? He will have had enough of trying to boss New York." Dana continued two days later: "I vonder vere I can get some hemb cheab.—Choe Buliter." He followed relentlessly with: "Judas Pulitzer is a Jew who denies his race and pretends that he is not of Jewish origin. He is ashamed of his birth and ancestry, and tries to repudiate them. He thus makes himself a Judas indeed."[17]

The scurrilous attacks were not one-sided. Pulitzer called the *Sun*'s editor "the champion liar of America, Coward Ananias Dana." He described him as "poor, despised and disgraced" and an "infamous blackguard." He also denounced Dana's "vigorous campaign of slander and malice" and charged him with venality and treachery.[18]

Dana's venom against "Hungry Joe," as he called the *World*'s owner, became sharper. When Fellows was elected, Dana was overjoyed. He was his masterful self the following morning:

> We wish, Pulitzer, that you had never come.
>
> Perhaps your lot will be like that of the mythical unfortunate of the race you belong to and deny . . . we mean the Wandering Jew. In that case, it may shortly please the inscrutable Providence which has chastened us with your presence, to give you that stern and dreadful signal—
>
> Move on, Pulitzer, move on![19]

Pulitzer had no such intention: "The editor accepts the hatred of Mr. Dana as a compliment. . . . Its circulation is three times that of the *Sun* and its influence is in proportion."[20] Before the week ended, he announced that the *World*'s average daily circulation was twice that of any other morning paper in America.

The excitement of the campaign, the attacks by Dana, and his own frenzied activity had shattered Pulitzer's nerves. His defective eyesight had become so bad that, on election night, when he called for proofs of the next day's editorial, he could not read the type. His doctors ordered Pulitzer to rest in California. He agreed but had no intention of leaving the newspaper business.

The *World* continued to gain strength despite his absence. He was on the West Coast when New York's Great Blizzard of March 1888 paralyzed the city and caused four hundred deaths. *World* reporters used snowshoes for street wear and formed brigades to cover stories in Westchester County, Long Island, and New Jersey. They even rescued several people, while New York remained virtually isolated from the rest of the world. Not until four days after the blizzard began did New York start to dig out.

Elizabeth Cochrane was a *World* reporter who used pseudonyms to obtain exclusive stories. She had spent ten days in an insane asylum on Blackwell Island (now Roosevelt Island) under the name of Nellie Brown by feigning madness. Her exposure of conditions there shocked the city into cleaning it up. On another occasion, she disguised herself as a wealthy married woman in Albany and succeeded in exposing lobbyist Edward R. Phelps, who bribed legislators at will. Miss Cochrane also posed as a saleslady, a beggar, and a Salvation Army lass. Her stories were the talk of Park Row's male counterparts, and she made the woman reporter one who could rank alongside them.

Her editor summoned her one day and asked, "Can you start around the world the day after tomorrow?" "I can start this minute," she replied.[21] On November 14, 1889, she sailed for Southampton, using the name of Nellie Bly, and determined to beat the record established by Phileas Fogg in Jules Verne's novel *Around the World in 80 Days.* She journeyed from Southampton to London and then to Amiens to visit Verne and his wife. Brindisi, Port Said, Aden, Colombo, Penang, and Hong Kong followed. She spent Christmas in Canton, returned to Hong Kong, and went on to Yokohama and Tokyo. She traveled on ships and trains, on burros and horses, and in jinrikishas and sampans. After 124 hours in Japan, she sailed for San Francisco on January 7, 1890, and crew members of the steamship wrote over the engines:

> For Nellie Bly
> We'll win or die.

The last leg of the journey began in San Francisco, when Nellie Bly boarded a special *World* train for the triumphant ride home. She was cheered wildly wherever the train stopped: Topeka, Chicago, Pittsburgh, Philadelphia, and Jersey City. She reached the *World* building on January 25, and the next day the paper devoted most of its space to her achievement. The front-page streamer read, "FATHER TIME OUTDONE!"

The journey had taken seventy-two days, six hours, and eleven minutes and covered almost twenty-five thousand miles. Babies, horses, and cats were named for Nellie Bly all over the country, and for days the main subject in Park Row's saloons and restaurants was Elizabeth Cochrane's achievement.

Park Row was the most widely known newspaper area in the nation in 1890. Not only were there seventeen papers in the city, but hundreds of thousands of their copies went out to all parts of the country. In addition, every important newspaper in the United States and Canada had representatives on Park Row.

The old *World* building owned by Jay Gould had long proved inadequate. In 1886 Pulitzer had closed a contract with R. Hoe & Company for three new double-patent printing machines that would print, cut, insert extra sheets, and fold at the rate of seventy-two thousand papers an hour. Less than a year later he opened an annex in Brooklyn, within a ten-minute access to his Park Row building via the Brooklyn Bridge. But Pulitzer was dissatisfied; he wanted a permanent home for his paper.

French's Hotel at Park Row and Frankfort Street, directly opposite the *Sun,* was up for sale. Pulitzer decided that the location, 63 Park Row, would be ideal. That was the hotel from which he had been ejected after the Civil War. Holding fast to the superstition that ten was his lucky number, he completed the deal for the property on April 10, 1888, his forty-first birthday, for $630,000 in cash. As soon as Pulitzer had decided upon the new home for the *World,* he remarked, "I want the tallest building on earth."[22]

Pulitzer's four-year-old son, Joseph Jr., laid the cornerstone of the new structure on October 10, 1889. Pulitzer could not attend the ceremonies. He was in Wiesbaden, Germany, because of his nerves and blindness. He cabled from his sickbed that day, "Let it ever be remembered that this edifice owes its existence to the public; that its architect is popular favor; that its cornerstone is love of Liberty and Justice; that its every stone comes from the people and represents public approval for public services rendered."[23]

The $2 million building, erected in Renaissance style and Venetian detail, opened on December 10, 1890. Nothing like it had been seen in New York, and everything concerning the structure had been paid for in cash. The 309-foot building towered above all others in the city and made the opposition newspapers envious. It was twenty stories high with a gilded dome of copper weighing 860,000 pounds, the first glimpse of New York sighted by the ocean voyager. A lighted globe, seventeen feet in diameter and showing the points of the globe, ornamented the broad sidewalk.

Pulitzer was not present when the doors of the building were opened to the public. He had sailed for Europe twenty-four hours before, his nerves unable to take the excitement. Less than two months earlier, he had announced his withdrawal as editor of the *World* and vested its entire control in an executive board. Bennett, who had watched the *World* surpass the *Herald*, paid tribute to his rival when he heard the news: "What the Greeleys and the Raymonds and the Bennetts did for journalism thirty years ago, Pulitzer has done today. . . . As for the *Herald*, we droop our colors to him. . . . Le Roi est mort, vive le Roi!"[24] Pulitzer's exile lasted only six months. He was dissatisfied with the performance of the executive board and again became active, despite his illness.

The magnificent Pulitzer Building hurt Bennett's pride. If he cared for anything, it was the great name of the *Herald*. The Commodore decided to leave Park Row, the first move away by a Giant from that famed canyon. He leased for thirty years a triangle formed by 35th Street and the intersection of Broadway and Sixth Avenue known as Dodge Place, later to be called Herald Square. Noted architect Stanford White drew up the plans for a two-story building copied after the Palazzo del Consiglio in Verona. The eccentricities shaping Bennett's life presented themselves in the new structure. A $200,000 clock with a deep-toned bell struck by two bronze figures adorned a portion of the roof. Bronze owls, run by electricity, blinked at night above the *Herald*'s portals. Bennett had fallen asleep on watch during a tour in the navy, and the hooting of an owl had awakened him in time to prevent his yacht from running into a reef. Now the owl was his talisman.

Pulitzer could not understand why Bennett had leased the land for the building instead of purchasing it outright. When they met in Paris, the *World*'s owner remarked, "I could not sleep nights if I thought another owned the ground upon which my building stood." "I shall not be here to worry about it," Bennett replied.[25]

Shortly after Bennett had moved his paper, an open space facing Herald Square was named Greeley Square. Ironically, if ever two men had hated each other, they were Horace Greeley and James Gordon Bennett the Elder.

Pulitzer, Bennett, and Reid were all absentee owners. Reid had been appointed minister to France in 1889, and his former secretary, Donald Nicholson, managed the *Tribune*. Upon his return, Reid participated vigorously in politics and was nominated for the vice presidency of the United States in 1892. All three watched the course of their papers closely but used different styles to control them. While the dictatorial Bennett employed an intra-office spy system, Reid ruled by moral force, expecting his men to obey orders as a matter of principle.

The wily Pulitzer pitted his chief employees against one another by pressure. No editor was more keenly aware of the work of each man on his staff than Pulitzer. Stories were selected from the best of each writer and sent to the blind publisher no matter where he was traveling. The more daring a reporter, the better the *World*'s owner liked him. He spoke harshly of editors and tolerantly of writers. When asked why, he replied, "I suppose it is because every reporter is a hope, and every editor is a disappointment."[26]

Despite his ailments, there was no slackening in Pulitzer's exertions. He bombarded the *World*'s offices with cables, memos, suggestions, complaints, and reprimands. Posted on bulletin boards were slogans such as "Accuracy, Terseness, Accuracy."

Crusades and stunts gathered momentum, and reporters continued to solve murders. Railroads, oil companies, and other trusts were exposed. Front-page sensationalism rolled along steadily, but the editorial page, liberal and unimpeachable, remained Pulitzer's delight. His favorite newspaper was the lofty-minded *Evening Post,* with a circulation of less than twenty-five thousand. When asked why he did not print a journal such as that, he replied, "Because I want to talk to a nation, not to a select committee."[27]

The *Sunday World*'s circulation exceeded four hundred thousand, far above that of any other paper in the country. Morrill Goddard was one of those responsible for this vast circulation. As a reporter, Goddard had discovered that the city morgue possessed stories of horror to shock readers, and when he became Sunday editor, he introduced sensational features that displeased Pulitzer but brought tremendous sales increases.

No paper in the country outsensationalized the *Sunday World.* A color press in the Pulitzer Building's basement had been allowed to rust because of the costliness of running it. Author Don Carlos Seitz, who labored long in the business department of the *World,* suggested a colored comic supplement. One page was devoted to a full-sized political cartoon in color, while another was given to a comic feature by Richard Felton Outcault in 1894 showing a yellow-garbed boy playing in *Hogan's Alley.* Outcault created both the *Yellow Kid* and *Buster Brown.*

Park Row had been used to weekly comic magazines, such as *Puck,* publishing colored comics. But the *World*'s innovation in using them in a daily journal caused newspapermen to speculate on its success, and trade journals took sides on its worthiness. The comics added to the success Goddard made of the Sunday edition. He stretched headlines across one and two pages, often accompanying them with half-page zinc photographs. No paper published more illustrations than the *Sunday World,* and articles were salted with sex appeal. Pulitzer shuddered at Goddard's doings. They represented the evil side of journalism, but the owner refused to restrain Goddard, since the circulation results were so pleasing.

Many newspapers were read to Pulitzer, and his intense interest in what was happening in the country led to his bringing off one of the *World*'s great successes. Great Britain and Venezuela quarreled in 1895 over a divisional line between the South American republic and British Guiana. Venezuelan President Joaquin Cresco cited the Monroe Doctrine and requested Washington's help. The United States proposed arbitration, but Great Britain refused. On December 17, President Cleveland asked Congress for a commission to determine the boundary. He denounced Britain's attitude as endangering the peace and safety of America and warned that it would be the duty of the United States to resist by every means in its power England's seizure of any territory that the commission decided was Venezuela's.

Pulitzer denounced Cleveland's message the next day: "It is a grave blunder to put this Government in its attitude of threatening war unless we mean it and are prepared for it."[28]

Jingoists cheered Cleveland's words. "Any American citizen, whether inside or outside Congress," wrote the *Sun,* "who hesitates at this conjuncture to uphold the President of the United States should be branded an alien or a traitor."[29] Other important New York newspapers took a different stance. The *Herald* urged international arbitration, and the *Evening Post* called the president's proposal for a commission ludicrously insulting and illogical. But it was the *World* that led the way in trying to end the crisis. Pulitzer's paper thundered, "War is not impossible. War, on the contrary, is being made every day more possible by the reckless and inconsiderate clamor of men who should know better, who fill the air with bombast about the pregnability of Great Britain's vast commerce and the impossibility of war."[30] Congress appropriated $100,000 to investigate the boundary dispute. It was a signal to England that the government stood behind Cleveland.

The *World* denounced the warmongers. All during that week before Christmas Day, Pulitzer cabled and telegraphed more than five hundred appeals to intellectual leaders in America and England, imploring them to send messages of goodwill and peace on earth if they felt inclined. The front page of the *World*'s Christmas Day issue was devoted to the harvest reaped by its owner. Messages from the greatest minds of both countries were published. The Prince of Wales and the Duke of York ignored traditional etiquette as they responded. Former Prime Minister William E. Gladstone cabled that only common sense was necessary.

American reaction was instantaneous. The *World* had succeeded in obtaining a nationwide clamor to avert fighting. Clergymen, educators, and businessmen stressed the necessity for preserving peace. The replies upholding the *World*'s stand influenced Cleveland to abandon his policy. Peace and arbitration societies of Great Britain recognized the paper's service on June 5, 1896. An arbitration treaty between Venezuela and Great Britain was ratified a year later.

Simultaneously, Pulitzer waged another battle against the Cleveland administration. The federal government's gold reserve had declined because of pro-silver agitation and the purchasing policies that resulted. To replenish this reserve, the Treasury, in February 1895, secretly sold a bond issue worth more than $62 million at 104½ to a syndicate headed by J. Pierpont Morgan. The market price of the bonds was 118, and the syndicate made a profit of at least $6 million. The *World* inveighed against the government for selling to a private group in defiance of the law, but the transaction had been consummated.

The gold situation improved for a while. Ten months after the deal, the *World* learned that President Cleveland and Treasury Secretary John G. Carlisle had approved another secret bargain with the syndicate, which would put $100 million on sale with the same profitable terms. The contract had not been concluded when the *World* appealed to the president to "Smash the Ring—Reject the Steal!" It urged Cleveland "to save the country from the mischief, the wrong, and the scandal of the pending bond deal."[31] The paper pleaded with the president to trust the people and offered to subscribe $1 million on its own account.

Cleveland denied that a secret deal was being negotiated, but two days later the issue was publicly announced. More than five thousand bids were received, but fewer than eight hundred were accepted. Among them was the *World*'s, which, at 114, was the highest for a large amount. The routing of the syndicate established the public's ability to buy government bonds on the open market.

Pulitzer was riding high. His success with the Venezuelan and bond controversies within two weeks had brought the paper to the country's attention more than ever. The *World* was at the peak of its triumphs, and the *Sunday World* was setting the pace for all other Sunday publications.

Pulitzer determined to keep his papers foremost in the nation's eyes, but a new figure with millions of dollars had entered the New York newspaper scene to challenge him. His name was William Randolph Hearst.

9

"Yellow Journalist"

DURING THE LAST DECADE of the nineteenth century, technology enabled presses to roll at a roaring speed and newspapers to print more copies per hour than ever. More advertising at higher rates meant increased profits, and the key to this was greater readership.

In late 1895, when the *World* scored its smashing successes, the *Morning Journal*, known along Park Row as the "washer-woman's gazette," was no longer owned by its founder, Joseph Pulitzer's estranged brother, Albert. He had found there was money to be made by providing chambermaids with spicy gossip and salacious news and paid little attention to politics and civic duty. After a trip to Europe early that year he doubled the size of the paper and raised the price to two cents. The move caused circulation to plummet from 135,000 to 30,000.

In May, Albert Pulitzer sold the paper he had established with capital of $25,000 to John R. McLean, wealthy publisher of the Cincinnati *Enquirer*, for $1 million. The Midwesterner attempted to make the *Journal* a respectable Democratic daily, but competition with the *World* and *Herald* was too stiff. In a vain effort to stem financial losses, he cut back the price to one cent on September 1.

Some months before, in Paris, William Randolph Hearst, owner of the San Francisco *Examiner*, had met with his paper's business manager, Charles M. Palmer, to discuss a plan considered earlier: a chain of papers across the United States. When Palmer offered McLean $180,000 for his *Journal*, the proposal was accepted. A German-language newspaper was included in the transaction, and the deal was consummated on September 25.

The new owner of the *Journal* was the only child of U.S. Senator George Hearst, who said of his son, "I've been watching him, and I notice that when he wants cake, he wants cake and he wants it now. And I notice that, after a while, he gets his cake."[1]

The elder Hearst was a forty-niner who had made a strike in Eldorado, California, after seven years. The real pay dirt came later when he and some of his partners bought an interest in the Ophir Mine, the best in the Comstock Silver Lode in Nevada. That made him a millionaire, and he returned to his native Missouri to marry Phoebe Apperson, a schoolteacher and daughter of a wealthy farmer. They lived in San Francisco's Nob Hill section, and their son was born on April 29, 1863.

Young Hearst entered Harvard at nineteen. He preferred history to other subjects. The stage and its people also appealed to him, and he appeared in a Hasty Pudding show at the university. In addition, he was highly successful as business manager of Harvard's humor magazine, *Lampoon.* His father had bought the San Francisco *Examiner* in 1880, and newspapers fascinated Will. He spent much time off campus at the Boston *Globe,* where he learned about its intricacies. When alone in his room, Will would spread Eastern newspapers on the floor, analyze them, and admire the New York *World.* He would tell his *Lampoon* associates that Pulitzer was running the best paper in the country, that he was studying his methods, and that he thought he had caught on to what Pulitzer was trying to do.

Hearst spent money lavishly at Harvard, and his efforts at having fun knew no bounds. In 1886, during his final year, he sent each of his instructors at Christmastime an impressively wrapped chamber pot with the recipient's name and photograph on the inside bottom. Authorities did not find the prank amusing, and his days at Harvard were over. He maintained throughout his life that he had not been expelled but rusticated, a term for suspension. He did not return to graduate.[2]

After his departure, Hearst worked as a reporter for the *World.* He was in New York less than a year, learning the way Joseph Pulitzer blended the sensational with the crusading to merchandise his successful product. His father offered to make him manager of one of his profitable mines or ranches, but the proposal was rejected. All Will wanted was to take over the money-losing *Examiner* in San Francisco, and the senator finally agreed. The younger Hearst assumed control on March 4, 1887, when its circulation was thirty thousand. Within days, the paper called itself the "Monarch of the Dailies." Hearst shook up the staff and brought in three *Lampoon* colleagues, including Ernest L. "Phinney" Thayer, who created the immortal "Casey at the Bat" for the journal. He paid high salaries to lure others from competing publications and hired Ambrose Bierce to write a column called "Prattle."

While in New York, Hearst met Samuel Chamberlain, who had worked for the *World* and the *Herald* and founded *Le Matin* in Paris. Chamberlain became the *Examiner*'s managing editor. Other writers and artists who joined the staff were Homer Davenport, T. A. "Tad" Dorgan, Edward W. Townsend, Arthur McEwen, and Winifred Sweet Black. Contributors included literary jewels: Mark Twain, Gertrude Atherton, and Joaquin Miller.

Hearst's employees were more than wage slaves; they were companions who enjoyed life with him. The doings on the *Examiner* became legendary in every saloon where newsmen congregated. Hearst provided the West Coast with journalistic sensationalism such as it had never seen. Editorial writer McEwen said, "We run our paper so that when the reader opens it he says 'Gee-whiz!' "[3]

Shortly after young Hearst took over, the *Examiner* devoted a fourteen-page special edition to a hotel fire and splashed it with articles and illustrations. Winifred Sweet Black, who also wrote under the names Annie Laurie and Winifred Black, faked a faint so that she could obtain admission into a city hospital and expose conditions. When a prostitute gave birth to a crippled child in jail, the paper conducted a "Little Jim" campaign, with sob stories that raised $20,000 by the time the child died.

The *Examiner* crusaded against crime, vice, and corruption. One of its targets was the blind Democratic Boss of San Francisco, Chris Buckley, a saloon-keeper who had been George Hearst's political backer. Despite the ties between his father and Buckley, young Hearst assailed the political leader, implying associations between the Boss and blackmailers and other criminals. In addition, Buckley had offended the *Examiner* by refusing to let municipal printing contracts flow its way. The Boss was indicted, and when public opinion stirred over his sheltering a bank robber in his saloon, he fled the country.

The *Examiner* staged its greatest battle against Southern Pacific Railroad. Collis P. Huntington controlled S.P., the strongest power in the state. The newspaper accused the railroad of franchise stealing, legislative bribing, and tax manipulations. Hearst was in Egypt in 1892 when the *Examiner* negotiated a $30,000 advertising contract with the line. Charges arose that he had sold out to Southern Pacific, which canceled the agreement with $8,000 still unpaid. But attacks against the railroad continued in the *Examiner* even while the contract was being honored.

In 1893, with the *Examiner*'s circulation more than double what it had been when Hearst took over, skeptics no longer called him "Wasteful Willie" because of the vast sums he had spent to build up the publication. The Chicago World's Fair opened on May 1 that year, and a month later he printed the largest edition of any daily published in the United States: a 120-page paper that mainly extolled the virtues of California. That broke the record set by Pulitzer when he celebrated his tenth anniversary as owner of the *World* with a one-hundred-page issue shortly before.

Hearst decided to make his mark on Park Row two years later. His father was dead, and his mother sold her interest in the Anaconda Copper Mining Company for $7.5 million to the Rothschilds of London. She gave her son the millions for his debut as a New York publisher. No man had ever invaded Manhattan's journalistic scene with as much money. Hearst's main goal was to overtake the *World* as the nation's greatest circulating daily. Some of the *Examiner*'s most talented members went with him.

The *Journal*'s quarters lay inconspicuously on the sixth floor of the *Tribune* building. The *Journal* had no Associated Press franchise, and no one on that paper was admitted into the *Tribune*'s composing room. Copy was sent up in little tin boxes running on wires outside the building. Sometimes, the wind blew the loose papers over the surrounding roofs. Without an AP franchise, the *Journal* procured the news however it could. Bits of special dispatches were pirated and blown into full-length articles. Charles O'Rourke's City News Association, which distributed "flimsies" to newspapers, supplied most of the routine local stories.

All this the mustachioed Hearst was ready to change. He retained the offices in the *Tribune* building but installed presses in nearby Gold Street. He raided writers from other newspapers, as Joseph Pulitzer had done after his arrival from St. Louis. They came from the *World, Sun, Herald,* and *Recorder.*

Most journalists on Park Row first thought of Hearst as a spendthrift, checkered-suit dude from San Francisco who would not last in the big city. *The Fourth Estate* announced his purchase of the *Journal* on October 10, but it was not until November 7 that Hearst permitted his name to appear in the *Journal*'s masthead as its proprietor.

Hearst emulated the *World* in makeup, size, and sensationalism from the start. That first issue announcing his ownership flung a challenge to other papers as it described on two-thirds of a page the wedding of the Duke of Marlborough to Consuelo Vanderbilt. Soon after, Hearst paid novelist Richard Harding Davis $500 to cover the Yale-Princeton football game, an unprecedented amount for reporting such an event. The fact was trumpeted throughout the city, and the edition sold out.

Pulitzer was not worried. His business manager, Solomon S. Carvalho, pleaded with him: "This young man Hearst from California, I think, is the first serious menace you have had since you came to New York." "Menace!" roared Pulitzer. "That kid! What can Hearst do? McLean was a businessman. He gave it up. He knew the value of money. Hearst doesn't."[4]

In his first three months in New York, the Chief—as Hearst was called—spent twice as much as the *Journal* had cost. Money was unimportant to the

Californian; he wanted circulation. The combined sales of the morning and afternoon editions of the *World* were five times that of Hearst's paper. He had a long way to travel to threaten Pulitzer, but before the year ended the *Journal* called itself the greatest one-cent paper in the world.

Until now, Hearst's corralling of the *World* staff had been done on a minor scale. However, a few days after the *World*'s triumph with the government-bond issue, he asked Morrill Goddard to join the *Journal*'s staff. Goddard protested that he would need his writers and artists. Hearst offered to hire any or all of them. Goddard hesitated; he knew his job with Pulitzer was secure, and he feared the newcomer to Park Row might turn his booming paper into a bust and destroy it within months. Hearst handed him a Wells, Fargo & Company draft for $35,000 and remarked, "Take all or any part of that. That ought to convince you I intend to remain in New York quite some time."[5] Goddard accepted, and he and his staff moved on one day's notice to the *Journal*'s office.

Pulitzer paled at the news, and he ordered Carvalho to get the men back. Carvalho pleaded with Goddard and promised higher pay. Goddard relented and returned with his staff. Hearst refused to concede defeat and offered more money. Twenty-four hours after the return to the *World,* Goddard and his associates marched down the street to the *Journal*'s quarters. Among the men Hearst lured from the *World* was Richard Felton Outcault, the artist creating wonders with the boy in the yellow nightshirt in the *Hogan's Alley* comic supplement.

Pulitzer was desperate. The *Examiner*'s bureau was in his building and had been used by Hearst for secret negotiations with Goddard. Pulitzer ordered the lease canceled. "I won't have my building used for purposes of seduction!" he roared.[6]

A Sunday editor was needed, and Pulitzer named a trusted special writer, Arthur Brisbane, to take over. Goddard's replacement was the son of Fourierist advocate Albert Brisbane. Through his father, he had joined Charles Anderson Dana's *Sun* at nineteen in 1883 and become prominent along Park Row for his coverage of the John L. Sullivan–Charley Mitchell prizefight in Chantilly, France, five years later. After Brisbane's return to the United States, Dana appointed him managing editor of the *Evening Sun.* He remained there until Pulitzer drew him away with higher pay in 1890.

Brisbane's mind was as inventive as Goddard's. Lurid features continued unabated in the *World,* while the *Sunday Journal* became more flagrant than it had been since Hearst's purchase. Headlines grew larger in both the *World* and the *Journal,* and streamers became popular in both newspapers. Illustrations showed more women wearing less. Sketches of the mythical scientific world abounded, as the papers found truth irrelevant in their efforts to shock, amuse, and amaze readers.

The *Journal*'s circulation soared to 150,000, only 35,000 less than that of the *World*. Pulitzer's business advisers pleaded with their boss to lower the price of the paper from two cents to one, and he agreed less than a month after Goddard switched papers. The *World* explained to readers that it was doing so because, although it already had more readers than any other news-paper on earth, it was not willing to let well enough alone.

Overnight, the morning *World*'s sales increased 88,000 a day. But profits declined with the loss in revenue, and Pulitzer raised his advertising rates. Later, Pulitzer ruefully said, "When I came to New York, Mr. Bennett reduced the price of his paper and raised his advertising rates—all to my advantage. When Mr. Hearst came to New York I did the same. I wonder why, in view of my experience?"[7]

The price drop sparked a devastating newspaper warfare that New York had seldom witnessed. Hearst's millions fought Pulitzer's profits. "Publicity, Publicity, Publicity," the *World*'s owner stressed in his columns when trying to destroy an evil. He believed publicity was the greatest moral factor and force in the universe. Now Hearst adopted the principle to force the *Journal*'s circulation to the top.

Throughout the city, billboards were constructed in every accessible spot, advertising the *Journal*'s greatness. Sandwich men paraded in business dis-tricts to laud the paper's efforts. Newspapers and trade publications carried advertisements describing its successful, meteoric rise. Bandwagons, deco-rated with *Journal* posters, roamed the streets to spread the paper's name. Registered voters received pennies in the mail with which to buy the *Journal*.

Park Row was astonished. Hearst continued raiding other papers, paying higher salaries than the newspapermen had dreamed of earning. City editor Richard A. Farrelly was promoted to managing editor of the *World*'s morn-ing edition in April 1896. A dinner to honor his success was scheduled for a Monday evening, but it was canceled abruptly. Farrelly had joined the *Jour-nal*'s staff the day before.

Carvalho, one of Pulitzer's highest-ranking aides, disagreed with his em-ployer over the raising of advertising rates and resigned to become Hearst's business manager. Pulitzer made feeble attempts at retaliation. He hired some of the *Journal*'s men but proved more successful in importing employ-ees from his *St. Louis Post-Dispatch*.

Hearst strove to employ almost anyone on the *World*, no matter how insignificant a job he held. Often he hired men to embarrass Pulitzer and promptly fired them again, knowing they would not all return to the *World.* The word was passed along Park Row. Writers began to demand contracts before they joined Hearst's organization, and he agreed. Then not being able to use these men, he tried to break their contracts by forcing them to accept menial work, including the care of lavatories.

The *Journal* still had no Associated Press franchise. Its offices were usually quiet until the first edition of the *World* was brought in, when the news could be copied. Then a chant ran through the newsroom:

> Sound the cymbal, beat the drum!
> The *World* is here, the news has come.[8]

When a big story broke in the city, shouted commands could be heard throughout the offices. Almost all of the staff would rush into Park Row to grab bicycles, carriages, and hansom cabs. Hearst would bound out of the building with his employees, usually heading in his gig toward the scene of the news. Along Newspaper Row the *Journal* became noted for its "wrecking crew," which raced en masse to get the story and attracted passersby who stopped to watch the antics.

Less than a year after its purchase, the *Journal* claimed that its daily sales had jumped to almost 379,000 and that it now had the largest circulation of any paper on earth printed in the English language. That rankled the *World,* which claimed the next day that *its* circulation was the largest in the world, with its Sunday sales alone more than half a million.

The presidential campaign of 1896 reached a peak that summer. Every important newspaper in the city except the *Journal* favored Republican William McKinley. The *World* balked at a Democratic candidate for the first time since Pulitzer had bought the paper. He felt that William Jennings Bryan was too radical with his free-silver policy, which was asserted to be the antithesis of sound money.

Hearst conferred with his editorial and business advisers, and they almost unanimously urged that he endorse McKinley. But the Chief would not take their advice. He believed that support of Bryan would lead to the *Journal*'s replacing the *World* as New York's leading Democratic organ and draw readers away from Pulitzer's paper. The day after the conference, the *Journal* came out in favor of the Great Commoner. The *Journal* assailed McKinley daily, but his campaign manager, Mark Hanna, was attacked even more vehemently. Homer Davenport drew cartoons of Hanna wearing suits of dollar signs and depicted McKinley as his puppet.

Fall had hardly arrived when Hearst plunged ahead in another direction to trim the *World*'s circulation and aid the Bryan campaign. The first edition of the *Evening Journal* was published on September 28, while the opposing papers were engaged in vicious mudslinging. Although McKinley won, the *Journal* claimed that it had distributed 1,506,634 copies of the election issue, with the morning edition alone accounting for 956,921. The Audit Bureau of Circulation was still years from existence, and there was no way to check the accuracy of those figures and verify that Hearst had reached a high mark of circulation in American journalism. But he had succeeded in having a paper whose average daily sales were second only to those of the *World*.

Before the campaign ended, the *Journal* scored an achievement that dealt another blow to the *World*'s supremacy. George Pancoast, one of Hearst's close aides, and R. Hoe & Company produced an improved press that could print from four to sixteen pages all in color. During October, the first color comics appeared in the *Journal*, described as "eight pages of iridescent polychromous effulgence that makes the rainbow look like a lead pipe."[9]

The "Yellow Kid" race was on in full force. George B. Luks drew the saffron-garbed boy in *Hogan's Alley* for the *World*, while Outcault sketched the youngster with exaggerated ears, queer toes, and long-flowing skirt for the *Journal*. Until now, in both the *World* and the *Journal*, Outcault's creation had appeared in a one-panel format, but on October 18 it showed up in the *Journal* in progressive panel narration, the first definitive comic strip. Edward W. Townsend, one of Hearst's *Examiner* employees, wrote the script. Outcault sought an injunction to prevent the *World* from running *Hogan's Alley* but failed. Never had the city seen so many "Yellow Kids," and through the competition, the forerunners of twentieth-century comic strips arose. The splashing of color in the Sunday sections of both papers produced a term that would boomerang because of its extreme sensationalism: yellow journalism.

The *Journal* invaded another area that had helped make the *World* great: crusading. While Pulitzer's paper campaigned for one-dollar gas for consumers, Hearst procured an injunction restraining the mayor and aldermen from granting a $10 million fuel-gas franchise to the Consumer's Company. The *Journal* cheered the move with a front-page streamer: "WHILE OTHERS TALK THE JOURNAL ACTS."[10] Three days later the city fathers withdrew the gas bill. Having tasted the fruits of successful crusading that resulted in increased circulation, the *Journal* proceeded to campaign for more reforms.

Hearst's paper provided food and fuel to the hungry and cold. Five wagons were kept busy all day in carrying supplies to the starving and sick.

The art department of the *Journal,* early 1900s. (*The Journal-American*)

Her rescue, orchestrated by the *Journal,* aroused anti-Spanish sentiments among the American public. (*The Journal-American*)

Pulitzer was anti-militant, but his rivalry with Hearst helped foment the Spanish-American War. (Author's collection)

Arthur Brisbane, busy at his
Journal, writing editorials
and giving out assignments.
(*The Journal-American*)

Park Row in the 1880s, before the *World's* gilded dome arose over the scene. (*Editor and Publisher*)

Henry Jarvis Raymond, founder of *The New York Times*. His principles animate the paper to this day. (Author's collection)

Adolph Simon Ochs, who revived *The New York Times*. (Author's collection)

William Randolph Hearst of the *Journal*. He knew no bounds, in newspaper publishing and in politics. (Courtesy the Hearst Corporation)

Charles A. Dana, editor of the *Sun*. He believed newspaper writing should be of high literary quality. (Author's collection)

Horace Greeley, in his active days as editor of the *Tribune*. (Author's collection)

James Gordon Bennett Jr. of the *Herald*. He created news, rather than waiting for it to happen. (Author's collection)

Park Row in its heyday, boasting more newspapers and publications than any other street in the world. (Author's collection)

Frank Andrew Munsey did not believe newspapers should exist if they were not economically sound. (Burr McIntosh; author's collection)

Upper left: George Jones. Upper right: Whitelaw Reid. Center: Charles Anderson Dana. Lower left: Jay Gould. Lower right: James Gordon Bennett Jr. (The J. Clarence Davies Collection, Museum of the City of New York)

NATURAL HISTORY.
THE SOUTHERN SAWBONES.

HIS dangerous animal is found in the latitude of Philadelphia.

It is carnivorous, subsisting principally upon boarding-house keepers, and devours poor widows in that line with the utmost voracity. While its palate rejects no tradesmen, it has a tooth single to tailors. It also feeds with keen relish upon the words of Governor Wise.

The habits of the Sawbones are foul and clinging. There is one weed that it continually chews, the juice of which oozes out at the corners of its mouth, and defiles its track. It is said by huntsmen—employed by the city authorities—that they are thus enabled to follow their game. It never goes to water; its eyes are wild, rolling, and red; its hair attains a length that laughs at the shearer; its whole appearance is fierce and shaggy. As it roams the streets at night, women and children flee, affrighted, while nothing but the knowledge that the creature is really a coward preserves the spirit of the men tremendous.

The Sawbones has never been domesticated; and the eminent African explorer, Mr. Du Chaillu, while on a recent visit to its chosen haunts, expressed the belief that it is a member of the Gorilla species, partly basing it upon a passion remarkable in both animals for brandishing great sticks, such as the branches of small trees, or silver-headed canes.

It is thought that the species will finally disappear before advancing civilization. Being acutely sensitive to changes of climate, every Northern blast drives away a large number. Not long since more than three hundred migrated in one drove. The community slept more soundly, and relaxed many precautions against the predatory incursions of the dreaded beast.

Damning with Faint Praise.

The *Tribune* reprints from the *London Examiner* the following opinion of Mr. Bayard Taylor:—

"A clever, cheerful man, who has run over much of the surface of the globe, and written many welcome books of travel. He is a gossip who never exceeds the bounds of discretion; he likes much to see lions, whether in the flesh or whether built of stone, but he has left in no country a man who has reason to be sorry for attention shown to him."

This is wholly out of proportion to Mr. Taylor's merits, and we wonder at the *Tribune's* want of consideration in reproducing it. It is of the same order of approbation that a letter of introduction after this style would be:—

DEAR SIR : This will introduce to you Mr. John Robinson. He is a person of decent manners, does not swear oppressively in company, and, if cautioned, will not soil your carpets with tobacco juice. He is fond of wine, but you may be sure that when he leaves your house, he will not carry away any of the spoons in his pocket, and will not be likely afterward to abuse, in public, any members of your family.

Yours truly, &c.,

The Squatter Sovereign of the Old World.

The Grand Lama.

Adjournment of Congress.

Pro Rogueing.

Important to Ladies.

CORRECTION.—The rumor to the effect that the new bonnets are sold by the yard is unfounded. They are, as yet, sold only by the foot.

The further report that the dressing-apartments of all the ball-rooms in this city have been enlarged for the accommodation of the aforesaid bonnets, is also erroneous. They are not yet enlarged, but are to be at an early period.

Weight for the Waggon.

There is, according to the *Newark Advertiser*, a man by the name of Will, in Monmouth County, N. J., who weighs four hundred and seventy-two pounds: he is a lively evidence of the truth of the adage that Where there's a Will there's a Weigh.

A Sensation Writer.

Louis Napoleon.

"BLOW, HERALD, BLOW!"

" HEAR THE TRIBUNE SPEAK."

The Age Progresses.

TO THE ENAMORED—Love Verses and Epistolary Correspondence, suited to amatory occasions, furnished on short notice. Portraits sent for personal descriptions faithfully returned. Strict confidence and inviolable secrecy maintained.—*Herald.*

We suppose the advertiser will soon announce that he " is ready, at all times to furnish the amount of affection to be bestowed upon any person of the opposite sex." And that, " if his male customers feel too bashful to place themselves under the matrimonial yoke, he will gladly offer himself as the substitute, at moderate prices."

The Lion and the Bear.

A speaker at the late shoemakers' meeting at Lynn strongly advocated the strike, and says it must be carried through with " lion hearts." From present appearances we judge that the strikers will not only have to be Lion-hearted, but Bear-footed also.

Artless Joke.

Clark Mills' Statue of Washington.

JONATHAN TO STEPHEN.

Waäll, Steve, haöw's bizniss, aöut yeöur way ?—
   A-fluctooatin' more or less ?
They say *your* trade is ruther brisk :
   Mighty onsartin though, I guess.

Fact is, the public's mighty queer,
   It favors enterprisin' chaps ;
W'at sot it so ag'in yeöu, Steve ?
   It's took a prejudice, perhaps.

You're all-fired smaärt, that's plain enough ;
   But so'thin's wantin'—I do'no—
A sort o' modesty, I guess,
   Or else your principles won't go.

'S'pect you've abaöut forgot me, Steve ;
   Likely I wa'n't no great acc'ount ;—
D'ye recollect the deestric' school
   We went to, once-t, up in Varmaöunt ?

We sot together 'baöut a year,
   And larned a thing or two, I *think ;*—
Remember them two pooty gals,
   Eüphemy Tubbs an' Almy Spink ?

Yeöu hed a takin' way, ye know ;
   Ye got along fust-rate with *one ;*
I mean Eüpheme, the light-haired gal,—
   Ye might 'a' hed her, sure's a gun.

O, yeöu remember well enough !
   Ye know ye kind o' waänted her !
Ef *I*'d 'a' be'n in your place, Steve,
   I'd a stuck to 'Phemy like a burr.

Ye would n't hev ketched *me* playin' smaärt,
   An' foolin' 'raoun' that Almy Spink ;
No sech peart, braöwn.complectid thing
   Could fetch *me* over with a wink.

Eüpheme, ye know, she up 'n' vaöwed
   Ye shouldn't fool with *her* no more ;
'N' ye did n't, nuther, did ye, Steve ?—
   Yeöu woozent eq'al to the chore.

Then Almy, bein spunky teöo,
   Jest up'n' said, " The hull 'r none !"
But yeöu *would* heng araöun' Eüpheme,
   An' so she dropped ye like a stun.

They say Time fetches things araöun'
   In sort o' circles. Naöw jes' look :
I swow ef yeöu aint ketched *ag'in,*
   On pooty nigh the same old hook !

This time it's so'thin's serious ;
   It ain't exactly idle sportin' :
You've sp'ilt yer only airthly chance
   By foolish Presidential courtin'.

I'm lately ruther apt to guess
   Old Bullion's language wa'n't all saöund ;
You recollect he told ye, once-t,
   " Your coat-tails hung teöo nigh the graöund !"

I s'pose he meant, Your pattern's small,
   Consid'rin' what ye want to deö ;
An' argyin' from w'at I've laärnt
   Most common folks think jes' so, teöo.

Ye've damaged everything ye've tetched ;
   On every p'int ye've hed yer say ;
Ye've bayed the moon of Treüth, quite smaärt :
   But naöw, poor dog, ye've hed yer day.

Of Course.

At the last meeting of the Sanitary Association, somebody asked what business-pursuit was, according to statistical evidence, most conducive to the health. We are happy to be able to answer that the statistics of the Inspecting and Guaging business show that the weighers always weigh a great deal more during a busy season than in a dull one.

" A Long and Successful Reign."
   The Deluge.

For much of the nation, Horace Greeley's voice was the one to listen to. (*Vanity Fair*)

Joseph Pulitzer of the *World*. His heart was with the people. (*Joseph Pulitzer by John Singer Sargent. Private collection. Photographed by Robert Holt III.*)

Park Row during the Civil War. (Author's collection)

Park Row between 1883 and 1889. (Author's collection)

This cartoon led Frank A. Munsey, portrayed as a grave digger, to fire J. Norman Lynd. (*Life*, October 5, 1916)

The statue of Horace Greeley, in front of the newspaper that he made famous. Installed in 1890, it was removed to City Hall Park in 1916 because it was considered dangerous to the subway section being constructed under the *Tribune* building. (Author's collection)

Joseph M. Patterson, founder of the *Daily News*, the most successful tabloid in America. (Courtesy of the *Daily News*)

The *Journal* also improved its news-gathering methods. It acquired a new International Code signal system that could be used at night. To prove its worth, the paper chartered two tugs equipped for an experiment, and off Sandy Hook, New Jersey, marine experts looked on as flags used in the code were distinguished plainly in the dark at a distance of almost two miles. Hearst ignored the fact that he was merely following in Pulitzer's footsteps as the *Journal* asserted in another front-page banner, "THE NEW JOURNALISM AGAIN VINDICATED AND VICTORIOUS."[11]

While the paper acclaimed the New Journalism, the Corbett-Fitzsimmons prizefight for the heavyweight championship of the world was scheduled for Carson City, Nevada, on March 17, 1897. Hearst signed the boxers to exclusive interview rights, but *World* correspondents talked with the participants, and former champion John L. Sullivan commented on the impending bout for Pulitzer's paper.

Twenty-five thousand people jammed Park Row and overflowed into City Hall Plaza on the day of the match to watch the results flashed upon newspaper bulletin boards. Outside the first floor of the Pulitzer building, a platform had been erected, containing a reproduction of the arena and ring two thousand miles away. Four-foot-high puppets identified as the fighters and their seconds could be seen from as far away as Broadway. Mr. and Mrs. John Till, renowned marionette operators, supervised telegraphic reports from Carson City. To prevent accidents, all trucks and wagons were barred from Park Row at the Brooklyn Bridge to the post office.

While the fight progressed, the string-manipulated manikins duplicated the actions of James J. Corbett and Bob Fitzsimmons, with each punch described by the telegrapher in the West. The match ended in the fourteenth round when Fitzsimmons knocked Corbett out with a blow that became famous in pugilistic history as the "solar plexus" punch. The crowd was about to disperse when the Tills repeated the last round—a forerunner of television replays.

The fight fans on Park Row were unaware of another battle that had been going on for years. The *Sun*'s publisher, William M. Laffan, had sabotaged the old New York Associated Press. Dana was president of the United Press, and it had garnered every important newspaper in the city, as well as many elsewhere. Meanwhile, the Associated Press of Illinois refused to be stampeded by the United Press, and its president, Victor F. Lawson, came to New York to lure papers from Laffan's organization.

The *World* was the first of the major metropolitan dailies to join Lawson's service. After that, other New York papers deserted the United Press, and the wire operation neared collapse toward the end of March 1897. During that month there were shades of the Moral War against the elder Bennett, this time against the *World*. The *Sun* and the *Journal* led the way in vitriol, with the *Times, Press, Advertiser,* and *Mail & Express* joining. Pulitzer contended that the *World* and *Herald* were the only two great and free newspapers in New York because they belonged to journalists who conducted their dailies on ideas of perfect freedom and independence. Editorials attacked Pulitzer's enemies as pharisees.

The blind publisher said that the *Times* had been a great paper under Raymond and Jones but that when it fell from the hands of dead journalists into the grip of living plutocrats, its fate was sealed. Turning to Hearst, Pulitzer called him a "silver king who with no principle or moral purpose in journalism, sought by sheer sensationalism to dazzle the town. . . . The *Journal*'s attempted rivalry of the *World* has not been the flattery of imitation, but the vulgarity of caricature . . . malice, assaults of greed and need."[12]

On the eighth day of Pulitzer's attack the *World* published a two-page article titled "Derelicts of Journalism." It contained many of the charges made during the preceding days, with Newspaper Row termed "Poverty Row." A diagram showed Park Row strewn with newspapers that had lost $10 million in the fourteen years since Pulitzer had arrived in the city. The *World* declared that the publications behind the vilification campaign were trust-controlled, dishonest dailies with owners representing Wall Street and corporations.

The *Journal* was called the "Behemoth of Deficits." It was described as having lost $2 million since Hearst's entry on the New York scene and as continuing to lose money. The *World*'s biggest guns were aimed at the *Sun*, which was accused of defending "every rogue since Tweed" and of defaming "every honest man who dared disagree with its vituperative editor."[13] Tables were printed showing the decline of the *Sun* and the growth of the *World* since 1883. Pulitzer charged that Dana was foremost among the mudslingers because he blamed the *Sun*'s setbacks on the *World*.

Throughout the attacks, the opposition fumed. Dana answered by calling Pulitzer a "villainous old Jew" who ran an "Academy of Crime."[14] The *Journal* described the *World*'s owner as "a journalist who made his money by pandering to the worst taste of the prurient and home-loving, by dealing in bogus news, such as forged cablegrams from eminent personages, and by affecting a devotion to the interests of the people while never really hurting the interests of their enemies, and sedulously looking out for his own."[15]

The *Herald, Tribune, Times,* and *Telegram* switched to the Associated Press.

Sixty-eight New England papers also deserted the United Press, as did other papers in the country. Only the *Sun* and the *Journal* were among the important papers that did not abandon the dying United Press for the Associated Press. Dana filed a bankruptcy plea for the U.P., and Laffan's control of a far-flung news association was over. The *Sun* did not return to the Associated Press fold. Instead, it developed its own Laffan Bureau, and the U.P. ceased rivaling the AP. Hearst, never a member of the sabotaged Associated Press, solved the problem by purchasing a moribund newspaper and merging it with the *Journal* to obtain its AP franchise. When he did, the *Journal* gloated:

> Yesterday the Journal destroyed all of Mr. Pulitzer's joy by consolidating with the Morning Advertiser, a newspaper which possessed an Associated Press franchise. . . . Poor Mr. Pulitzer, foiled Mr. Pulitzer, ridiculous Mr. Pulitzer, Mr. Pulitzer, of the cowardly and cornered New York World, member— together with the Journal—of the Associated Press.[16]

Dana had no love for the type of journalism provided by the *World* and the *Journal*. He called it the "popocratic press" and struck at both when the *World* referred to Hearst as the silver king:

> . . . the *New York World* is as much a progenitor of the *New York Journal* as Beelzebub was of the whole race of dung-flies. . . . There is not an offensive feature, or a contemptible trick, or an audacity of indecency on the part of the younger establishment, which has not been borrowed directly from the repertory of the pioneer or suggested by one of the *World*'s exploits.[17]

The race of time had passed by Dana. The New Journalism captivated the imagination of the masses with its brand of sensationalism, widespread news coverage, and extensive use of illustrations and photographs. He disapproved of the use of photography in newspapers, believing it to be an ill-fated fad. He also frowned on typesetting machines, feeling that the setting of type by hand possessed individuality similar to that of writing a letter by hand. In addition, Dana balked at putting bylines over stories. He insisted that each article should carry enough weight to bear the stamp of its own personality, but he retained his acumen for recognizing outstanding work.

The *Sun* had long printed on its front page the slogan "If you see it in the *Sun*, it's so." Its editor in chief, Edward P. Mitchell, showed editorial writer Francis Pharcellus Church a letter received from an eight-year-old child, Virginia O'Hanlon. She wondered whether there really was a Santa Claus, and her father had told her to write the *Sun* to find out. Mitchell thought it might lead to a worthwhile editorial. Church reluctantly wrote an answer, and the result was published on September 21, 1897, under the heading "Is There a Santa Claus?" Dana was elated when he read that editorial. "Real literature," he exulted. "Might be a good idea to reprint it every Christmas—yes, and even tell who wrote it!"[18]

Dana was seventy-eight when that literary gem, the most reprinted editorial in American journalism, appeared. In less than four months he was due to observe his thirtieth year as the *Sun*'s editor, but he did not live to mark the anniversary. On October 18 a two-line announcement—following his desire—appeared in his paper: "Charles Anderson Dana, Editor of *The Sun*, died yesterday afternoon." No further obituary of him was printed in the *Sun*. He passed away at a moment when Arthur Brisbane, indebted to Dana for his first job, was proving an outstanding force in the New Journalism dimming the radiant *Sun*.

Pulitzer named Brisbane managing editor of the *Evening World*, but he did not stay long in the post. Unhappy over a number of matters, including not being allowed to sign his name to editorials, Brisbane went over to the enemy in September. He earned from $10,000 to $15,000 a year on the *World*, but he proposed to Hearst that he take charge of the new *Evening Journal* and be paid $200 a week plus a dollar a week increase for every thousand circulation he added. Before a year passed, Brisbane earned $50,000, the largest salary paid an employee in journalism up to then.

Brisbane joined the *Journal* at a time when Hearst was attempting to provoke war between the United States and Spain. Strife had existed between Cuba and Spain for decades, and in the early nineties Hearst's *Examiner* had urged the country to intervene. A rebellion broke out on the island some months before Hearst bought the *Journal*, and soon after the purchase, that paper replaced Dana's *Sun* as the most vociferous on Park Row seeking Cuban freedom.

The *Journal* dubbed Gen. Valeriano Weyler, the new Spanish governor in Cuba, "Butcher." Reports of atrocities on the island dominated its front pages as Hearst appealed for intervention. Stories told of Spanish jailers taking Cuban captives from forts and prisons to be shot, of families tossed into fever-ridden concentration camps, of mutilated mothers and slain babies, and of dead Cubans thrown to the buzzards.

Pulitzer detested jingoism; his Civil War experiences had given him a hatred of the battlefield. But Hearst's driving agitation spurred the *World* into competition, and Pulitzer's correspondents in Cuba steadily produced exclusive stories. When *World* reporter Sylvester Scovel incurred the wrath of Weyler and was arrested, the *World* warned that he stood in "imminent danger of butchery by a decree of a drum-head court-martial."[19] Readers were aroused, mass meetings glorified the correspondent, and state legislatures the country over approved resolutions demanding his release.

Bennett believed a war between the United States and Spain was inevitable. To his homes in France came some of the world's notable figures. He gathered information from them that led him to believe that not only would such a struggle occur but that Japan, when ready, would seize the opportunity to strike at the United States.

Four New York newspapers maintained reporters in Cuba: the *World*, *Journal*, *Herald*, and *Sun*. Pulitzer's staff included author Stephen Crane. Hearst sent Richard Harding Davis and artist Frederic Remington to Havana. Remington saw little need of remaining in Cuba, and he wired the Chief, "Everything is quiet. There is no trouble here. There will be no war. I wish to return."[20] The word spread that Hearst cabled back, "Please remain. You furnish the pictures, and I'll furnish the war." The Chief made no comment about that report, but years later told his son, William Randolph Jr., that he had never sent such a cable.

Whenever a news item from Cuba appeared in the *Journal* offices, Hearst scrutinized it closely, hoping to discover an incident that would shock readers. Davis reported that a police matron had searched a girl suspected of carrying secret dispatches in the privacy of her room aboard the American steamer *Olivetta*. When the story appeared, it was accompanied by a Remington illustration showing a young girl standing naked before three men. Davis vehemently denied that the woman was unclothed and searched by men. He said that Remington had drawn an imaginary picture of the scene.

When McKinley had campaigned for the White House, he believed the United States should intervene to give Cuba independence, but as president-elect, he seemed to have changed his attitude. The *Journal* warned that if the United States did not take action, McKinley's administration would become discredited and despised, and the country would never forgive him.

Journal correspondent George Bryson wired his office in New York that eighteen-year-old Evangelina Cisneros, daughter of a Cuban insurgent, had been assaulted in the Isle of Pines penal settlement by the new military commander and transferred to a prison in Havana. Hearst jumped at the chance of arousing the nation over her plight: "The unspeakable fate to which Weyler has doomed an innocent girl whose only crime is that she has defended her honor against a beast in uniform has sent a shudder of horror through the American people."[21] The *Journal* followed up that statement by saying that she was reared in seclusion and was as ignorant of the world as a cloistered nun.

The paper telegraphed Weyler, asking mercy for Miss Cisneros, and it also appealed to prominent women in the United States to petition the pope and Spain's queen regent on her behalf. The sympathy of American women, including that of McKinley's mother, overflowed for the señorita. Consul-General Fitzhugh Lee, the respected nephew of Gen. Robert E. Lee, investigated the case. Upon his return from Cuba, Lee said that a stupid impression prevailed about the conditions in which Miss Cisnero dwelled. He said she had two clean rooms, was well-clothed and fed, was not subjected to cruelties and indignities, and would have been pardoned long before if not for the hubbub created by American papers. Lee also said he believed her name was now on the roll for pardon.

Women in the United States, who had sympathized with Evangelina Cisneros, considered Lee's findings a canard and refused to believe the story. "This girl," Hearst told Sam Chamberlain, "must be saved, if we have to take her out of prison by force."[22] *Journal* reporter Karl Decker and two others, William McDonald, an American businessman in Havana, and Cuban insurgent Carlos F. Carbonell, hatched a plan to free her. To make certain that bribed guards would not be blamed, the rescuers sawed bars from the girl's prison window. They dragged her out and smuggled her aboard a steamship bound for the United States. Miss Cisneros and Carbonell, who became a member of Lee's staff, were married in Baltimore eight months later.

The *Journal* hailed the rescue as the greatest journalistic coup of the age and explained that, since all other methods had been unavailing, the paper had decided to secure her liberation through force. It acknowledged the action was illegal but added, "The *Journal* is ready to stand all the consequences of what it has done."[23] The paper quoted McKinley's mother two days later: "I am greatly pleased at the release of Miss Cisneros."

The *Times* could not see the rescue through Hearst's eyes. It pointed out that the young woman had been charged with lending material aid in armed rebellion to constituted authority and that she had been convicted after a trial. The *Times* also said that she had been accused of plotting with others to assassinate a high official. It added that the rescue was indefensible and that "if acts like this are to be committed, international relations become impossible, and war is the only condition in which nations can exist."[24]

The fury in the United States against Spain abated with the señorita's rescue. Weyler was returned to Spain, which announced part autonomy for the Cubans. Then, when it seemed that Hearst had failed to attain his goal of war, the *Journal* intercepted a letter that plunged the country into a new fervor.

Depuy de Lome, Spanish minister to the United States, wrote a letter to a friend in which he discussed McKinley's annual message to Congress. In disapproving of the address, he described McKinley as "weak and catering to the rabble, and, besides, a low politician who desires to leave a door open to himself and to stand well with the jingoes of his party."[25] The letter was stolen and taken to the *Journal,* which defended McKinley in a story with a front-page streamer: "THE WORST INSULT TO THE UNITED STATES IN ITS HISTORY." The minister immediately cabled his resignation to Spain, and the *Journal* banner read, "JOURNAL'S LETTER GETS DE LOME HIS WALKING PAPERS."[26]

The battleship *Maine* blew up in Havana Harbor five days later, February 15, 1898. The *Journal* and *World* published extras, vying with each other to produce the largest and most terrifying scareheads. Day after day the *World* and *Journal* played up the *Maine*'s destruction with banner headlines, diagrams, illustrations, and photographs accompanying shock stories. The *World* wired its Key West, Florida, correspondent to hire divers and investigate the explosion. The *Journal* was not so cautious: "THE WARSHIP MAINE WAS SPLIT IN TWO BY AN ENEMY'S SECRET INFERNAL MACHINE."[27] Hearst offered a $50,000 reward for information leading to the conviction of the guilty parties.

His banners stirred readers: "WAR! SURE! MAINE DESTROYED BY SPANISH"[28] . . . "THE WHOLE COUNTRY THRILLS WITH THE WAR FEVER"[29] . . . "NEW PROOFS THAT TREACHERY DESTROYED THE BATTLE SHIP MAINE"[30] . . . "WAR MAY NOW BE DECLARED."[31]

Some of the *World*'s headlines were equally sensational: "IS SPAIN AFRAID OF THE *WORLD*'S PUBLICITY?" . . . "GEN. MILES SAYS WE ARE UNPREPARED FOR WAR BUT *WORLD* INVESTIGATION PROVES OTHERWISE" . . . "FIFTY PHYSICAL PROOFS THAT THE MAINE WAS BLOWN UP BY A SUBMARINE MINE OR A TORPEDO."[32]

Most other papers in the city frantically strove to hold their own against Hearst and Pulitzer. Edwin Lawrence Godkin of the *Evening Post* was appalled by their moves: "The lies of our two New York lying journals have really been a source of enormous gain, as far as we can learn. It has been found that the more wonderful and incredible their stories, the fouler their imputations . . . the more absurd and delusive their cartoons, the more eagerly they are bought and read."[33]

The Hearst newspapers pulled out more stops in March: "We have a government owned by Wall Street gamblers, and a President owned by an Ohio bribe-giver Mark Hanna. . . . A good war might free Cuba, wipe out Spain, frighten half to death the meanest tribe of money-worshipping parasites that has ever disgraced a decent nation."[34]

Less than two weeks later the *Journal* wrote: "If you oppose interference in Cuba by the United States, you are either a coward and a disgrace to those responsible for your birth or a poor ignorant thing not worth bothering about."[35]

A Spanish commission investigating the destruction of the *Maine* concluded that an internal accident had destroyed the battleship. An American naval court of inquiry, however, blamed the sinking on an external explosion. (Almost eighty years later another naval investigation, supervised by Adm. Hyman Rickover, found no evidence to support that allegation.[36])

McKinley prepared to address Congress. Stewart L. Woodford, the U.S. ambassador to Madrid, informed the president that Spain would agree to American demands if it could do so with dignity. McKinley delayed the speech and asked for more time to negotiate with Spain. That provided another *Journal* headline: "PEACE WITH SHAME." There was no question how the paper felt toward the president: "When we have done with Spain, the question will be what to do with McKinley. He will drag along through his term the most despised man ever elected to a great office."[37]

The same kind of name-calling hurled at Lincoln prior to the Civil War now focused on McKinley: "He has confessed himself weak, cowardly, shuffling, deceitful, cringing, dull brained, incapable even of expressing his paltroonery in intelligible language."[38]

The *World* at first agreed with McKinley that it was unwise to rush into a needless conflict, but Pulitzer's antimilitant spirit vanished in the circulation battle with Hearst. The *World* changed its mind in less than a month: "It is indeed time for action, and if Spain does not yield to our just demand, it is time for Force, or war, if it must be so called, 'short, sharp and decisive.' . . . To be short and sharp in war is to be merciful as well as economical."[39]

Hearst went ahead with a memorial to the Americans who had lost their lives on the *Maine*. The *Journal* solicited the names of notables it could quote, but former president Cleveland replied to the paper, "I decline to allow my sorrow for those who died on the *Maine* to be perverted to an advertising scheme for the New York *Journal*."[40]

A front-page interview in the Hearst paper quoted Assistant Secretary of the Navy Theodore Roosevelt: " 'It is cheering to find a newspaper of the great influence and circulation of the *Journal* tell the facts as they exist and ignore the suggestions of various kinds that emanate from sources that cannot be described as patriotic or loyal to the flag of this country.' "[41]

Roosevelt repudiated the interview the next day. He told the Associated Press that the report was "false, fictitious and fraudulent from the first word to the last." Roosevelt denounced the reporter's conduct as "infamous" and said the paper should have known the interview was a lie "if for no other reason than that I have never given a certificate of character to the *Journal.*" Pulitzer was overjoyed. Roosevelt's refutation was headlined on the front page of the *World,* which described the *Journal* as a newspaper "whose war news has been written by fools for fools."[42]

The shadow of impending war spread itself over the United States. Washington statesmen denounced yellow journalism, and rumors circulated that Spanish ships would sail from the Mediterranean to attack Adm. George Dewey in Manila Bay before two U.S. monitors could reach the Philippines. Hearst informed James Creelman, a correspondent in London, that if the Spanish fleet started for Manila, he wanted to buy a big English steamer and have it taken to the Suez Canal where she could be sunk and obstruct the passage of the Spanish warships: ". . . I understand that if a British vessel were taken into the canal and sunk under the circumstances outlined above, the British Government would not allow her to be blown up to clear a passage and it might take time enough to raise her to put Dewey in a safe position."[43]

Spain severed relations with the United States, and Congress formally declared on April 25 that war had existed for four days. The *World* and *Journal* spared no money or energy in covering the fighting. Brisbane's genius for typography, including four-inch streamers on the front page, drove the *Journal* on to far more than a million copies a day, while the *World* approached the figure.

Headlines goaded the public with misleading facts. Brisbane exhausted all the metal type and resorted to wooden headlines. On the editorial page, he produced leaders in short, pithy, one-sentence paragraphs for the masses in common, down-to-earth English that they could grasp and visualize. Illustrations and photographs stirred the imagination of immigrants unable to read the paper.

The war of yellow journalism—the private war between Pulitzer and Hearst—had blossomed into warfare between nations. While Brisbane remained on the home front, Hearst chartered a steamship and a fleet of tugs and sailed to the war zone with correspondents, artists, and photographers. He acted as a reporter during some of the fighting. When a Mauser bullet smashed the arm of his correspondent Creelman at El Caney and he was lying on the grass, the Chief appeared, took down his story, and remarked, "I'm sorry you're hurt, but wasn't it a splendid fight? We must beat every paper in the world."[44]

The *World* reported that a Hearst dispatch boat was detained by military personnel when it was suspected that reporters aboard had surreptitiously obtained government documents and planned to take the vessel to a port where they could wire the information back home. The *World* reported the incident under the headline " 'Zeal' by Theft in News-Gathering Thwarted at Port Tampa."[45] Hearst immediately filed a $500 million libel suit against Pulitzer's company, denouncing the story as a malicious falsehood.

On the same day, the *Journal* published an item that made the *World* a laughingstock. Editorial writer Arthur McEwen doctored a report that appeared in a dispatch from a staff correspondent. Planted among San Juan casualties was the name of Col. "Reflipe W. Thenus," described as a distinguished Austrian artillery officer. The *World* reprinted the name, and the *Journal* revealed that "Reflipe W. Thenus" was actually "We pilfer the news" in a scrambled arrangement.

Godkin condemned the actions of both papers: "A yellow journal office is probably the nearest approach, in atmosphere, to Hell, existing in any Christian state. A better place in which to prepare a young man for eternal damnation than a yellow journal office does not exist."[46] As the war progressed, he blasted Hearst, saying that a "blackguard boy with several millions of dollars at his disposal has more influence on the use a great nation makes of its credit, of its army and navy, of its name and traditions, than all the statesmen and philosophers and professors in the country."[47]

Extras were plentiful during the war, and often the *Journal* printed as many as forty a day, a record the *World* did not match. Newspapers, including Bennett's *Herald*, competed for exclusives. The greatest beat of the war came when the *World* announced Dewey's victory at Manila on May 7. Not only had Pulitzer's paper scooped all others, but McKinley and the secretary of the navy also first learned of the victory in telegrams from Pulitzer's paper. The end of the war in July saw both the *World* and *Journal* with circulations of more than a million a day. Secretary of State John Hay echoed their sentiments by calling it a "splendid little war." It had been short and not too far away, and it offered much freedom for the front-line reporter.

The war hurt both Hearst and Pulitzer. Hearst had been forced to spend the millions his mother had given him, and the *Journal* dismissed more than one hundred employees after the shooting stopped. Despite its record circulation, the *World,* for the first time under Pulitzer, showed a loss. With the conflict over, he ceased indulging in strident yellow journalism.

That was not so with Hearst. In the years that lay ahead he would wield much good for the nation, but as the elder Bennett became the most horse-whipped editor, Hearst would become the target of more vituperative attacks than any other person in American journalism. In addition, he would become the most controversial publisher the nation had known.

10

Little Man in the Big City

NEW YORK CITY, growing as if with an uncontrollable pituitary gland, stepped into the twentieth century as the most populous city in the nation. Immigrants arrived in unprecedented numbers to escape from European poverty and tyranny and to walk expectantly along the streets believed to be paved with gold. Skyscrapers were on the horizon, and subway construction was under way that would eventually doom the noisy overhead "El." The dollar signs of Wall Street and the antics of New York's high society—its "400" leading families—turned the world's attention and ambitions toward the big city.

Outside of New York, attention was paid to editorials in such newspapers as Joseph Medill's *Chicago Tribune*, William Rockhill Nelson's Kansas City *Star*, and Henry Watterson's Louisville *Courier-Journal*. Also heard was the voice of a small-city editor in Kansas: William Allen White of the *Emporia Gazette*.

Park Row, however, was the nation's newspaper capital. The *Evening Journal* and *Evening World* prepared for the new age by competing to present McKinley with the first daily of 1901. The *World* relied upon a Pennsylvania Railroad train to take its paper-entrusted messenger to Washington. Only reporter Langdon Smith was aboard a special *Journal* train that raced against it and arrived in the capital in four hours and fifteen minutes, the fastest time made between New York and Washington. The next day that paper's banner read, "THE JOURNAL, THE FIRST NEWSPAPER OF THIS CENTURY.—MCKINLEY." Not to be outdone, the *World* ran the first copy off the presses at two seconds past midnight, and its headline read, "THE FIRST NEWSPAPER PRINTED ON THE WESTERN HEMISPHERE IN THE 20TH CENTURY."

The *Journal*'s train reached Washington earlier, but Smith had to wait in the White House anteroom while Pulitzer's paper was the first given to McKinley. The president was smarting over the *Journal*'s criticisms of him and did not want Hearst's publication to receive the honor.

The morning *World* reverted to the now-pallid sensationalism that had seemed so startling before Hearst's entry into New York. It greeted the new year by transforming itself for one day into tabloid form, supervised by Britain's Alfred Harmsworth. The editor of the London *Daily Mail* called it "the busy man's newspaper." He had been invited by Pulitzer to produce a twentieth-century daily. Assisted by *World* employees, who appeared at work in evening clothes out of respect for the Briton, Harmsworth (later Lord Northcliffe) produced a paper on January 1 with pages less than half the length of those in the regular issue. He wrote that every item in the edition was made to be read within sixty seconds, because people in the new century would be too busy to peruse drawn-out articles: "I claim that by my system of condensed or tabloid journalism hundreds of working hours can be saved each year."[1]

The tabloid sold an additional one hundred thousand copies of the *World.* Magazines praised the issue, but editors of dailies elsewhere and subscribers were of mixed opinions. The Springfield *Republican* called it "a queer newspaper hash, wherein a fine chopping had dissipated flavors that ought to be manifold and distinct and left a decidedly dry and stringy result."[2] Inventor Thomas Alva Edison said he believed the idea was an innovation that all great newspapers must adopt.

The tabloid's size was as old as New York penny journalism. The papers that Day and the elder Bennett had established in the 1830s had been little larger. Also, Frank A. Munsey had established New York's first modern tabloid when he took a six-month option on the morning New York *Star* in February 1891 and renamed it the *Continent.* Munsey believed that passengers on the elevated railroad could read a tabloid, unlike a full-sized newspaper, without disturbing other riders. However, after only four months and a loss of $40,000, Munsey returned the paper in June to the man who had given him the option, railroad magnate Collis P. Huntington. The *Continent* was renamed the *Morning Advertiser* and put under the editorship of Col. John A. Cockerill, Pulitzer's right-hand man, with whom he had split.

The *Advertiser* was the paper later purchased by Hearst for its Associated Press franchise. With the greatest circulation in the country, the *Evening Journal* continued on its blatantly yellow course. Grotesque, motley ink smeared readers' hands and ruined gloves touching the sheet, which was condemned for being too sensational, vulgar, and unreliable. Circulation was uppermost in Arthur Brisbane's mind, and to gain it, he defended yellow-journal tactics. "I expect," he scoffed, "that before long somebody else may come along and run a paper that will be more radical than ours, and will attack our papers for being too conservative."[3]

Brisbane not only directed the newspaper but also dictated the size of the

headlines on major stories. He devised various methods of increasing the
evening edition's sales. One was "putting the paper to bed" at 7:00 A.M. so
that it could be bought before noon in places as distant as Albany, more than
150 miles away. Readers were not perturbed because it contained only the
news of the day before. They wanted the paper for its regular features:
Brisbane's editorials, advice to the lovelorn as dispensed by Beatrice Fairfax
and Dorothy Dix, Ella Wheeler Wilcox's poetry, and T. A. "Tad" Dorgan's
sport stories.

Brisbane achieved great popularity among the masses with his editorials.
His philosophical discussions of marriage and babies, diatribes against the
use of alcoholic beverages and tobacco, and discourses on the universe and
morality elicited more comment than any steady stream of editorials since
Greeley's day. They were written in language that was understood by the
semiliterate and unreflecting.

Brisbane's salary became a legend. College graduates the country over
swamped Park Row newspapers to seek jobs; convinced they could write
better editorials than Brisbane, they were willing to accept far less than the
one thousand dollars he received weekly. They seemed unaware that most
cub reporters were hired at fifteen or twenty dollars a week, while no other
newspaper employee was paid a salary even approaching that of the *Evening
Journal*'s managing editor and chief editorial writer.

Park Row was glorified in fiction, and much of it referred to newspapermen as journalists who trapped criminals and exposed public evils, rushed
out editorials that aroused statesmen, and created stories in haste that were
printed under banner headlines. The derelict newspapermen, morbid and
miserable, who haunted the Row's saloons were seldom described.

Dana's *Sun* had been the setting for many of the early romantic stories
about the nation's great newspaper area, but the success of Pulitzer and
Hearst changed that. With the onset of the twentieth century, their newspapers were the leading attractions for Park Row's observers. No other editors
appeared who could produce a more radical daily, but publisher Adolph
Simon Ochs had arrived on Newspaper Row, and his success was being
talked about for other reasons. Although he shied away from outlandish
attempts to attract readers, he understood the principles that brought fame
and notoriety.

The five-foot-seven Ochs was shorter than most of the publishers who
had made Park Row so popular. He arrived in New York in 1896 from
Tennessee, well-grounded in journalism. Under his guidance the decrepit
Chattanooga *Times* had become the most successful newspaper in the region.

Ochs was born of Jewish parents in C
father, Julius, and his mother, Bertha, h;
Germany but met for the first time in 1
she was shopping in his dry-goods store.
less than three years old. Adolph was the
two boys and three girls. The multitalen
in the Mexican War and as a captain on
Army during the Civil War. His wife di(
issue and was embarrassingly pro-Confe(

142

to house his pape
few months af
banks, yet
profitab
colla

After the Civil War ended, the Ochs f
see, where it hoped business opportunities might be good, but the post-
bellum economic distress of the South kept the Ochses in poverty. To help
out, eleven-year-old Adolph became a carrier for the Knoxville *Chronicle* at
twenty-five cents a day. At fourteen, he left school and became a full-time
employee at the paper. One of his jobs was that of a printer's devil. He liked
the newspaper atmosphere so much that three years later he went to work as
a compositor and part-time reporter on the Louisville *Courier-Journal*. He
was homesick, however, and six months later returned to Knoxville, where
he became a printer on the *Tribune*.

Ochs was nineteen when, in the fall of 1877, *Tribune* colleague Franc Paul
launched the Chattanooga *Dispatch* and brought him into the newspaper as
business solicitor. The project collapsed within a few months, but it provided
Ochs with the determination to control an operation whenever possible. He
borrowed $300 from a bank and, with $250 of it, purchased a half-interest
in the Chattanooga *Times*, circulation 250 daily, with a right to buy the other
half in two years. In less than a year his name appeared on the masthead as
publisher. After purchasing Associated Press service, he was left with $12.50
working capital. Two years later, as editor and publisher, he had transformed
the moribund Chattanooga *Times* into a journal eagerly patronized by towns-
folk.

With the Chattanooga *Times* a profitable venture, Ochs married Effie
Wise, the daughter of Cincinnati Rabbi Isaac M. Wise, on February 28,
1883. Their honeymoon took them to Washington, where they were received
by President Chester A. Arthur. Ochs's newspaper, following a conservative
course, brought him into association with leading politicians.

A real-estate boom prompted Ochs to invest much of his earnings in land
near Chattanooga, where he planned to establish a suburban community to
be called Timesville. A real-estate collapse in the late eighties wrecked that
hope. Undismayed, he prepared to erect the largest building in Chattanooga

...r, but the crash of 1893 threatened him with bankruptcy a ...er the six-story building opened. Ochs borrowed heavily from ...he needed more money. The Chattanooga *Times* was highly ...e, and he arranged a $300,000 bond issue on the property to use as ...eral for his loans.

Ochs decided to gamble on the purchase of another journal to increase his income. Friends advised him to strike out for New York City. After studying the Manhattan field, he wrote friend Casper H. Rowe: "There is going to be a great change in the newspapers in New York in the next five years, for I believe in less than five years Mr. Dana will die of old age, Pulitzer of nervous prostration and Bennett of riotous living."[4]

At first, Ochs considered purchasing the New York *Mercury,* but after months of negotiations, the deal fell through in March 1896, when the paper's owners were unable to assure him that the *Mercury*'s United Press service could be transferred to a new owner. That month, on his thirty-eighth birthday, he received a telegram from Harry Alloway, an acquaintance and a Wall Street reporter for the financially ailing New York *Times.* Alloway said Ochs had an opportunity to buy cheaply the paper that Henry Jarvis Raymond had founded.

Ochs believed that the *Times* offered the greatest journalistic opportunity in the country. He was in Chicago when he mentioned the Alloway wire to Herman H. Kohlsaat, publisher of the Chicago *Times-Herald.* Kohlsaat thought this was Ochs's big moment, but the Southerner replied that he might not be big enough for the job. "Don't tell anybody," Kohlsaat said, "and they'll never find it out."[5]

Times publisher George Jones had died in 1891, and in his will had admonished his heirs never to sell the paper. Profits declined, and they raised its price from two cents to three. Circulation dropped, and the heirs decided to unload the journal and asked a million dollars for it. Editor in chief Charles R. Miller and other staff members feared the *Times* might fall into the hands of someone who would destroy its integrity. They raised a million dollars, but one subscriber failed to come through with his pledge of $50,000. The Jones heirs, however, sold the paper for $950,000 in April 1893 to the New York Times Publishing Company, with Miller as its president. The estate retained ownership rights to the building and equipment, while the new owners purchased only the paper's name and goodwill.

The panic of 1893 hurt the *Times.* Advertising decreased, and the new company was forced to obtain $250,000 through debenture notes. When Ochs received the Alloway telegram, the paper had sunk to the lowest financial level it was ever to know. Arriving in New York, Ochs learned the *Times* was running at a weekly deficit, as it had been doing for three years. A syndicate headed by a group of *Times* stockholders wanted to merge the paper with the weak New York *Recorder*, but Miller and Edward Cary, minority members of the board of directors, objected to the plan and placed the *Times* in receivership.

The losses Ochs had incurred in his nonjournalistic ventures had sharpened his business acumen. After Miller talked with him, he and other stockholders favored the Chattanoogan's taking over the paper. Charles R. Flint, who controlled three of the five directors, suggested that Ochs manage the proposed reorganized company at a salary of $50,000 a year. Ochs declined and countered with his own offer, which was accepted. A new organization, the New York Times Company, was created with a capital of ten thousand shares at $100 each. Ochs invested a borrowed $75,000 and received 1,125 shares. He was promised the paper's controlling interest at the end of three successive years during which the journal lost no money.

The receivership was lifted on August 13, 1896, and five days later the paper was under Ochs's management, with Miller retained as editor in chief. Ochs took over a publication printing nineteen thousand copies a day, with actual sales of only nine thousand. When he expressed the hope of increasing the circulation shortly, he was met with "Increase! Mr. Ochs, if you could keep it from going down any further you'd be a wonderful man!"[6]

He had to keep it from going down. His paper back in Chattanooga, as well as his other investments, depended upon his latest gamble. Ochs had no intention of competing with the *World* or *Journal*. Pulitzer and Hearst garnished their news with appeals to basic—and baser—emotions and spent more money than he had ever made. His paper would rely strictly on news and use no artificial means of increasing circulation. There would be no contests for children or housewives, no weekly novelettes or song sheets easily detached from the rest of the paper, no stimulating sex stories, no tales of fantasy that might label the *Times* as sensational.

Ochs abhorred comic strips, although one appeared ten years later. It was called *The Roosevelt Bears* and was published every Sunday for four months in 1906 in admiration of President Roosevelt, for whom Ochs had great respect. The strip vanished because it was considered too high class for anyone's taste.

In the beginning, Ochs did not plan to ignore all the techniques employed by Pulitzer and Hearst. Headlines would increase in length and width commensurate with the importance of the story. Photographs, too, would be displayed, although he had no desire to sprinkle them freely throughout the paper. His main competition would come from the conservative newspapers. Ochs recognized that among them a gap existed that his *Times* could fill. The *Sun* stressed its literary brilliance in preference to covering all the news. The *Tribune* catered to a small, sturdy, wealthy Republican following and was the party's foremost organ in the nation. The *Herald* was published for the stratum of society that had bitterly condemned Bennett's father. It appealed especially to the gentlemanly sporting elements, epitomized by the polo-playing, yacht-racing groups.

The city lacked a conservative Democratic publication that reported all the news. This was the opening for the *Times,* as Ochs was ready to adhere to the high character Raymond and Jones had established for the paper. The day after he became its publisher, Ochs made clear that he would continue to follow their principles. He said the *Times* would give all the news without fear or favor, regardless of party, sect, or interests involved. He added that the paper would become a "forum for the consideration of all questions of public importance, and to that end to invite intelligent discussion from all shades of opinion."[7]

Honest advertising became a part of Ochs's practiced doctrine in his efforts to operate the *Times* as a respectable paper. He barred objectionable advertising leading to fraud or misrepresentation, and patent-medicine advertisements with unsubstantiated claims were restricted.

Less than a month after Ochs took control, the *Times* inaugurated a magazine section that contained articles and photographs printed on a quality of paper usually reserved by other publications for special events. Patterned somewhat in makeup after the *World* and *Journal,* the magazine section omitted their sensationalism and provided information only. Before the second month ended, the first book-review section in American newspapers came off its presses and treated the criticism of books as news. The *Times*'s slogan, "It Does Not Soil the Breakfast Cloth," gave way to one the paper ever after retained: "All the News That's Fit to Print."[8] The motto was displayed in an electric sign at Madison Square.

Along Park Row, where skeptics questioned the possibility of success for Ochs, the slogan was criticized as insolent and presumptuous. He was delighted by the attacks and, to enhance publicity, offered $100 for a phrase of ten words or less that was more acceptable. The *Times* spelled out its philosophy, saying it wanted a motto that avoided sensationalism, revolting details of scandal, unfounded attacks on public persons, and reckless assaults on private interests. What it wanted was a slogan that appealed to the intelligent and thoughtful and distinguished the publication as one for the home and one that upheld morality, inspired patriotism, and encouraged good citizenship.

Thousands of suggestions were received, and the *Times* listed 150. Although the prize was awarded to D. M. Redfield of New Haven, Connecticut, for "All the World's News, but Not a School for Scandal," the paper held fast to the slogan that had upset Newspaper Row.

Ochs defended the gold standard, and editorials criticized William Jennings Bryan, the Democratic presidential candidate who had run a free-silver campaign. The publisher was accused of operating the *Times* as a Wall Street sheet. Pulitzer, in his astounding "Derelicts of Journalism," had asserted that J. P. Morgan and August Belmont were among those who actually controlled the *Times*. These two owned $25,000 each of the old company's debentures but had no authority.

When William Laffan's United Press collapsed, Pulitzer, holding a veto power over the granting of an Associated Press franchise to any of the city's other morning papers, consented to the *Sun*'s, *Herald*'s, and *Tribune*'s becoming full-fledged participants. However, fearing Ochs and foreseeing his potentialities, he permitted the weak *Times* only a Class B franchise, thereby restricting its services, although the Chattanooga *Times* was a member of the Western Associated Press. Not until 1900, when the Chicago *Inter-Ocean* won a case against the AP and the veto was ruled monopolistic, did the *Times* gain full membership.

Ochs struggled as the *Times*'s circulation rose slowly. He scooped all other papers in the city with its publication of photographs on Queen Victoria's jubilee in 1897. Fifty pictures appeared in the magazine section at a cost of $5,000 that was paid to an official photographer at the procession. Despite this triumph, the *Times* found itself at the end of Ochs's first year with a circulation of little more than twenty thousand and a deficit of $68,000.

The outbreak of the Spanish-American War saw the *Times* dependent upon regular news services for coverage. Unlike the wealthy owners of the *World, Journal,* and *Herald,* Ochs could not afford boats or special writers and artists. He had no money for frills, and at the end of the conflict was faced with ruin. His paper's advertising was still poor, although daily circulation had risen to twenty-five thousand in his second year. Ochs needed twice that to show a profit. Unfortunately, not only had the circulation grown, but so had the annual deficit—to $78,000. He could have eliminated the loss by accepting a Tammany offer amounting to $150,000 to print city government advertising, but Ochs did not want the public to believe the *Times* had sold out to Tammany leaders because of its struggle.

The moment had come for a drastic move. That October, Ochs amazed his associates by reducing the paper's price from three cents to one. They would not have been surprised to have seen him increase the price to five cents. No other conservative daily in the city charged less than three, and it was assumed that only a yellow sheet would sell for a penny. He declared in a front-page editorial that he did not intend to step into the field dominated by Pulitzer and Hearst and that only the price and not the character of the *Times* was being changed: "It puts before the people of New York a clean newspaper of high and honorable aims. . . . Should the results of the step we are now taking, after a fair trial, prove unsatisfactory we should not hesitate to reestablish the price of *The Times.*"[9]

The move paved the way for success. A one-cent clientele, disgusted with the fakes perpetrated by the yellow sheets, was hungry for his type of paper. The small-town publisher had stumbled upon a market in the big city eagerly awaiting a paper like the *Times* and at the price charged. Ochs had gambled upon his business judgment and succeeded.

Ochs was making a big profit by 1900 and had obtained full control of the paper. The *Times* gained added prestige in March when French commissioners granted Ochs exclusive rights to publish a daily newspaper on the grounds of the forthcoming Universal Exposition in Paris. He announced that the paper would run from eight to thirty-two pages a day and be printed from the latest web-perfecting press that could turn out fifty thousand complete newspapers an hour.

Ochs's brother George managed the Paris issue's operation, with a complete printing plant. On its first day, May 31, a sixteen-page paper was produced. Eight pages contained original matter, and the other eight were of facsimile reproduction of the May 21 and 22 issues of the parent paper. It was a surprise to Parisians, who were not used to seeing papers of more than eight pages.

When the exposition edition made its debut, an editorial in the New York *Times* said that the primary objective was that of all exhibitors, a business one, but that the paper in France would contain the substance of all the news of the United States as well as that of Europe on the morning of publication.

Copies of the special edition were distributed without charge at the exposition. They were also available at newspaper kiosks in the French capital and were generally sold throughout Europe. The paper continued to publish through October 31 and paved the way for the *Times* to provide the first real challenge to Bennett's dominance in the foreign-news field.

The *Herald*'s prominence abroad had started with Stanley's finding of Livingstone in Africa almost three decades before. Oswald Garrison Villard, who became publisher of the *Evening Post* after the death of his father Henry in 1900, wrote that the *Herald* with its international reputation was unsurpassed by any journal in the world. American expatriates were accustomed to reading Bennett's Paris *Herald*, founded in October 1877, which blended news of the United States and Europe with the activities of high society. But they were impressed by the *Paris Times*, as were thousands of visiting Americans who lived outside the New York paper's distribution area.

During the exposition, Adolph Ochs not only visited Paris but also met with members of the Walter family, owners of the prestigious *Times* of London. They discussed a mutual alliance that called for their New York and London papers to exchange special correspondence. The reciprocal agreement was put into effect in 1901, less than a year later, and lasted for more than a decade. On that first day, nine stories appeared on the front page under the credit line of *London Times-New York Times Special Cablegram*. The arrangement gave Ochs's paper the exclusive right in America to the entire news service of its London namesake. The alliance put his daily in touch with every source of important news over the habitable globe and provided a service second to none in value and completeness.

Ochs offered the public uncolored news that was more objective than that of most papers. Unhampered by political or Wall Street domination, his publication usually published the news as it evolved. It possessed no desire to extend itself by campaigning against the evils of politics and monopolies. Ochs left the crusading against injustices mainly to Pulitzer and Hearst, who were propounding the social issues of the day and urging improvement of conditions for the masses.

The *Times* was a business, not a battlefield for reform. With the new century, it was on its way toward becoming the greatest news-reporting conservative paper in the country. Just as Pulitzer insisted on accuracy, Ochs objected to the slanting of news, and whenever the *Times* was accused of unfairness, he personally looked into the matter. He turned a moribund newspaper into one that became a national daily, but with success appeared the moments of despair that had bedeviled other Giants of Park Row.

11

Politics and the President

WHILE THE *Times* was leading Ochs out of his financial straitjacket, sensational newspapers stirred the imagination and wrath of the public and Park Row's newspapermen. Hearst knew no bounds. He started the *Chicago American* in July 1900 to aid Bryan's second presidential campaign, and Arthur Brisbane went to the Windy City to get the publication under way. The Midwestern opposition hired thugs to terrorize the Californian's newsboys, but Hearst used his rivals' tactics to combat them. With enough money at his call, he also hired hoodlums. The newspaper war continued until the police, alarmed by its expansion, halted the battling.

In New York, Hearst, with Brisbane back as his strongest aide, fought the trusts and endeared himself to the laboring classes who reverently bought his paper. Enemies of the *Journal* assailed the yellow tactics of fake pictures and interviews. The masses did not object, and profits rolled in.

The *Journal*'s attacks upon McKinley were in full force. In Kentucky, governor-elect William Goebel was shot before taking office and died on February 3, 1900. Columnist Ambrose Bierce, without Hearst's knowledge, penned a poem the next day in his editorial-page article "The Passing Show":

> The bullet that pierced Goebel's chest
> Cannot be found in all the West;
> Good reason: it is speeding here
> To stretch McKinley on the bier.[1]

The elder Bennett's hint of murder for Lincoln had set a precedent carried on in the *Journal*'s pages. More than a year after the Bierce quatrain appeared, the evening edition fired another blast at McKinley: "If bad institutions and bad men can be got rid of only by killing, then the killing must be done."[2] Not long after, Brisbane wrote, "Did not the murder of Lincoln, uniting in sympathy and regret all good people in the North and South, hasten the era of American good feeling and perhaps prevent the renewal of fighting between brothers?"[3]

The *Journal*'s lambasting of McKinley reached its climax on September

6, 1901, when psychopathic anarchist Leon Czolgosz shot the president in the Temple of Music at the Pan-American Exposition in Buffalo. Hearst's foes seized upon the shooting to condemn him. Rumors spread that Czolgosz was caught with a copy of the *Journal* issue containing Bierce's poem in his pocket. The *Press* wrote, "At the door of the New York Journal and its kind shall the people of the United States lay the atrocious crime against William McKinley, President of the United States."[4]

The *Journal*'s next-door neighbor, the *Sun*, lashed out most viciously at Hearst. It denounced him for vilifying the president and reprinted the Brisbane column of June 1, 1901, in which assassination was seen as sometimes worthwhile. No paper in the city was more closely aligned to Wall Street financiers than the daily run by Paul Dana, the late editor's son, and publisher Laffan. The *Journal*'s denunciations of the money barons had embarrassed the *Sun*, and it echoed the *Press* in accusing yellow journalism of paving the path of agitation that led to McKinley's death eight days after the shooting.

The *Journal* struck back at the attacking newspapers in a two-page editorial:

> Why is the *Journal* hated and howled at by papers like the New York Sun? Primarily because the *Journal* stands for the Democratic idea—because it has steadily stood and still stands, for the rights of the common man as against the privileges of the larcenous man. . . . Who are they against whom the *Journal* has fought? CHIEFLY THE PREDATORY, RICH, THE CRAFTY AND THE ABLE WHO PILE UP MONSTROUS FORTUNES BY PILLAGING INSIDE AND OUTSIDE THE FORMS OF LAW.[5]

Hearst was hanged in effigy twice within a week in East New York, Brooklyn. In the second hanging, his figure was accompanied by a placard reading, "Willie Hearst, Red Journal."[6] Libraries, reading rooms, and social clubs banned Hearst's newspapers. With the boycott of his publications spreading throughout the country, the *Journal* changed its attitude toward McKinley. A full-page editorial the day of his death eulogized, "FAREWELL TO A GOOD AMERICAN." "Death has crowned him as a martyr," wrote Ella Wheeler Wilcox.

Theodore Roosevelt addressed Congress for the first time as president in December and indirectly assailed Hearst when he spoke of McKinley's killer:

> This criminal was a professed Anarchist, inflamed by the teachings of professed Anarchists, and probably also by the reckless utterances of those who,

on the stump and in the public press, appeal to the dark and evil spirits of malice and greed, envy and sullen hatred. The wind is sowed by the men who preach such doctrines, and they cannot escape their share of responsibility for the whirlwind that is reaped.[7]

The *Journal*'s circulation continued to drop as the attacks mounted against its publisher. To prove his patriotism, Hearst adorned the outside of the paper's building with a large picture of McKinley, and the *Journal* was the first daily to cover its offices with black crepe paper. He also changed the name of his morning edition from the *New York Journal and Advertiser* to the *New York Journal and American* in November and, finally, to the *New York American.*

Not everyone condemned Hearst. One reader wrote *The Journalist* magazine that his papers had created a "tremendous reading public which did not exist before. They have caused millions of people to think, a factor of such value that it cannot be overestimated."[8] He added that Hearst had not allied himself with the privileged classes but had devoted his energy to the uplifting of the masses.

By this time Hearst was ready to make his first plunge into politics. In 1902 it looked as if Tammany would run Brisbane for Congress, but Hearst had similar aspirations, and Brisbane bowed out. The Chief was convinced he was destined for the presidency, and Capitol Hill would be his first step. Hearst made a deal with Tammany boss Charles Francis Murphy that the paper would support Tammany in return for the backing of his candidacy. That fall Hearst was elected representative of the city's Eleventh Congressional District, a guaranteed Democratic stronghold.

Congressman Hearst was almost forty when he married twenty-one-year-old Millicent Willson, daughter of a clog dancer. They had met while she was appearing in the chorus line of *The Girl from Paris,* a musical playing at the Herald Square Theatre.

Hearst was too aloof in Congress to be a mixer with the majority of Democrats. When he made one of his infrequent appearances on the floor of the House, unheard-of scenes occurred. If the publisher wanted a bill passed, he did no speaking himself. Instead, the "Hearst Brigade" of six men, playing the political counterpart of his *Journal* "wrecking crew," did his bidding. Congressmen came to his seat, and he whispered orders. When they returned to their places, they threw verbal bombshells into the Republican side. The Chief never changed his position. He sat on the small of his back with one knee in the air and made no plea himself for any of his measures.

Hearst tried unsuccessfully to tack a rider of an eight-hour working day onto a naval appropriation bill, and he placed GOP lawmakers on record as against the proposal. His papers in New York, San Francisco, Los Angeles, and Chicago could point proudly to his progressive efforts. His resolutions, highly publicized in his publications, included trying to strengthen the Sherman Anti-Trust Act, giving the Interstate Commerce Commission power to set railroad rates, establishing a parcel-post system, and creating national control of telegraph operations.

Hearst failed to obtain the Democratic nomination for president in 1904. Cecil A. Lyn, a Republican national committeeman from the Lone Star State, scoffed at Hearst's hope: "No man who parts his hair in the middle can ever carry Texas." The *Times* commented the next day on the Texan's remark: "Perhaps, if he had thought harder, he might find some more rational ground for opposing Mr. Hearst's presidential aspirations than the manner in which Mr. Hearst chooses to wear his hair."[9] That fall Hearst successfully ran for reelection to Congress.

The *Journal* moved out of the *Tribune* building and into the Rhinelander structure on Williams Street, east of Park Row, in 1905. That year Hearst decided the road to the presidency lay through his becoming mayor of New York City. The *Journal* conducted a campaign rarely paralleled in the country. Hearst ran on a ticket sponsored by the Municipal Ownership League, an organization he had built up for such purposes. Samuel Seabury and other liberals, convinced of his progressiveness, backed him in his fight against political corruption. On the same ticket were Seabury, running for Supreme Court justice, and Clarence J. Shearn, Hearst's chief legal adviser, campaigning for district attorney.

Muckraking was the order of the day, and the *Journal* and *American* mercilessly berated trusts. Hearst's foes denounced him as a socialist and an anarchist, although he believed he adhered to the democracy of Jefferson, Jackson, and Lincoln. Posters pasted all over the city pictured him waving a red flag. Supporters of Hearst appealed to women by decorating billboards with photographs of the Chief and his eighteen-month-old son, George.

At first, Murphy thought Mayor George Brinton McClellan Jr., son of the Civil War general, would be reelected easily. As Hearst's advisers, reporters, editors, and legal assistants beat the drums of publicity, it seemed his opponent was Murphy and not McClellan. Wrote the *American*, "Murphy, the most hungry, selfish, and extortionate boss Tammany has ever known, is fighting for his life and his plunder."[10] The steaming Murphy gave orders that under no condition was Hearst to be elected.

Impartial straw polls taken by the *Herald* and *World* showed voters favoring the publisher. On the day after the election, the *American*'s front-page banner shouted, "W.R. HEARST ELECTED MAYOR."[11] The Chief was victorious, but he was never to serve. Murphy's henchmen heeded an order from the Boss to keep Hearst out of City Hall and dumped ballots favoring the publisher into the East River.

The *Journal* and *American* bellowed that their owner had been elected. An editorial signed by Hearst read, "All Tammany's fraud, all Tammany's corruption, all Tammany's intimidation and violence, all Tammany's false registration, illegal voting and dishonest count have not been able to overcome a great popular majority. The recount will show that we have won the election by many thousands of votes."[12]

Cartoons depicted Murphy in prison stripes. Brisbane warned in a caption underneath one, "Every honest voter in New York WANTS TO SEE YOU IN THIS COSTUME. You have committed crimes against the people that will send you for many years to State prison if the crimes can be proved against you."[13]

The crimes could not be proven. A recount showed McClellan ahead by more than three thousand votes. Murphy had taken no chances and directed the printing of new ballots favoring his candidate. Once more Hearst had failed in his advance toward the White House, but he was not ready to forget his dream of being president.

Hearst sought to become governor of New York State in 1906 and was endorsed by his own Independence League, formerly the Municipal Ownership League. Murphy supported him this time. Despite the mayoral loss, Hearst had returned to politics stronger than ever, and the Tammany leader sensed the Chief's popularity with the masses. He could forget for the sake of politics how Hearst had threatened to send him from Delmonico's to Sing Sing, but other Tammany men could not. The Boss met with his district leaders and pleaded on his knees that they stay loyal to the whole ticket. In Buffalo, Murphy rammed through Hearst's nomination at the Democratic convention.

The Republicans named as their gubernatorial candidate attorney Charles Evans Hughes, who had conducted a state inquiry of one of Pulitzer's targets, the gas trust. While this investigation proceeded, the *World* launched one of its great crusades in which Hughes was to play a major role. It was against the sacrosanct insurance companies, with Pulitzer's paper first attacking the Equitable Life Assurance Society, in March 1905. Before the scandal ended more than a year later, Mutual Life and New York Life were also exposed for spending policyholders' money for bribery and political corruption, to a total of more than $5 million.

The fight was the first instance of a newspaper's daring to attack the powerful insurance firms. With Pulitzer's editor in chief Frank I. Cobb in the vanguard, and small stockholders and policyholders joining in the clamor for action, the paper bombarded Governor Francis W. Higgins with demands for a probe.

Reluctantly, Higgins called for a report from State Insurance Superintendent Francis Hendricks. Three copies of the study were locked in a safe, but Louis Seibold, a *World* reporter, obtained one of them, and the paper amazed the nation when it splashed the revelations over more than five pages. A joint legislative committee was appointed, with Hughes its chief counsel.

Involved in the scandal were the presidents of the three insurance companies. Other names that cropped up during the investigation included U.S. Senator Chauncey M. Depew, George Perkins of J. P. Morgan & Company, Jacob H. Schiff of Kuhn, Loeb & Co., Elihu Root, and E. H. Harriman. Hearings resulted in the resignations of the corporations' leading officers, and only pressure from high GOP places averted jail terms.

The *World*'s long struggle ended thirteen months later when the governor signed the final two of twelve insurance-reform bills and a perjury measure. In the last of 202 articles on the corruption, the *World* wrote that public opinion "has destroyed one huge form of public corruption. It can destroy others. It can blot out all public iniquity, which requires the connivance of Government and the maladministration of law."[14]

Hughes's new prominence made him the Republicans' candidate for governor, and Pulitzer endorsed him despite his party affiliation. Formidable assistance came from an unexpected source, the *Herald,* which did not want Hearst elected to the state's highest office. Bennett, as always, remained the absentee owner, living in France. He had disliked Hearst ever since the Chief had cabled Bennett years before and asked if the *Herald* were for sale. The inquiry had infuriated him. Bennett had replied tersely: "Price of *Herald* three cents daily. Five cents Sunday."[15]

Relations remained cool between Hearst and Bennett until late 1906, when open warfare erupted. R. F. Outcault, the "Yellow Kid" creator, had left Hearst in 1901 for the *Herald* and introduced his popular *Buster Brown* comic strip to readers the following year. Lured by the Californian's money, Outcault returned to Hearst, and *Buster Brown* began appearing in the *American* in January 1906. Bennett's paper took the case to court, and in March it was decided that Outcault could keep the characters but not the strip's name, while the *Herald* could use both the name and characters.

After Hearst's decision to run for governor, Bennett directed his paper to oppose the candidacy vigorously. The *Journal* retaliated by aiming its guns at the *Herald*'s "Personals" column, which appeared on the front page and contained advertising from prostitutes and brothels. The paper was accused of turning the "sorrow of poor young girls" into money. Such advertisements included the following: "Affable trained masseuse, with assistants, gives Swedish, general massage; baths, select patronage"; "Young widow, having cozy apartment, would appreciate gentleman of means"; "Newly opened elegant parlors; massage, refreshing baths; manicuring, expert operators."[16]

That October, with the election approaching, a federal grand jury indicted Bennett and the *Herald* for sending indecent matter through the mails. Brisbane wrote that hereafter Bennett would be known as a man who dared not return to his own country, but Bennett did dare to come back. He quietly returned to the United States, pleaded guilty, and was fined $25,000. A $5,000 fine was levied against the *Herald* itself and $1,000 against Manley W. Gillam, its advertising manager.

The enraged Bennett ordered that Hearst's name never appear in his paper. When election advertising worth $42,000 was sent to the *Herald,* Bennett rejected the copy because Hearst's name appeared in it once: "The paper is mine. I would not admit that man's name to its columns for $42,000, for $420,000, nor for the full value of the Hearst estate. If Hearst dies, goes to jail, or is elected President of the United States, I want no mention of him made in the *Herald.*"[17]

The battle of the two publishers was not over. Hearst described himself as a defender of labor and an enemy of corporations that he denounced as the "Plunderbund." He also called himself the friend of the mechanic, businessman, letter carrier, farmer, and mother. Hearst said his foes were John D. Rockefeller, J. Pierpont Morgan, Thomas F. Ryan, and August Belmont. He claimed the New York Central Railroad had been fined $108,000 because of his crusade against rebaters. Hearst pointed to his fights against the ice, coal, beef, and gas trusts. He cited his success in obtaining eighty-cent gas for the city and told of his efforts to procure an eight-hour-working-day law, as well as emphasizing his opposition to coolie labor.

On the day after Bennett and the *Herald* were indicted, a *World* bombshell revealed that, although Hearst championed the eight-hour day, men were working ten hours daily at his South Dakota mine, while other mines paid the same amount for eight hours. Bennett's reporters, meanwhile, had completed an investigation of Hearst's enterprises and were ready for the public. Disclosures began showing up in the *Herald* on October 27, shortly before Election Day. The headline read:

HEARST ESTATE IN
PLUNDERING DEALS
IN WALL STREET

Many Syndicates Participated
In and 'Exposed' When
the Money Was Made.

PUBLIC THE LOSER
TO 'PLUNDERBUND'

Transactions Revealed with Shipyard
Trust, Tobacco Trust and Third
Avenue Road Wreck.

The Hearst estate, with the Chief as the main beneficiary, was depicted as a heavy stockholder in traction companies, trusts, and underwriting syndicates—groups that the candidate had denounced time and again.

Although Hearst claimed to be labor's staunchest friend, the *Herald* reported he had broken up a reporters' union at his San Francisco newspaper. In his New York plant he had hired private detectives early in 1902 and placed them throughout the composing room until his printers threatened to strike en masse. Hearst was accused of setting up a complicated system of corporations to avoid personal liability. Not only was he evading federal taxes through the scheme, but he had never paid New York State taxes, despite owning one of the city's most profitable publications. Furthermore, to keep his promise to Tammany, he had, through his campaign manager, thrown every labor-union candidate off the Independent League ticket.

In one campaign speech after another, Hearst fought back against the newspapers that sought his defeat. He alluded to Bennett's indictment for printing obscene and indecent advertisements and called Laffan of the *Sun* the mortgaged menial of J. P. Morgan. Hearst also charged that Ochs was indebted to the traction trust and life-insurance companies even for the building in which the *Times* was printed. In addition, he accused Pulitzer of investing his money in coal stocks and Vanderbilt roads and in following the tips of Wall Street speculators more than he did the people's interests.

President Roosevelt was aware that Hearst's election meant the publisher would seek the White House next. He did not want the Chief elected governor and sent Secretary of State Elihu Root to Utica, New York, to speak for him. Root said the president felt the selection of Hearst would be an injury and a discredit alike to honest labor and honest capital. He added that Roosevelt was thinking of the publisher during his first address to Congress when he spoke of reckless utterances leading to McKinley's death. Furthermore, said Root, he was authorized to say that what Roosevelt thought of Hearst then, he thinks of him now.

Hughes defeated the Chief, although voters approved all other Democratic-Independence League candidates. The day after the election, the *Journal*'s headline read, "Hearst to the People: 'I WILL FIGHT IN THE RANKS'." The publisher stated that he would carry on the battle against the plunderbund.

Hearst did not run for the presidency in 1908. Bryan was the Democratic choice, but without Hearst's support. Hearst's Independence League Party operated now on a nationwide scale, and it nominated Thomas L. Hisgen, a Massachusetts manufacturer, for the nation's number one position, and John Temple Graves of Georgia, one of Hearst's writers, as his running mate. Hisgen received 83,628 votes, the least of five presidential candidates.

During that campaign the Chief caused a sensation throughout Park Row and the nation by raking the muck flowing through politics and big business. Four years before, two minor employees of the Standard Oil Company at 26 Broadway had stolen letters from the corporation's vice president, John D. Archbold, who became known as the firm's "Great Corruptionist." The letters were offered to various newspapers, which refused them, until the *American* finally bought them.

Hearst said nothing about the correspondence until 1908, during which more letters were purloined from Archbold's files, photographed in the *American*'s offices, and surreptitiously returned. Hearst finally made the disclosures while campaigning for Hisgen's election. They revealed that Republican Senator John Benson Foraker, in addition to others, had received thousands of dollars to demonstrate and vote against legislation that displeased Standard Oil.

Hearst told a Columbus, Ohio, audience that he had obtained the letters from "a gentleman who has intimate associations with this giant of corruption, the Standard Oil, but whose name I may not divulge lest he be subjected to the persecution of this monopoly."[18] Foraker retired from office before the year ended, but the finger of infamy continued to be pointed at other political figures.

As the Chief kept up his disclosures, letters were published that showed Archbold had endeavored to bribe magazines, newspapers, teachers, lecturers, and "every medium of publicity for political and financial purposes."[19]

Roosevelt announced that although he had criticized Hearst in the past, the publisher now rendered a public service of high importance. The election was unaffected by the revelations because both Republicans and Democrats were implicated. After it was over, Roosevelt invited Hearst to the White House and asked if any of Archbold's correspondence involved him. Hearst replied there was none that he intended to publish at this time.

Why Hearst had waited four years to expose the corruption remained a mystery. Some said he had blackmailed the participants, including the Rockefellers, who began to advertise in his papers for the first time. Others maintained that he had waited for a propitious moment.

Hearst continued printing Archbold's letters until October 5, 1912, when *Collier's Weekly* published an article titled "Mr. Hearst's Forgeries." Written by Arthur H. Gleason, it disclosed that, while many of the Archbold documents in Hearst's possession were genuine, others were forged. Gleason's story appeared at a time when a Senate committee was investigating political campaign contributions. Hearst testified before the panel and swore that neither he nor any of his employees had paid anything for them. This contradicted the assertion of the two persons who had stolen the correspondence and always maintained they had been paid $12,000. Foraker testified the next day and also refuted Hearst. He said his investigator had learned that three editorial employees of the *American,* including city editor John L. Eddy, had paid $34,000 for the letters.

Hearst had not given up hopes of being elected to public office. In 1909 he ran again for mayor of New York, this time on a Civic Alliance ticket. His Democratic opponent was Judge William J. Gaynor, supported by Boss Murphy. The Hearst papers hurled an endless barrage of invectives against Gaynor, who won anyway. The result did not quiet the *Journal* and *American,* which continued blasting away at Gaynor. Without mentioning names, Gaynor told *Editor & Publisher* that some newspaper proprietors in the city were so corrupt that they didn't hesitate to say any falsehood with regard to those in office.

Less than two weeks later, James J. Gallagher, a dismissed dockworker, shot the mayor as he boarded a ship bound for Europe. While Gaynor recovered in the hospital, Hearst said he was sorry the mayor had been shot but that his experience "did not abate his evil temper nor his lying tongue. The criticism of Mayor Gaynor's public acts by the Hearst papers has been temperate and truthful, dignified and deserved, unprejudiced and in the public interest."[20]

The White House had become an impossible dream for Hearst, despite his money and power. Once people forgave the yellowness of his paper and remembered only that he had crusaded on their behalf; now they no longer had unshakable faith in him. Their hopes had been shattered when his covert dealings came to light.

Hearst had lost his enthusiasm for the people's rights. Being called a radical had paid off in circulation that brought increased advertising, but as early as 1906 he did not want to lose any of it by crusading for progressive laws. Patent-medicine advertising was a great source of revenue for the Hearst papers. When the Pure Food and Drug Bill came up before Congress that year, he could not afford to defend the legislation. The public clamored that he do something about that type of advertising, and he did. He ran the ads as news or editorials and collected on the basis of advertising rates.

That was a great discovery for the *Journal*. Since publishing advertisements in the form of editorials was profitable, why not increase the income that way in other areas? The *Journal* was a poor medium for theater advertising, and Hearst and his advisers hit upon another plan. Brisbane wrote, "We want our readers to understand that if they read about a play in this newspaper IT IS BECAUSE IT IS A GOOD PLAY, AND ONE THAT . . . WOULD AMUSE THEM OR INSTRUCT THEM."[21] Nothing in the city was read more eagerly than a Brisbane editorial. For $1,000, a theatrical advertiser could now buy a full-page advertisement and an editorial by Hearst's top aide.

Pulitzer was having his troubles with Roosevelt. The president denounced him in a special message to Congress on December 15, 1908. In October, while the publisher was away, the *World* charged that an American syndicate headed by lawyer William Nelson Cromwell had purchased the French rights to build the Panama Canal for $3.5 million. Since the U.S. government had paid $40 million to acquire the property, the financiers were accused of reaping a profit of almost $37 million. The paper linked President-elect William Howard Taft's brother Charles and Douglas Robinson, the president's brother-in-law, to the operation. Cromwell had approved the story, but along with it was his denial of the charges.

The Indianapolis *News*, picking up the story from the *World*, created the first furor. On the day before the presidential election, it demanded to know who had received the $40 million. On December 6 Roosevelt replied to the accusations in a letter made public. He denounced the *News,* called its editor Delavan Smith a liar, and declared that the government had paid the money directly to the French. He also denied that Taft's brother or Robinson had anything to do with any profit reapers.

The *World* asserted that J. P. Morgan & Company had obtained the money and described Cromwell's role in the affair. The paper charged Roosevelt with deliberate misstatement of facts in his attack upon Smith and called on Congress to investigate the scandal.

In the special message to Congress, Roosevelt claimed that the paper's accusations were a libel not only on the president-elect's brother and Robinson but also upon the U.S. government. He charged that Pulitzer was the real offender and should be prosecuted. Roosevelt also said the attorney general was considering the form in which the proceedings would be brought against him.

Park Row was amazed. Not since the days of President Cleveland and the Venezuelan crisis had the government tried to take legal steps against the blind publisher. He wanted no more headaches. His shattered nerves were causing more pain than ever. Roosevelt, however, had uttered strong words, and he would fight them. Pulitzer answered the president's charges through an editorial written by Cobb:

> If *The World* has libelled [*sic*] anybody we hope it will be punished, but we do not intend to be intimidated by Mr. Roosevelt's threats, or by Mr. Roosevelt's denunciation, or by Mr. Roosevelt's power. . . .
>
> No other living man ever so grossly libelled the United States as does this President who besmirches Congress, bulldozes Judges, assails the integrity of courts, slanders private citizens, and who has shown himself the most reckless, unscrupulous demagogue whom the American people ever trusted with great power and authority. . . .
>
> So far as *The World* is concerned, its proprietor may go to jail, if Mr. Roosevelt succeeds, as he threatens; but even in jail *The World* will not cease to be a fearless champion of free speech, a free press and a free people.
>
> It cannot be muzzled![22]

A District of Columbia grand jury returned indictments against Pulitzer, managing editor Caleb Van Hamm, and night editor Robert Lyman. Other indictments were levied against the Press Publishing Company operating the *World* and Smith and Charles R. Williams of the Indianapolis *News.*

A federal judge in Indianapolis dismissed the proceedings against Smith and Williams, but the *World* was not so fortunate. It had erred in failing to obtain proof that Charles Taft and Douglas Robinson had been involved with the syndicate. To combat the government's case, De Lancey Nicoll became the *World*'s chief counsel. The issue of a free press was at stake. If a national libel law existed, every paper in the nation would be in the government's power.

The U.S. Supreme Court ended the controversy by ruling in the *World*'s favor in January 1911. In reviewing the history of the libel suit, the *World* reprinted what it had written just a year before: "As the Panama case now stands there is nothing to prevent a future Roosevelt from making another assault upon the freedom of the press in order to gratify his own personal malice."[23]

Pulitzer had won again, although the question of who had received the millions was never answered. However, the indictments had worried him, and his health became worse.

All his life he had fought—for bread, for his papers, for the people. Although he could have done even more, no paper in the nation boasted a more liberal record. But there was that blacker side of the *World*. Pulitzer regretted the description of yellow journalism flung at his paper during the circulation war with Hearst. His publication also had been banned from homes, clubs, and libraries. Since the end of the Spanish-American War he had tried to regain prestige, but some people could not forget.

Pulitzer felt strongly that journalism was a profession and not a trade or business. As early as 1892, he had proposed journalistic education on a professional basis to Columbia University president Seth Law, who rejected his idea.

Pulitzer reopened negotiations on a projected school in 1902. By that time, Nicholas Murray Butler was Columbia's president, but he and the university's trustees hedged. They looked skeptically on journalism as a profession, and Butler feared public reaction because of the yellow journalism taint associated with the *World*. However, a compromise was reached.

They agreed on a school to be founded after the blind publisher's death. Pulitzer endowed Columbia with $2 million for that purpose and for scholarships and prizes in journalism and literature. The delay enabled the University of Missouri to establish the first school of journalism in the world in 1908.

Pulitzer's will enjoined upon his three sons, Ralph, Herbert, and Joseph Jr., the duty of preserving, perfecting, and perpetuating the *World*. He wanted to see that paper conducted as it had been under him—for public service—and he prohibited its sale.

Pulitzer was sixty-four years of age when, after being given Veronal because of stomach pains diagnosed as indigestion, he died aboard his yacht, the *Liberty,* in the waters of Charleston, South Carolina, on October 29, 1911.

Hearst forgot his bitter, costly struggles with the *World*'s owner when he heard the news:

> Joseph Pulitzer was the founder and foremost exemplar of modern journalism—the great originator and exponent of the journalism of action and achievement. . . .
>
> Joseph Pulitzer was a democrat in doctrine and in deed. He came from the people, understood the aims and aspirations of the people. . . .
>
> In his death journalism has lost a leader, the people a champion, the nation a valuable citizen.[24]

12

News at Any Price

PULITZER'S DEATH cast a lingering gloom on Park Row. Not often had a publisher so influenced journalism or campaigned so vigorously for people's rights. Crowding the back room of Perry's drugstore in the Pulitzer Building, newspapermen speculated on the paper's future. They wondered if Ralph Pulitzer, oldest of the three sons and president of the company issuing the *World*, could carry on the tradition established by his father. Their fears were dispelled when Frank Cobb, the paper's militant chief editorial writer, was named editor. He was as aggressive and liberal as his late employer.

Hearst's screeching *Journal* alone exceeded the circulation of the *World*. Led by Arthur Brisbane, the *Journal* was the best money-maker among the Chief's expanding chain of newspapers encircling the country. Its claimed daily sale of almost eight hundred thousand copies, twice that of the *Evening World*, was the greatest in the land.

Brisbane was proud of the typographical sensationalism he employed to boost circulation. Speaking in Geneseo, New York, he called himself "the yellowest journalist in the world. If I am not, I want to be." He said that Hearst frequently remonstrated against his tactics and that more than once he thought he would be discharged, until other papers imitated his style. Brisbane added that, on one occasion, when a group of Presbyterian ministers criticized his garishness, he responded, "I told them that when God gets ready to send a storm he creates ugly black clouds which are typified in the paper in black type; lightning is the red type that they frequently use and the colored supplement on Sunday is the rainbow."[1]

When it came to his editorials and columns, Brisbane had nothing to fear from the publisher. Hearst was aware that any man who could be forced to write to order was not worth having. Brisbane devoted his column to any subject that appealed to him. Although his coverage of prizefighting while on the *Sun* had elicited much praise, he abhorred pugilism. When heavyweight boxing champion Jack Johnson defeated former titleholder Jim Jeffries, Brisbane ridiculed the bout. He wrote of a chimpanzee at the Bronx Zoo that was about a foot tall and weighed only sixteen pounds when full of milk, and he pictured the simian telling both men:

I've got a brother at home in the jungle could lick you both with one hand. . . .

What IS fighting, anyhow? You two fight each other, and my brother could beat you both for he could deal a blow that would knock you both senseless. But a zebra could KICK my brother senseless, and the lion could kill the zebra, and a falling tree trunk could kill a lion.

I should think you man monkeys, that walk so straight on your hind legs and get milk and peanuts and sugar so easily, would be ashamed to use your fists.[2]

When New York's business district had formed its northern limit at 14th Street and the city ended at 59th Street, communication with the rest of the world centered in lower Manhattan. Construction of the Brooklyn Bridge and the main post office opposite Park Row enabled publications to distribute newspapers easily, quickly, and cheaply from the area. But Park Row's reputation as the center of the newspaper district began to erode with the rapid growth of New York in the early years of the twentieth century.

Railroad terminals moved uptown with the construction of Grand Central Terminal and the Pennsylvania Station. Theaters, banks, and clubs all headed toward the 42nd Street vicinity. The city's first subway, the IRT, was completed in 1904 and proved a boon to Manhattan and Bronx residents. Its construction had pleased Pulitzer, who campaigned for transportation that could take riders from City Hall to Harlem in fifteen minutes.

The success of the *Times* meant a further disintegration of Park Row. Commodore Bennett had moved his paper to Herald Square in 1893, and Adolph Ochs was next to leave Newspaper Row, taking his publication farther uptown than any New York daily. At first, he had wanted to build his new *Times* home near Madison Square at 23rd Street and Fifth Avenue. A friend, Henry Morgenthau Sr., advised him, however, that a more suitable business axis would be where Broadway crossed Seventh Avenue at 42nd Street. The publisher accepted his suggestion and bought property there.

On January 18, 1904, the cornerstone for the building was laid at Longacre Square, which, in less than three months, was officially renamed Times Square. Almost a year later, on January 2, the presses rolled for the first time in the trapezoid edifice, which, with its 419-foot height, was the loftiest building in the city and the tenth highest tower in the world. The *Times* continued to prosper so much in the new location that by early 1913 it was in even larger quarters at 229 West 43rd Street. Conservative as the paper appeared on the editorial page, its news policy enhanced the paper's reputation for hard-hitting reporting and exclusive features. The managing editor was Carr Vattel Van Anda, former night editor of the *Sun*.

Guglielmo Marconi invented wireless telegraphy before the end of the nineteenth century, and Bennett invited him to report the America's Cup races for the *Herald* in September 1899. The Commodore, however, lost interest in the invention when he realized it would hurt his Commercial Cable Company business. Hearst also turned his attention to the wireless. On January 19, 1903, the first messages were sent eastward across the Atlantic, from South Wellfleet, Massachusetts, to London, by President Roosevelt to King Edward VII and from Hearst to the editor of the *Times* of London. The publisher congratulated him on the new bond of communication between their countries.

However, regular transatlantic service was not inaugurated until 1907, after Ochs seized the opportunity to support the Italian's invention. Under Van Anda, the *Times* received the first wireless message sent westward across the ocean by Marconi. Limited to fifty words, it was transmitted from Clifden, Ireland, to Glace Bay, Nova Scotia, and then to New York. Approximately ten thousand words were sent that first day, and Thomas Alva Edison told a *Times* reporter, "Give Marconi ten years and he will be sending over the Atlantic 1,000 words a minute and will be receiving at the same rate of speed."[3] Five years later, all records for wireless dispatches were broken when the *Times* received a message from London in just ten minutes, breaking the previous best time of fifty-five minutes.

Aviation was in an early stage, and the *Times* showed its astuteness by scooping Newspaper Row on a story that should have gone to the *World.* Early in 1909, when a centennial celebration was planned in honor of Robert Fulton's journey down the Hudson aboard the *Clermont,* the *World* offered $10,000 to the first pilot who made the 150-mile flight from Albany to New York. As time passed, the paper extended its offer. It grew impatient as Glenn Curtiss, winner of an international speed trophy at Rheims, France, delayed his attempt to capture the prize. Finally, when he left Albany in a biplane in May 1910, the *Times* beat the *World* by hiring a special train to trail Curtiss the entire distance.

The actual flying time from the state capital to Governors Island was just under three hours, but another two hours were spent on the ground—once near Poughkeepsie where autoists supplied Curtiss with gasoline, and the second time at Broadway and 214th Street in Manhattan, where motorists provided him with oil. When Curtiss made his second stop, *Times* reporters were the only ones from any paper to greet him. Along the route, bulletins were dropped off the train as it sped past stations, and they were also posted on *Times* bulletin boards and telephoned to major hotels and clubs. Curtiss set a speed record by averaging more than fifty miles an hour.

Ochs skimped on nothing that might produce better news stories. Other papers so envied the progress made by the *Times* that they did not hesitate to steal its exclusive reports. In March 1912 the *Times* served notice that it had obtained copyrighted American rights to publish the story of Norway's Roald Amundsen, discoverer of the South Pole, and warned that it would prosecute any infringement. The *Times* devoted five full pages to the Amundsen report in April, but the *American, World, Sun,* and *Press* helped themselves to the story. That was because the London *Daily Chronicle* had British rights to the Amundsen narrative, and the difference of time between London and New York permitted a fast-enough cabling of the news so that the copyright violators kept pace with Ochs's paper.

The *Times* sued for contempt, and it called the *World* and *American* the worst offenders. The *American* retorted that the *Times* published "all the news that's paid for."[4] "All the news that's paid for!" mimicked the *Times*. "Well, it is certainly better to print all the news that you have paid for, and no other, than it is to print all the news that can be stolen, or all the news that's paid for by somebody else."[5]

Bradford Merrill, treasurer of the Star Company publishing the *American,* asserted in an affidavit that the *Times* had not come into court with clean hands and had stolen several stories from the Hearst paper. Van Anda called the allegation false and said that the only time the *Times* had reprinted an *American* story—a letter from radium discoverer Marie Curie—he had received permission from Merrill and given credit to the *American.* The *Times* lost the suit on a technicality. It had not deposited two copies in the copyright office or in the mail addressed to the Register of Copyrights by midnight preceding publication of the Amundsen account.

Van Anda gained more Park Row respect, as well as the plaudits of the public, when the "unsinkable" 45,000-ton *Titanic* struck an iceberg the night of April 14, 1912, on its way to New York. More than two thousand persons were aboard the world's largest and most luxurious ship on its maiden voyage. At least fifteen hundred of them, including many notables, perished in the worst disaster in marine annals.

That was on a Sunday night, and the first reports were confusing. One wireless message, reported to have come from the steamship *Virginian,* stated that she was towing the White Star Line queen with hopes of beaching her in the vicinity of Cape Race, Newfoundland. Other messages of a reassuring nature, including bulletins from the White Star, were accepted at face value by news associations and printed without question by newspapers on both sides of the ocean. By late Monday, the truth was flashed around the world that the greatest vessel built had sunk and that the Cunarder *Carpathia* was on its way to New York with survivors.

Once it was revealed that the *Titanic* had gone to the sea's bottom, relatives of passengers were in despair, and bedlam monopolized newspaper offices from Park Row to Times Square. The *Evening World* obtained the earliest first-hand story. Aboard the *Carpathia* was Carlos F. Hurd, a correspondent for the *St. Louis Post-Dispatch*. He tried to wire the story to the *World* from the moment the *Carpathia* rushed to the *Titanic*'s aid but was balked by the ship's officers. He then wrote his copy and attached it to a life preserver. When the *Carpathia* sailed into the bay, he spotted a *World* tug, but crewmen forestalled his tossing the preserver overboard. However, passengers formed a ring around Hurd to protect him from the ship's men, enabling him to hurl the preserver to the tug as the *Carpathia* passed quarantine and paving the way for a *World* scoop.

Newspapers rented tugboats that sailed as far as Providence, Rhode Island, to obtain news "over the rail." When the *Carpathia* neared the Cunard pier in Manhattan, the dailies combined to hire rooms in the Hotel Strand opposite the dock at the foot of 14th Street. Van Anda perfected a system that brought his paper complete news coverage without delay. The *Times*'s suite of rooms was connected by telephone to the paper's editorial room uptown. Newspapermen sat near each of the many telephones in both places to handle specified phases of the story, four reporters were stationed on the pier, and eight more cruised through the crowd awaiting the rescue ship's arrival. When one of them rushed into the *Times*'s rooms at the Strand, he was directed to a telephone connecting him with the rewrite man in charge of that feature.

The *Times*, with a front-page, three-line streamer and fifteen pages of news on the disaster, led the field in satisfying the public's eagerness for information. Most of the newspapers ignored the fact that they had been deluded by the White Star Line's first announcement that the *Titanic* was safe, but *The Globe and Commercial Advertiser* apologized for its share in spreading misleading reports: "They were published by all newspapers in good faith. But good faith is not an excuse for such a stupendous error. The first duty of the whole press, of every newspaper, of all news agencies, is not to publish what is untrue."[6]

Not often had a New York newspaper apologized for printing erroneous information. Its publisher, Jason Rogers, believed in decent journalism and advocated honest circulation as a means of selling advertising. The *Globe* was announcing that its daily sales were 138,000 when he disclosed that the paid circulation was actually 103,000. Fighting for an organization that would verify the claims of newspapers, Rogers traveled throughout the country, promoting his idea. The Audit Bureau of Circulation arose in 1914 from his efforts and provided authority to circulation statistics for the first time.

Little more than a month after Woodrow Wilson's election as president of the United States in 1912, Whitelaw Reid, the *Tribune*'s owner and ambassador to Britain, died at the age of seventy-five. The paper had shrunk considerably in circulation and profits since Horace Greeley's day, and Reid had not kept pace with the journalistic metamorphosis wrought by Pulitzer and Hearst. While they wooed the far more numerous working class, Reid maintained the *Tribune* as a journal for conservative middle- and upper-class Republicans. He kept the paper's price at three cents, believing the "one-cent craze" would vanish.

For some twenty years after the panic of 1873, Reid and New York Typographical Union No. 6 carried on a dispute. It began over his wage-cutting policies and his anti-union stand that culminated in a printer's strike at the *Tribune* in 1883. Not until 1894 did Reid and the "Big Six" reach an agreement. One key factor in the conflict with the union was the publisher's use of machinery. The union was aroused when three Barr-patented typesetting machines were installed in the composing room. The printers were also upset when Reid installed Ottmar Mergenthaler's first twelve Linotype machines.

Reid's attention also turned to diplomacy and politics. He was appointed minister to France in 1889 and three years later ran for the vice presidency of the United States with Benjamin Harrison, only to see Cleveland elected decisively.

Reid was appointed ambassador to the Court of St. James's in 1905, and when he went to London, regents ran the paper until his son, Ogden Mills Reid, a Yale law student, could take over the management.

The owner's refusal to change the paper's news and makeup policies as well as infuse more money into the *Tribune* handicapped the regents. Salaries and the number of employees dwindled, and the Tall Tower, once a spectator's delight, became shabby. Whitelaw Reid finally reduced the *Tribune*'s price from three cents to one in 1909, but the paper's circulation remained below fifty thousand until his death.

The younger Reid became editor in chief three months after his father died. He realized that the paper had to alter its traditional ways or disappear

from Newspaper Row. With his wife, Helen, working with him, they insti-
tuted modern makeup techniques and injected life into the *Tribune's* features.
They hired such writers as Heywood Broun, Robert Benchley, and Franklin
Pierce Adams, whose initials F. P. A. preceded his column, "The Conning
Tower," and cartoonists H. T. Webster, creator of *The Timid Soul,* and Clare
Briggs.

The outbreak of war in Europe in August 1914 saw the *Tribune* struggling
to compete with the *Times.* Before the conflict erupted, disagreement between
Ochs and Lord Northcliffe, who had taken over the *Times* of London, ended
the arranged exchange between their papers. Nevertheless, because of its
growing foreign coverage, in the first month of war the New York *Times*
published in full the British and German White Papers. Although *Times*
columns were open to both sides, supporters of Germany viewed Ochs as
pro-Ally, and the cry of "British gold owns it!" was flung at his paper.

The *Times* opposed an administration bill proposing the purchase of in-
terned foreign ships. A series of letters written by someone whose real identity was never learned indicated that British money influenced the *Times's*
stand. Van Anda and Charles Miller, the paper's editor in chief, were called
before a U.S. Senate committee. Ostensibly, questioning was to focus on the
paper's opposition to the ship measure, but the senators primarily wanted to
know whether Britons had financial interest in the *Times.* Van Anda, at
Ochs's direction, produced a list of all stockholders. It showed that Ochs
owned 62 percent of the *Times* and Miller 14 percent, with the remainder
held by persons connected with the paper and none of it by any foreigner.

At the next session, Miller called the proceedings inquisitorial. He warned
that if they were adopted as a policy they would reduce the press of the
United States to the "level of the press in some of the central European
capitals, the press that has been known as the reptile press, that crawls on its
belly every day to the Foreign Office and to the Government officials and
Ministers to know what it may say or shall say—to receive its orders."[7]

Miller termed *Times* readers a grand jury and said the paper felt that the
panel would be quick to discover if the *Times* were influenced by anyone
outside the office. The *World* agreed with Miller that the questioning was
highly improper and that it indicated someone outside of the *Times's* office
was trying to edit the paper.

The most pacifistic among New York papers were those owned by Hearst.
He had been desperate to plunge the United States into a war with Spain
before the turn of the century, but now he railed against Wall Street bankers
for trying to embroil the United States in the European war. He implored

Congress to place an embargo on munitions and opposed any loan to Britain and France.

Almost twelve hundred people, including women and children, died when the Germans sank the *Lusitania* in May 1915. The outraged *American* insisted the attack was not an act of war but "a deed of wholesale murder."[8] But less than a month later, Hearst in a signed editorial wrote that whether it was armed or not, the British vessel was "a spoil of war, subject to attack and destruction under the accepted rules of warfare."[9] He added that the destruction of the ship was an indictment not of Germany's warfare alone but of war itself as war was now waged on land and sea.

Hearst's opposition to the war did not stop his International News Service. It was described as reporting first and most vividly all the big news of the world war and possessed, through its associations with European newspapers, the "greatest news gathering organization the world has ever seen."[10] *Harper's Weekly* investigated and disclosed that not only had the wire service faked many of the stories but also that many of its acclaimed eighty war correspondents were nonexistent. The more that America's sympathy swung toward the Allies, the more Hearst strove to divert America's attention away from Europe. Within a month after the disclosure of the imaginary correspondents, the magazine exposed another fabrication by Hearst.

On September 26 and October 3, 1915, the *American* ran double-page installments "literally translated" from a Japanese book titled *The War between Japan and America.* The book was characterized as Japan's most popular, with more than a million copies sold. It was reported as having been issued by a powerful society, the National Defense Association, with Count Okuma, Japan's premier, as its president and high cabinet officials as other members. The articles contained plans for the invasion and conquering of the United States, including the capture of the Philippines, Hawaii, and California and the destruction of the Panama Canal. Mexico was described as a great and powerful ally that would help Japan against the United States when the time came.

Acting upon a request from *Harper's Weekly,* Japan's consul-general in New York cabled his foreign office. The reply pointed out that the book had actually been published two years before, at a time when a California alien-land question was hotly discussed, and that the actual title was *The Dream Story of the War between Japan and the United States.* In addition, no National Defense Association existed; it had been a reporter's creation. The magazine also disclosed that the Japanese version had no plans to destroy the Panama

Canal, and instead of a million copies being sold, only a few thousand had been purchased.

Wilson sent Brig. Gen. John "Black Jack" Pershing to pursue Mexican bandit leader Francisco "Pancho" Villa in 1916. Hearst, seething over Villa's raid of his Babicora ranch, clamored in a signed editorial for the country to invade Mexico. He maintained that U.S. authority in the country south of the border was the right of humanity and that if the United States had no right in Mexico, it had no right in California or Texas.

The British government banned Hearst's International News Service from using its mails and cables the following year, citing a garbling of messages and breach of faith. The manager of INS immediately charged that the crackdown resulted from the wire service's not printing the kind of news that the English desired to have published in the United States. He added that INS intended "to continue printing the news, all the news, and nothing but the news."[11] France followed suit before the month was over; Canada barred the Hearst papers in November, and Newfoundland did the same in December.

Restrained in Europe, the INS pirated Associated Press stories. It bribed employees of the Cleveland *News* to furnish it with AP stories from the banning nations. The AP obtained a federal court injunction to stop Hearst, and the case went to the U.S. Supreme Court. The Chief did not deny the facts but maintained the move was necessary because of the prohibition abroad. The final action affirming that his organization was guilty was handed down in May 1919. The AP was too fearful to take any further action against the powerful and wealthy Hearst.

When the United States entered World War I on April 6, 1917, Hearst's battle cry was "America First!" as it had been for almost three years. But Hearst was not the type to follow meekly in any path he chose not to travel. Five days after America declared war on Germany, he warned, "Stripping our country of men, money and food is a dangerous policy. Our earnest suggestion to Congress is that it imperatively refuse to permit the further draining of our food supplies and our military supplies to Europe."[12]

Hearst appealed to Congress to establish universal military service and to undertake a 100 percent effort in conducting the war. He acknowledged that before America's entry into the war, he had advocated peace until the United States could be adequately prepared. But now, he said, the only thing that could be done was to create complete preparedness at the earliest possible moment.

Despite those words, his hostility toward the British remained. He charged that the painful truth was that the United States was being used as a reinforcement of England's warfare and future aggrandizement. He struck again at Tokyo, warning that while the Allies were busy in Europe, Japan would come out of the war more of a menace to the United States than ever.

Hearst also continued to campaign for the annexation of Mexico, even though the United States was fully occupied in fighting Germany. The *American* described the Mexican government as being worse than Prussian militarism. Conceding that the war in Europe might prevent America from giving the necessary attention to Mexico now, the paper added that "nothing will solve the Mexican situation except the eventual intervention of the United States, and nothing will so benefit the people of Mexico as well as the people of the United States as to have our democratic government make Mexico a part of our federation."[13]

Hearst's sharpest critic on Park Row was the *Tribune*. Wholly pro-British, although not controlled by British interests, the *Tribune* resented the vicious attacks against England. It charged that Hearst's German-language newspaper, discontinued a year after America joined the Allies, "practiced almost every one of the methods of obstructing the war and dampening national enthusiasm."[14] The *Tribune* printed a series of six articles written by Kenneth Macgowan and headlined "Coiled in the Flag, Hears-s-s-st." Macgowan reported that in the first year of U.S. participation in the war, Hearst's journals had assailed the Allies seventy-four times, praised Germany seventeen times, and spread antiwar propaganda on sixty-three occasions.

While the series was running, the *Tribune* found an ally in Theodore Roosevelt. He attacked Postmaster-General Albert Burleson for naming Reid's paper as a publication that criticized the administration's conduct of the war and felt Washington's displeasure, although it had consistently upheld the nation's efforts. The former president named the Hearst papers as the prime example of failure by the administration to proceed against newspapers that opposed the war, attacked the Allies, or directly or indirectly aided Germany:

> By turning to the New York *Tribune* of May 8, 1918, Postmaster-General Burleson will find an ardent tribute made by the former German correspondent of the *Koelnische Zeitung* to Mr. Hearst and Mr. Hearst's editor in chief, Arthur Brisbane, for having been "auxiliaries of valued influence" to Germany, especially because of "the editorials in the Hearst newspapers."[15]

Defenders of Hearst charged that the *Tribune* was the mouthpiece of Great Britain in America. Whitelaw Reid had married Elisabeth Mills, daughter of California multimillionaire Darius Ogden Mills. Their daughter Jean was the wife of an Englishman, and Mrs. Reid's father was pictured as pouring out money to cover the deficits of the *Tribune*. Hearst's supporters printed letters from Wilson's private secretary James P. Tumulty, Secretary of the Navy Josephus Daniels, Secretary of the Treasury William G. McAdoo, and Secretary of War Newton D. Baker praising the Hearst papers for their war efforts.

A rare editorial blunder toward the end of the war embarrassed the *Times* more than it had been chagrined in almost sixty years, since William Henry Hurlbert's botched-up article "The Defensive Square of Austrian Italy." Once again, Austria was involved. With Allied victory apparently close at hand, the Austro-Hungarian government asked for "non-binding" peace negotiations, and the message arrived at the *Times*'s office on Sunday, September 15, 1918. Ochs was at his home in Lake George, New York, when Van Anda notified him of the proposal and said that Miller was writing an editorial on the subject for Monday's issue. The article began:

> From Vienna, the quarter in which for three years the Allies have felt that the movement for peace would originate, comes the first veritable peace offer, and it comes in a form which the Allies may honorably accept in the confident belief that it will lead to the end of the war. . . .
>
> We cannot imagine that the invitation will be declined. . . . [W]e must conclude that only the madness or the soulless depravity of some one of the belligerent Powers could obstruct and defeat the purpose of the conference.[16]

Unlike the *American* and *Journal,* the *Times* had proven itself vigorously anti-German throughout the war years, and no one dared doubt its patriotism. Now its loyalty was questioned. The *Times* received more than three thousand telegrams and letters of protest. Some of them canceled subscriptions, and the Union League Club of New York debated barring the paper from its rooms.

Almost every daily in the city volleyed condemnation at Ochs. The *Evening World* wondered if the *Times* had suddenly gone mad and been bought by German money. The morning *World* called the editorial a "white flag" and an emblem of surrender. The *Herald* was equally acrid:

> When this nation goes to war it goes to war to win. What Austria-Hungary proposes, and the *Times* so blandly approves, would be the beginning of defeat for civilization, to uphold which the American people have gone to war. . . .
> We are not going to surrender.
> *We have just begun to fight!*

In addition, the *Herald* quoted Wilson as saying that there was only one possible response to the Austrian proposal: "Force, force to the utmost, the righteous and triumphant force which shall make right the law of the world and cast every selfish dominion down to the dust."[17]

The *Globe* charged that Hearst himself, in the worst days of his pro-Germanism, had said nothing better calculated to serve the interests of the kaiser. It wondered if some new influence had come upon the *Times* that it should encourage the peace drive Germany had started just when its military defeat was impending. The *Tribune* was equally puzzled. It said that the peace offensive was now Germany's most dangerous weapon and could not understand how it could sway the *Times,* which had been so unfaltering in support of the cause.

The criticism astounded the *Times*'s staff. This was Miller's first slip during the four years of fighting in Europe, and the usually perceptive Van Anda had also failed Ochs; yet neither could explain the lapse. The uproar left the dazed Ochs so upset that he thought of retiring from management to save the paper from destruction. But Ochs refused to blame his subordinates and shouldered the responsibility alone.

That second year of American participation in the war was fraught with excitement in other directions on Park Row. The extravagant, eccentric Bennett died at the age of seventy-seven at his villa in Beaulieu, France, in May. The *Times*'s rise to supremacy in the foreign news field saw the downfall of the *Herald.* Its circulation dropped from a high-water mark of more than five hundred thousand in 1906 to less than one hundred thousand in 1916. In the last two years of the Commodore's life, the paper showed deficits.

Bennett had dissipated a fortune of at least $30 million, and unsubstantiated reports said he had come to New York for the last time before the United States entered the war in an unsuccessful effort to have Ochs take over the *Herald.* During the summer of 1916 he endeavored to increase the paper's circulation by reducing its price from three cents to one. The move boosted sales, but they continued to lag far behind those of the *Journal, World,* and *Times.* By the time of his death, even the *Evening Telegram* was losing money, although the war made his Paris *Herald* profitable for the first time in years.

Bennett had published his papers to suit his whims, and one of them was spoofing the *Times* and *Sun* by printing their slogans. For almost eleven months, "All the News That's Fit to Print" appeared in the front-page, left-side ear of the New York *Herald,* while "It Shines for All" showed up daily in the right-side ear. The Commodore directed his publications with an autocratic hand and permitted no other control. Years before, he had eliminated the post of managing editor from both the *Herald* and *Evening Telegram,* and committees composed of various department heads ran the papers.

Occasionally, the *Herald* had proved itself humane. Through the paper, Bennett had contributed $100,000 to start a fund for the relief of the Irish during one of their famines and had raised $300,000 more. The *Herald* expended thousands for its free-ice fund to aid the city's poor and popularized the diphtheria antitoxin in the United States.

The Commodore opposed Germany from the start of the European war. In September 1914, when it looked as if the Germans would engulf the French capital, Bennett refused to be stampeded. His Paris *Herald* appeared daily, although other publishers in the City of Lights fled to Bordeaux. That month, when it was announced that the Battle of the Marne had saved Paris, the bachelor Bennett married the Baroness de Reuter, an American born Maude Potter in Philadelphia and the widow of a member of the family that had founded the British news agency.

Despite his tyrannical treatment of employees, the Commodore held most of them through the years by saying that they would be remembered in his will. None of them, however, was singled out. Instead, the will directed that the executors take measures to establish a James Gordon Bennett Memorial Home for New York Journalists in memory of his father. The will specified that any old or infirm indigent newsman who had worked for a Manhattan daily for at least ten years would be eligible for admission, with preference given to his employees. Bennett also directed that capital stock of the New York *Herald* and his Paris paper not be sold or parted with unless it was absolutely necessary, but should be transferred to the projected home.

Park Row was overwhelmed; provisions were at last made for journalists down on their luck, but newspapermen were doomed to disappointment. Almost all of Bennett's vast fortune was gone at the time of his death. The will requested that annuities totaling $153,000 be paid to twenty-one persons, including $2,000 to Mrs. Carrie Wright who, as Carrie May, had been his fiancée forty-one years before. The memorial home that Bennett envisioned never came into existence, although former *Herald* and *Evening Telegram* employees received pensions of thirty to fifty dollars a month.

Park Row had barely recovered from its surprise of the proposed home when another publisher aroused attention. Dr. Edward Aloysius Rumely of the New York *Evening Mail* was arrested in July 1918 by government agents and charged with perjury because he had sworn falsely that the *Mail* was an American-owned newspaper. Rumely had purchased the paper from Henry L. Stoddard three years before, with $735,000 secretly received from the German imperial government. At the time, Stoddard was unaware of the deal with the Germans and continued to own bonds in the company. When Rumely took over, Stoddard warned him that the paper must be aggressively patriotic or the bonds would be foreclosed at maturity.

Rumely, however, switched the paper from a pro-Ally to an anti-British policy. The *Mail* was the only paper in the city besides Hearst's to attack the British violently. It began losing money, and the Germans were forced to help out with an extra $626,000. Stoddard announced the day after Rumely's arrest that he and Paul Block, second-largest bond holder of the *Mail,* had assumed control of the paper and would conduct it as a loyal publication. Rumely was sentenced to a year and a day in a federal penitentiary, but a stay of execution was granted, and President Calvin Coolidge commuted the term to one month in 1924.

The denizens of Park Row were also stunned when, two months after Rumely's arrest, the *Evening World*'s brilliant but sadistic city editor, Charles E. Chapin, murdered Nellie, his wife of almost thirty-nine years. He shot her in the head as she lay asleep in their Hotel Cumberland room, then wrote, "Don't Disturb" on a sheet of paper and fastened it to the door with one of her hat pins. Financial problems stemming from heavy losses on the stock market had plagued the sixty-year-old Chapin for years, and he feared exposure, disgrace, and possible loss of his position. Chapin had contemplated suicide but told authorities that he did not have the heart to leave his feeble wife alone, with no one to care for her, after they had been "such good pals." He was sentenced to twenty years to life and died in Sing Sing prison in December 1930.

The city editor had reveled at his work on the *World* and gloated whenever a major disaster occurred in which many people perished. Author-humorist Irvin Shrewsbury Cobb, a star writer for the *World,* wrote that the only one Chapin worshiped "except his own conceitful image was the inky-nosed, nine-eyed, clay-footed god called News."[18] The hard-boiled Chapin had terrorized his staff and, without any Newspaper Guild to protect them, fired at least one hundred men, most of them under forty, without warning or explanation during his twenty years as city editor. When Cobb heard that Chapin would not be in to work one day because of illness, he uttered a sentence that became legendary among newspapermen: "Dear me, let us hope it is nothing trivial."[19]

The gossip flowing from Chapin's action had subsided when, less than a week before the end of World War I, a blunder stirred not only Newspaper Row but also the general public. It was a false report of an armistice sent by Roy W. Howard, president of the United Press.

Howard, an accredited correspondent, was in Brest on November 7 when he called on Adm. Henry B. Wilson, commander of U.S. naval forces in France, to check an unconfirmed report of the armistice. At that moment Wilson was reading an official wire from a naval attaché of the American embassy in Paris announcing that an armistice had been signed at 11:00 A.M. The admiral handed a copy of the official dispatch to Howard and gave him permission to send the message to New York. Howard immediately cabled the United Press office in the Pulitzer Building: "URGENT ARMISTICE ALLIES GERMANY SIGNED ELEVEN SMORNING HOSTILITIES CEASED TWO SAFTERNOON SEDAN TAKEN SMORNING BY AMERICANS."

Two hours later the admiral received another message from the attaché stating that the first had not been confirmed. Wilson notified Howard, who wasted no time cabling a correction. However, Navy censorship in New York, acting on the orders of Secretary of the Navy Josephus Daniels, a director of the rival Associated Press, held up Howard's correction for twenty hours after it had arrived in New York.

The denial of an armistice came too late for a pent-up populace that had been waiting to tear loose. All over the city, and especially on Park Row and in Times Square, where newspaper bulletins flashed the news, November 7 was celebrated as few days had been. Ticker tape floated down Broadway and Wall Street. The rarely ruffled J. P. Morgan, with an armful of ticker tape, sat on the window ledge of his office at 23 Wall Street and showered the crowd below when he heard of Germany's "surrender." More girls were kissed by soldiers and sailors in New York than on any previous day in history. Signs hung over closed stores: "Closed for the Kaiser's Funeral" and "Now is the time to hock the Kaiser and lose the ticket." The merrymaking continued for hours with little slackening. Many of the rejoicers refused to believe that the armistice was false, and in towns, villages, and cities all over the country it was cheered as enthusiastically as in New York.

When the actual armistice was announced four days later, Victory Day was celebrated throughout the United States in characteristic American fashion. The *World*'s banner read: "JOYOUS CITY OUTDOES DAY WHEN IT GOT JOYOUS TOO SOON."

13

The "Grave Digger"

JOSEPH PULITZER'S FEAR that the *Times* would overshadow the *World* became a reality at war's end. Ochs's publication was hailed as a "newspaper of record," and its circulation of almost four hundred thousand surpassed the *World*'s in 1919 for the first time, second only to that of the *Evening Journal*. In addition, the *Times*'s advertising linage was ahead of that of every rival on Newspaper Row. The *World* reaped wartime scoops by the score, but to the *Times* went the Columbia University School of Journalism's first Pulitzer Prize gold medal for "its public service in publishing in full so many official reports, documents, and speeches by European statesmen relating to the progress and conduct of the war."

Only 3 percent of the *Times*'s annual income was distributed to shareholders; the remainder was used in developing and expanding the paper. Ochs wrote on the twenty-fifth anniversary of his taking control of the paper that it had gone from running a weekly deficit to grossing $15 million a year.

Its success led to criticism of the paper. Walter Lippmann of the *New Republic* and a friend, Charles Merz, selected the *Times* to test its accuracy and honesty of news because it was considered America's leading newspaper in the publishing of foreign news dispatches. They analyzed the coverage of the Bolshevik Revolution during its first three years. The results, published in the *New Republic* in August 1920, found that the *Times*'s stories were biased and inaccurate. Atrocities that had not occurred were reported, casualty figures were far out of line with the truth, and on ninety-one occasions the Bolshevik regime was reported near collapse.

The survey by Lippmann and Merz (later editor in chief of the *Times*'s editorial page) temporarily undermined the paper's reputation for fairness. The analysis disturbed Ochs, and Walter Duranty, second in charge of the paper's Paris bureau, was transferred to Moscow. The *Times*'s coverage of the Soviet Union changed.

Park Row's disintegration as the nation's greatest newspaper street was also marked by the increasing crowds on election night in Times Square, instead of on Newspaper Row as formerly, to see the latest results posted there. Another setback came when William C. Reick, who had purchased the *Sun* papers in 1911, moved them to the old American Tract Society building at 150 Nassau Street four years later. Busy as they were with war news, *Sun* employees took time out for a "farewell dinner" to the building where Dana had reigned for almost thirty years. Remembered were not only the men who had made the *Sun* so popular but also the office cat, which had made readers laugh when it was blamed for mistakes in the paper. Reick sold the daily the following year to a man whose reputation for buying and destroying journals caused newspapermen to tremble.

As had others in the *Sun*'s history—including Benjamin Day and Dana— Frank Andrew Munsey had a New England background. He was born on his father's farm near Mercer, Maine, on August 21, 1854, to Andrew and Mary Munsey. They had four daughters and two sons but little money. Frank was number four among the six children. The Munseys moved twice when he was a boy, and it was while they were living on a farm in Bowdoin that his father went off for three years to fight with the Twentieth Maine Regiment during the Civil War. As the older son, it was Frank's role, from age seven to ten, to be practically in charge of the homestead.

When Frank was fourteen, the Munseys moved to Lisbon Falls, Maine, where he obtained work in a grocery store. Years later, he believed that running a newspaper was no different from operating a grocery store. He also worked in the local post office, where he mastered the art of telegraphy. His formal education was meager, and it was finished by the time he was sixteen, except for a few months at a business college in Poughkeepsie, New York.

Munsey became manager of a Western Union office in Augusta, where he learned the fundamentals of business and politics. His main desire was to publish a magazine in New York City. People in the state capital were pessimistic about his chances of success, but a stockbroker promised to back him with $2,500, and a friend in New York agreed to supply him with another $1,000. Munsey himself had $500, but when he arrived in Manhattan at the age of twenty-eight, he had only $40 left; the rest had been invested in manuscripts written by Horatio Alger Jr. and others. He expected to feature the stories in a weekly for juveniles that he planned to call *The Golden Argosy*. Munsey spent the remainder of his cash for a boardinghouse room, which he also used as an office with an eight-dollar table, two chairs, paper, pens, and ink.

The Maine stockbroker reneged on his promise to Munsey, who also never received any money from his friend. He took his plan to a publisher, and an arrangement was made for the weekly to come out in his name with

Munsey retained as editor and manager. On December 2, 1882, the first issue of his dream saw publication, a little more than two months after his arrival in the city.

Shortly after the magazine was launched, Munsey encountered his first major failure. His publisher went bankrupt and gave Munsey the goodwill of the weekly in lieu of $1,000 owed to him. His funds amounted to only a few dollars, but to keep *The Golden Argosy* alive, a friend in Maine lent him $300, and Munsey struggled under the burdens of work and debt. He was everything from office boy to editor and publisher, lived abstemiously, and labored long days in his sparse office to build up the distribution and advertising of the publication. Working eighteen hours a day, he used nights in his rented room to write serial stories by candlelight. One of them in particular, "Afloat in the Big City," appealed to the public.

With credit and nerve, Munsey unleashed a daring, innovative sales promotion of his magazine throughout the country, giving away sample issues and prizes. Success began to reward his prodigious efforts, and by 1887 he was able to pay off his creditors. The astute Munsey, however, did not stick with his now-successful formula. He believed that the clamor for juvenile publications had peaked, and so his magazine changed direction. It was retitled simply *The Argosy*, losing its *Golden* touch.

The man from Maine next started a publication for adults, *Munsey's Weekly*, and two years later he converted it into a more profitable *Munsey's Monthly*. Just a few months before he made that change in 1891, Munsey plunged into another dream, trying his hand at a daily newspaper. He took a six-month option on the New York *Star*, owned by Collis Huntington of Southern Pacific Railroad fame. Munsey renamed it the *Continent* and turned it into a tabloid, filling it with pictures and human-interest stories. But the tabloid was ahead of its time, and less than five months later, after losing $40,000, he returned the *Continent* to its former owner.

Munsey made an extraordinary move in the magazine field during the panic of 1893: he slashed the price of his monthly from twenty-five cents to ten. At that time periodicals such as *The Century*, *Harper's*, and *The Atlantic* each cost thirty-five cents, while *Scribner's* and *Cosmopolitan* sold for a quarter. The ten-cent price enabled it to attain a top circulation and large profits. Samuel S. McClure, who had founded *McClure's Magazine* five months before and charged fifteen cents, told writer Lincoln Steffens, "There's only one better editor than I am, and that's Frank Munsey. If he likes a thing, then everybody will like it."[1]

The price slash was so revolutionary that it caused the American News

Company to refuse to distribute the magazine because it would cut the delivery charge. Munsey wrote letters to newsdealers, at Charles Anderson Dana's suggestion. He also organized his own distributing firm, Red Star News Company, and appealed to the public in *Sun* advertisements. A compromise was reached with American News, and Munsey was set on the path to great wealth. He soon told Dana, "I'm going to buy the *Sun* one of these days."[2] By 1905 he had a million-dollar-a-year publishing income.

Munsey branched out in the magazine field as the years passed by, and he owned and combined other magazines. All of them eventually lost their separate identities in other publications. Munsey also launched the Mohican grocery chain, which expanded throughout the East until he owned seventy-five stores in New England, New York, New Jersey, and Pennsylvania. These retail units were based on the policies of mass sales, low prices, elimination of warehouses, and few expenditures for fixtures and decorations. He extended his sphere of business to include hotels, banks, and real estate.

Munsey became acquainted with J. Pierpont Morgan and invested heavily in the stock of the United States Steel Corporation. During the panic of 1907, when others sold, he bought more shares and amassed more millions of dollars. Possessing at least three hundred thousand shares, he was reportedly the largest single holder of U.S. Steel stock.

Despite his success in the magazine world, Munsey still yearned to be triumphant in the newspaper world. In November 1901 he bought both the Washington *Times* and the New York *Daily News*, an evening sheet identified with Tammany Hall and appealing to love-sick chambermaids. Munsey turned it into a higher-class publication and alienated many of its readers. Two years later, in another blow to Park Row's glamour, Munsey moved the *News* to 141 East 25th Street, where the mechanical department of *Munsey's Magazine* was located. After carrying the daily at a loss for three years, he gave up its ownership to the acting manager, and two years later the paper disappeared.

Munsey was not to be deterred. Some months later he bought the Boston *Journal* and disclosed that his dream was to own a chain of a thousand newspapers in a thousand towns. His next newspaper ventures included the launching of the Philadelphia *Evening Times* and the purchase of the Baltimore *Evening News*. At the same time he revealed that he had reduced the number of papers he hoped to own to five hundred: "There is no business that cries so loud for organization and combination as that of newspaper publishing. The waste under existing conditions is frightful. . . . For one thing, the number of newspapers is at least sixty per cent greater than we need."[3]

Munsey refrained from acquiring more dailies for four years, but in September 1912, despite two failures in New York, he made his third purchase in the big city. He paid Henry L. Einstein a million dollars for the New York *Press*, a paper supporting President Taft for reelection. Munsey wanted that daily to advance Roosevelt's candidacy on the Progressive ticket, nicknamed the "Bull Moose Party" because of the former president's comment that he was "as strong as a bull moose." He believed that Roosevelt could be elected and would continue a tariff that protected the American wage against the cheap pay abroad.

Munsey denied that George W. Perkins, a close friend and a member of J. P. Morgan and Company, or any other person was instrumental in his acquisition of the *Press*. He also said that no other person had anything to do with the purchase of any of his publishing properties and that they were independent of Wall Street, politics, and banks.

Despite Roosevelt's defeat, Munsey held on to the *Press*, a money-maker published on Spruce Street near the *Tribune*. However, his dream of owning five hundred papers began to fade. He started unloading other dailies because of heavy losses. The first to go was the Boston *Journal*, which he sold the next year, and he shut down the Philadelphia *Evening Times* the following year. In 1915 he sold the Baltimore *Evening News* to its manager, Stuart Olivier, and abandoned his plan for a newspaper chain. Munsey acknowledged that he had bought the Baltimore paper with that in mind. He sold the Washington *Times* to Arthur Brisbane in 1917, not because the paper was losing money, but because "Mr. Brisbane paid me a bigger price than it was worth to me."[4]

Even as he sold these papers, Munsey aimed again at the New York City market and in June 1916 paid Reick almost $2.5 million for the morning and evening editions of the *Sun*. The purchase fulfilled his prediction that one day he would own the *Sun*, the first successful penny paper in America. Munsey immediately merged the *Press* with the morning *Sun*. At the same time, he reduced the *Sun*'s price to one cent and provided it with a coveted Associated Press franchise. He wrote that he appreciated the responsibility that came with taking over the papers but that the man responsible for the *Sun* must square it with current conditions and requirements.

Munsey credited Reick for the development of the *Evening Sun*, and he remained with the organization. So did Edward P. Mitchell, who long had been Dana's chief editorial writer. Ervin Wardman, publisher and editor of

the *Press,* and Keats Speed, its managing editor, also stayed with the amalgamated paper. Munsey admitted that the *Press* had not attained a profitable
advertising revenue despite its impressive rise in circulation, but he predicted
the merger would give it the prestige it might not have had in fifty years.

Munsey delivered another death stroke to Park Row in November 1919,
when he moved the *Sun* properties out of the area to the old A. T. Stewart
building at 280 Broadway, at the corner of Chamber Street. In the past,
Newspaper Row's great editors strove to make their dailies the kind that
would attract nationwide attention and respect. But Munsey applied to the
newspaper industry the strategy used by U.S. Steel and other gigantic commercial enterprises—that of reducing overhead expenses and increasing production.

Prohibition went into effect on January 16, 1920, but just two days before
John Barleycorn's legal hibernation, another bombshell struck Park Row's
ranks. Munsey purchased the *Herald, Evening Telegram,* and Paris *Herald*
for $4 million from the executors of the James Gordon Bennett estate. He
now owned the papers that had made Dana and the Bennetts the nation's
most discussed newspapermen during their heydays.

The *Sun* and *Herald* had been the first successful penny newspapers in the
United States, and no newspaper had done more than the *Herald* to modern-
ize American journalism. From Park Row to Times Square and in other
cities, newspapermen shuddered at what Munsey might do with his four
New York dailies: the morning and afternoon *Sun*s, *Herald,* and *Evening
Telegram.* He could not tolerate papers that did not pay their own way, and
the *Herald,* despite its prestige and revered name, was losing money because
of low circulation. Its presses were antiquated, and new equipment would
cost more than a million dollars. If Munsey decided to merge the *Herald*
and *Sun,* he would field a strong threat to Ogden Reid's *Tribune* as the city's
ranking Republican organ. Furthermore, amalgamation would boost the fal-
tering morning *Sun.*

Munsey was delighted by his possession of the *Herald.* He had known
Bennett, and the Commodore's life had set an example for him. He could
spend money with Bennett's abandon or treat his employees just as harshly.
Lanky, gray, and mustachioed as Bennett had been, Munsey was pleased to
hear that he resembled Bennett in appearance and pose. Unwittingly or not,
Munsey also emulated Bennett in his will. Just as the Commodore had
bequeathed an annuity of $2,000 to his fiancée of almost half a century
before, Munsey specified an annuity of the same amount to Mrs. Hart E.
Pryor, to whom he had been engaged fifty years earlier when she was Annie

Downs in Gardner, Maine. The feeling he held for Bennett, however, was not reciprocated. Bennett scornfully looked down upon the New Englander as "the grocer."

The Commodore had specified in his will that he wanted the paper's name retained in case it were sold, and Munsey said he would carry out Bennett's desire. "So far as concerns any act of mine, the name *New York Herald* is immortal," Munsey said.[5] The *Herald*, however, was not to continue as in the past. Less than two weeks after the purchase, Munsey wrote that the *Sun* and *Herald* would become one newspaper, *The Sun and New York Herald*, and would be issued from the Stewart Building. He said that pride has no place in economics, and to continue the *Herald* as an independent entity would be contrary to all the laws of economics and sound business.

Before the combined papers appeared on February 1, 1920, Munsey reassured his readers that the *Herald* would live both in name and character. But the winds that attended the *Herald*'s course proved unfavorable. Departments that had brought prestige to the old paper vanished. Cartoons disappeared from the paper, and sports, real estate, and shipping news, as well as music, art, and social reports, all lost the flavor they had had in Bennett's paper.

One of Munsey's first acts as *Herald* owner was to fire artist J. Norman Lynd. The dismissal reflected the publisher's unrelenting memory toward those who he felt had slighted him. More than three years before, Lynd had drawn a full-page cartoon for the humor weekly *Life* in which Munsey appeared as a grave digger, burying newspapers and magazines he had scrapped. Author Gene Fowler, a well-known Park Row figure, summed up the sentiment of Newspaper Row's denizens: "To say that Munsey was unpopular with newspaper workers, hundreds of whom he had thrown out of work without warning, would be like saying of a convict who has spent thirty years in solitary confinement that he is not a gossip."[6]

The merger did not help circulation. By fall it had dropped considerably. Munsey resumed his paper-shuffling crusade. On October 1 he broke up *The Sun and New York Herald*. The morning paper became simply the *Herald*, and the *Sun* replaced the *Evening Sun*, which was jettisoned as the afternoon paper.

Munsey's peculiarities were well-known among newspapermen. Although a cigarette smoker himself, he barred smoking in his newspaper buildings because it bothered him to see men idling at their desks, puffing away. After the *Herald* was moved to 280 Broadway, the elevator operator became one of the most popular men with the staff on the fifth floor. He would alert them whenever Munsey approached, and when he showed up, cigarettes, cigars, and pipes were out of sight. Paradoxically, although Munsey could not stand men smoking in his offices, he gave large sums of money during World War I to the *Sun* Tobacco Fund for American soldiers and sailors abroad.

Although nominally a Republican, Munsey considered himself an independent. He waged editorial campaigns even when they meant the loss of circulation. He opposed America's entry into the World Court and the League of Nations and waged a battle against the Fordney-McCumber high-protective tariff bill. Munsey's stand against the tariff measure caused him to be denounced by Senator Frank R. Gooding in 1922. The Idaho Republican charged on the chamber floor that the publisher was fighting the measure because of his investments in Europe and that he had "turned his hounds loose on senators trying to protect American industries and American labor."[7]

Munsey personally directed a fight against a bonus for all veterans of the war. His lieutenant, Wardman, issued a pamphlet in which he defended Munsey's stand. He wrote that with the single exception of the president himself, his boss had done more effective work in the fight against the "$5 billion bonus raid" than any other individual in the country.[8]

The pamphlet prompted a harshly critical editorial against Munsey by a three-year-old New York tabloid, the *Daily News,* which was being run by Joseph Patterson of Chicago. Munsey was accused of being unsympathetic, heartless, and mercenary. The *News* wrote that his wealth came largely from U.S. Steel stock and was greatly increased by the war, which was "fought by soldiers using steel weapons":

> Many thousands were killed and many more thousands were wounded and prevented from earning their living again. Steel stockholders profited enormously—profiteered, it is claimed. Hundreds of thousands returned to find their places filled by others, some of them slackers—this, too, in establishments the owners of which, like Mr. Munsey, gained great wealth from the war.[9]

The editorial, coming shortly after the attack in the Senate, triggered a sharp reaction from Munsey. In a signed *Herald* article, he opposed "handing a bonus to the young men of the country for doing the thing that is their right and duty to do—the protection of their country." He added that the bonus degraded the American soldier, called the *News* attack inaccurate, and said that few of his millions came from the buying and selling of stock. He also said that he had not owned a share of Wall Street securities in about a dozen years, adding, "I made no money whatever, directly or indirectly, out of the war or anything associated with the war."[10]

Munsey's destruction of newspapers continued. He paid a reported $3 million for America's oldest daily, the *Globe and Commercial Advertiser*, consolidated it with the *Sun*, and, at the same time, obtained an Associated Press franchise. The *Globe* had started life as the *American Minerva* in 1793 under the editorship of Noah Webster, creator of *Webster's Dictionary*, and had an unbroken record of publication. A liberal journal possessing an AP franchise, the *Globe*, which had introduced a radio section to the city press, was on the market when Munsey bid for it.

The consolidated evening paper appeared in June 1923 as *The Sun and The Globe*, with only 22 of the *Globe*'s 125 editorial employees retained. Among those who lost their jobs were Robert L. Ripley, later of "Believe It or Not" fame, Henry F. Pringle, and humorist H. I. Phillips. Under a formal agreement, Henry J. Wright, the *Globe*'s editor in chief for many years, remained, but Munsey was determined to control the editorial page himself. He finally forced Wright to resign through the use of snubs, insults, and interference. On taking over the *Globe*, Munsey said that small units were no longer competitive in industry, transportation, commerce, merchandising, and banking, and that newspapers disregarding this economic law invited disaster.

The merger increased the *Sun*'s circulation and advertising. Munsey had finally created a successful daily by combining the outstanding features of both papers. The amalgamation brought a quick reaction from Brisbane in his popular *American* column, "Today":

> Frank Munsey, who is to newspapers what Herod was to babies, has bought the New York Globe. . . .
>
> Sometimes he builds a paper up to gigantic successes. About the Globe, he is uncertain. He may kill it, combining it with the Evening Sun; he may spare it for awhile.
>
> Just now he is saying "Eeney meeney miney mo" to decide its fate.
>
> Whether he makes a thing go magnificently, or slaughters it because it refuses to go at all, Munsey defies criticism, for he is able to tell his life history in six words:
>
> "Forty years, forty failures, forty millions."
>
> He has worked the forty years and more; he has had the forty failures and more; he has GOT the forty millions and more.[11]

Munsey decided he wanted no more of journalism in Baltimore and sold his two remaining dailies there to Hearst.

Too many papers were still published in New York to please Munsey, and he looked around for another daily to buy, convinced that his policy of consolidation would improve his own properties. The *Evening Mail,* owned by his friend Henry Stoddard, caught his attention. Stoddard agreed to sell his paper if he received more money than Munsey had paid for the *Globe.* When asked why, the *Mail*'s owner replied that the *Globe* had disparaged his journal. "That's a hell of a basis for a price," Munsey complained, but he paid Stoddard $2.2 million—$200,000 more than he wanted to spend.[12]

Munsey merged the *Mail* with the *Telegram,* which had a smaller circulation but more advertising. The amalgamated publication appeared in January 1924 as *The New York Telegram and Evening Mail.* Munsey wrote in the combined journal the next day that, if pressed, he could take over another paper or two.

When the first official circulation figures of Munsey's latest acquisition were printed, the *Journal* gloated. It pointed out that the combined circulations of both the *Mail* and the *Telegram* a year before had been 255,000 and that it was now no more than 200,000. In contrast, said the *Journal,* its own circulation was almost 700,000. It scoffed at so-called "class" papers, saying that the *Mail* and *Globe* had been such evening papers and had died. In a veiled challenge to Munsey, the *Journal* said that for twenty-six years it had been first in evening circulation in New York City and in the United States, and it intended to remain in first place.

The elder Bennett had created a sensation in his *Herald* with his modernization of the American newspaper. His son had scored a sensational coup with his making of news in Stanley's finding of Livingstone. Now Munsey created his own sensation with the *Herald*—its sale.

While rivals improved their business, the *Herald* could not escape losses. The deficit was reported to have been $750,000 in 1923. Even the *Tribune,* the only competing morning Republican daily and a paper smaller than the *Herald,* boasted of increased advertising.

Meanwhile, the morning Democratic opposition, the *Times, American,* and *World,* was more successful than either the *Herald* or *Tribune,* although the *Herald*'s Sunday edition was improving because of a new radio supplement. Munsey, always a great advocate of promoting a publication, had spent more than $200,000 over eight weeks in advertising the section in 176 newspapers from Bangor, Maine, to Birmingham, Alabama. As for his two evening papers, the combined circulation of the *Sun* and *Telegram-Mail* was less than it had been when people were buying the *Sun, Globe, Telegram,* and *Mail* separately.

Munsey considered the idea of the *Herald*'s appealing to the same clientele as the *Tribune* a duplication of effort and a display of inefficiency. He had endeavored to buy the *Tribune* before purchasing the *Mail* but had been turned down by the Reids. Convinced their paper was returning to more prosperous days, they had taken the *Tribune* out of Park Row in April 1923 to a new seven-story home on West 40th Street. With the journal founded by Horace Greeley gone from the corner it had known for eight decades, the only major dailies remaining on Park Row were the Pulitzer papers, the morning *World* and *Evening World*.

Following four days of intensive negotiations over combining the *Herald* and the *Tribune*, and less than two months after the merger of the *Telegram* and *Mail*, Munsey was invited to dinner by Whitelaw Reid's widow. Her son Ogden and his wife, Helen, were also present. The elderly Mrs. Reid was insistent that the paper meaning so much to her late husband should not leave the family. When Munsey said, "You buy the *Herald* or I'll buy the *Tribune*," she replied, "I'll buy the *Herald*."[13]

Munsey reluctantly agreed to part with the *Herald* if its name were kept in the paper's title, and the Reids consented. Munsey denied reports that they paid him $4 million, and Ogden Reid merely said the price exceeded $2 million, with the Paris *Herald* included in the transaction. Reid also said that the two outstanding causes contributing to the merger were rising newsprint costs and higher wages demanded by labor unions.

The amalgamation left six hundred men and women in various departments without jobs. About forty members of the *Herald*'s editorial staff were transferred to the *Sun*, including drama critic Alexander Woollcott, reporter Alva Johnston, and sports writer W. C. McGeehan. Reid's paper retained twenty-five of the *Herald*'s staff, including assistant night city editor Stanley Walker and reporter Herbert Asbury.

On March 18, 1924, the last day before the merged papers were printed as one, Munsey wrote in the *Herald* that it had become "but a starved shadow of its great days." He maintained that his work of amalgamating dailies was as sound a piece of economics as the merger of competing railroads, banks, or manufactures.

Of all of Munsey's mergers involving dailies in New York, this proved the most successful. Of the total of eighteen papers he had owned, only the *Sun* and the *Telegram* remained. The new *Herald Tribune* increased its circulation sharply, more than doubling sales.

Less than half a year after the merger, a hoax threatened to destroy the dependable reportorial name that the *Herald Tribune* was establishing. With

Prohibition in force, the paper received a tip in August that liquor was sold to parties aboard a large ship in the Atlantic, beyond the twelve-mile limit and somewhere between Bay Shore and West Hampton, Long Island.

Among those who had lost their jobs in the *Sun-Globe* merger was twenty-six-year-old Sanford Jarrell of Topeka, Kansas. He had joined the *Tribune* and, when a rumor of the rum ship was received, was assigned to verify the report. After a two-day absence, during which he kept in touch with his office from Bay Shore, Jarrell returned to New York with what he said were the facts of the oceanic vessel. The *Herald Tribune* splashed the copyrighted story on the front page. The article made vivid reading:

> Fifteen miles off Fire Island, beyond the pale of the law, is anchored a floating bar and cabaret that is the playground of the rich and "fast." It is a large ship, more than 17,000 tons. On board are silverware and other fittings, marked with the name of the *Friedrich der Grosse*, a former North German Lloyd liner.
>
> A Negro jazz orchestra furnishes the music to which millionaires, flappers and chorus girls out of work whirl on a waxed floor with the tang of the salt air in their lungs. A heavily manned bar serves both men and women. An excellent cuisine lends tone. Drinks of every conceivable character may be obtained at prices that melt the fat wallets of the customers. Revels de luxe are in vogue, especially over the week end.
>
> The ship flies the British ensign. The musicians are of the Alabama variety and play collegiate airs. Yachtsmen bent on gay parties go out there daily and anchor in the vicinity of the ship, which caters royally to their whims and fancies.[14]

Jarrell added that on the poop deck of the pleasure craft, convivial guests toasted a reproduction of the Statue of Liberty at midnight. He told of a five-dollar cover charge to clamber aboard the vessel and of a red-haired girl named Irene having the time of her life and shouting at 3:00 A.M., "This is an epic lark!" Drinks were reported as exorbitant, with two dollars charged for a sloe gin buck, a rye highball, or a mint julep, and that a movie, *The Thief of Baghdad* with Douglas Fairbanks, was shown at midnight.

Another story of the floating cabaret appeared the following day, and Jarrell wrote that federal authorities might make inquiries of British Prime Minister Ramsay MacDonald as to the craft's identity. He also said that after he broke the story, Coast Guard officers had received orders from Washington to hunt down and report on the steamship. The Coast Guard cutter *Seneca* was reportedly dispatched to find the palatial saloon. W. V. E. Jacobs, captain of the Coast Guard port, doubted Jarrell's story. He could not believe that his men, who patrolled deep waters from Cape Cod to Cape May, would have overlooked the ship.

Other papers felt themselves beaten by the *Herald Tribune*. They assigned their own men to find the ocean paradise, but the search turned up nothing. The *World* reported that the fisher folk of Bay Shore knew nothing of the floating booze and jazz palace, although Jarrell had written that it could be seen from Fire Island.

The *Herald Tribune* answered its rivals by comparing Jarrell to Columbus: "It has been the lot of the pioneer ever to find on his return from a successful quest that those who remained at home the while were seeking to belittle his discovery."[15] Ogden Reid posted a note on the paper's bulletin board, saying Jarrell would receive a one-hundred-dollar bonus.

Jarrell was sent back to Bay Shore and Fire Island to gather additional details of the liner, but his reports were so vague that the *Herald Tribune* became suspicious. The paper investigated, and soon it became apparent that Jarrell had never visited the liquor-laden vessel on which he had said he spent a night.

Despite close questioning, he insisted that his story was true, although admitting to embellishing details. He promised to straighten out the matter and departed. Instead of returning, he sent a confession to his office that the story was a hoax and submitted his resignation. The paper refused to accept the resignation and, in a front-page story, said he had been dishonorably dismissed.

Jarrell's monumental fake ended his career in New York. He traveled West, worked on a number of newspapers, and also freelanced. He died at the age of sixty-five in his Long Beach, California, apartment from inhaling the fumes of an unvented heater. On the day his death was reported in the papers, January 31, 1962, a one-page fictional story, "Lovers' Quarrel," appeared in the New York *Daily News* under his byline.

The *Herald Tribune* did not lose readers because of Jarrell's deception. Before the first year of the merger ended, the paper had balanced its budget, something not accomplished in twelve years. Although the *Tribune*'s new structure had been planned to allow for twenty years of normal growth, the acquisition of the *Herald* necessitated the construction of a twenty-story connecting building on West 40th Street in 1925.

Munsey had said he could take on more newspapers if necessary, but in getting rid of the *Herald*, his favorite paper, he had made his last merger. He had destroyed seven newspapers in Manhattan alone and was said to have invested about $20 million in his publishing efforts. In addition, he had carved a permanent niche for himself in New York journalism as the greatest force of newspaper destruction America had known. Except for the editorial page and typographical appearance of his papers, Munsey had shown little interest in them.

He was seventy-one years of age when, three days before Christmas in 1925, he died after being stricken with appendicitis and peritonitis. During his lifetime, his benefactions were many. Bishop William T. Manning of the Cathedral of St. John the Divine approached Munsey and asked for money to build the cathedral. "I will give $100,000, if you find nine others who will do the same thing," replied the publisher.[16] Munsey's gift served as an incentive to others, and within ninety days nine others had contributed identical gifts.

At his death, Munsey's estate was estimated at $40 million. The will made bequests to some relatives and left $10,000 to $50,000 to each of almost twenty top employees, but most of his millions went to the Metropolitan Museum of Art. The gift surprised its president, Robert W. de Forest: "So far as I know, he had never shown any special interest in the museum except by becoming an annual $10 member."[17]

Munsey's two remaining papers were also bequeathed to the museum. William T. Dewart, president and treasurer of the *Sun* company as well as Munsey's executor, bought the *Sun* and *Telegram* from the Metropolitan for about $10 million. He also mutualized the newspaper properties along lines that he knew Munsey had been considering before his death so that employees could buy stock.

Dewart sold the *Telegram* in February 1927 for $2.5 million to the Scripps-Howard chain, which was invading New York City for the first time. He said the *Telegram* was not sold to the highest bidder, but he felt that Scripps-Howard would best serve the future of the paper and the interests of the community. Within twenty-four hours after the purchase, the *Telegram*'s Associated Press service was discontinued, and additional United Press wires were installed.

Statesmen the country over, headed by President Calvin Coolidge, Chief Justice William Howard Taft, and Secretary of Commerce Herbert Hoover, eulogized Munsey. Most newspapermen reacted differently. Author Allan Nevins, an editorial writer for Munsey, wrote in *McNaught's Monthly* that those who praised him as a foremost leader in the field of journalism and those harshly critical of him were both wrong. Nevins said that his character was above reproach and that he was incapable of a sharp bargain or a dishonest transaction. Munsey was childlike in many acts, added Nevins, and that in wrecking newspapers he sometimes had the small boy's pleasure of smashing a plate-glass window.

William Allen White, renowned editor of the *____* understanding:

> Frank Munsey, the great publisher, is dead.
>
> Frank Munsey contributed to the journalism of his day the packer, the morals of a money changer and the manners of an un____ and his kind have about succeeded in transforming a once-noble ____ into an eight per-cent security.
>
> May he rest in trust![18]

GER"

mporia Gazette, was not so

191

talent of a meat
dertaker. He
rofession

ıus"

devastated Newspaper Row,
Hated for his wartime preach-
Nations, he was yet hopeful of
continued to elude the blan-

...y in operating behind the front lines.
He patted Tammany's back or defied the Hall according to his motives, and some Hearst-supported men, such as Mayor John Francis Hylan, were at his beckoning. His hopes of reaching the White House were thwarted by a formidable party foe, Alfred Emanuel Smith, who was born on Manhattan's Lower East Side. A strong Tammany man, he served twelve terms in the state assembly and became sheriff of New York County in 1915.

When Hearst sought the gubernatorial nomination in 1918, Smith opposed him and won. Smith appointed Robert L. Luce to the State Supreme Court, replacing Clarence E. Shearn, Hearst's attorney for many years. The *American* immediately attacked the governor, and Smith answered that the reason for the assault was that the publisher had wanted someone else named. Hearst replied he would never ask for any appointment or other political favor because he was not convinced Smith was sincere about his professions of progressive principles. He added that Smith was too close to Tammany and certain public-service corporations to make him an ideal public official.

The attacks against Smith continued for months, with the *American* and *Journal* accusing the governor of being in league with the Milk Trust. They claimed that the city's milk supply was contaminated and blamed him for tenement children's starving because they were deprived of it. Smith challenged Hearst to a debate anywhere in the state: "He can get up on the platform and he can ask me any question he likes about my public or about my private life, if he will let me do the same."[1]

Smith proposed a debate in Carnegie Hall, but Hearst refused the invitation. The *American* scoffed at the meeting, saying the audience would be composed of Tammany henchmen, who would probably vote for Smith under Boss Murphy's orders, and of Milk Trust and Traction Trust representatives. On the night of the scheduled debate, Smith appeared at Carnegie Hall despite Hearst's absence. He explained that he knew the man to whom he issued the challenge and that Hearst did not have a drop of good red blood in his body. "And," added the governor, "I know the color of his liver, and it is whiter, if that could be, than the driven snow."[2]

Smith insisted that Hearst opposed him because he had refused to grant political favors and described him as a professional falsifier and character assassin. He called Hearst a "cuttlefish" editor who sought shelter behind the *American*, which he described as the "Mud-Gutter Gazette."

When Smith ran for reelection in 1922, Murphy wanted Hearst on the slate as a candidate for the U.S. Senate, but Smith replied, "No matter how long I live, you will never find my name on the ticket with that bastard."[3] Hearst withdrew his candidacy, and the governor reluctantly agreed to allow a friend of the publisher, city Health Commissioner Dr. Royal S. Copeland, to run for the Senate on the ticket. Smith was reelected but ran unsuccessfully for the presidency against Herbert Clark Hoover in 1928.

Hearst, clipped in politics, remained the master in spread-eagling sensationalism. The *American* maintained an air of dignity, but the *Journal* continued to appeal to the semiliterate masses in the low-income brackets, and its headlines retained their flamboyant colors. It appeared certain that no rival would threaten the *Journal*'s circulation claim of number one in the nation. But that was before six-foot, forty-year-old Joseph Medill Patterson invaded Manhattan's journalism.

As did Hearst, Patterson trained for New York's newspaper arena before heading East. He and his cousin, Robert Rutherford McCormick, managed the *Chicago Tribune*, a paper made one of the nation's most important by their grandfather, Joseph Meharry Medill, a staunch supporter of Abraham Lincoln. Circulation wars were common in that Midwestern city, but they turned deadly when McCormick hired Max Annenberg away from Hearst's Chicago *American*. At least twenty-seven newsdealers were killed during 1910, 1911, and 1912, and hundreds of newsdealers, newsboys, and thugs were reported seriously injured before the bloodshed ended.

Patterson was born of Scottish-Irish parents in Chicago on January 6, 1879. He had one sister, Eleanor, known as Cissy, who merged the Washington *Times* and *Herald* after buying them from Hearst in 1939. Joe went to school in the East, attending Groton prep in Massachusetts and Yale. After his junior year at the university, he dropped his studies to cover the Boxer Rebellion in China for the Hearst publications in 1900, but he returned to graduate with an A.B. the following year. He became a reporter on the Tribune, where his father, Robert Wilson Patterson Jr., was the company's president, editor in chief, and creator of the Tribune's title, "The World's Greatest Newspaper." Joe's salary was $15 a week, meaningless because of a yearly allowance of at least $10,000 from his family.

He married Alice Higinbotham, with whom he was to have three daughters and an adopted son. But marriage could not quell the restlessness that distinguished him from other wealthy young men. He disliked the Tribune's conservative stand on public issues, preferring the whooping Hearst papers and their bellows. He believed that no smarter newspaperman than Hearst lived in the world.

Patterson considered himself a reformer and turned to politics. At twenty-four he was elected as a Republican to the Illinois House of Representatives, where he favored municipal ownership of streetcar lines, a stand his father opposed. During a debate on the subject, Joe participated in hurling books, chairs, and ink pots. When he learned that he had gained his seat through a deal his father made with the state Republican committee, he resigned from the legislature and switched to the Democrats.

Patterson severed his connections with the Tribune in 1905 to stump for the Democratic mayoral candidate, Judge Edward F. Dunne. His father objected to the move, considering him a chump for doing so. After Dunne was elected, Joe was appointed commissioner of public works. He saved the city money by compelling corporations, including Marshall Field—where his wife's father was a partner—to pay for privileges they enjoyed.

Convinced that municipal ownership did not go far enough and that nothing short of socialism could correct political and economic ills, Joe resigned his post. He joined the Socialist Party and purchased ten shares of stock in the Socialist Workers Publishing Society. His conservative father warned that if he ran for mayor on the Socialist ticket, it would be without his support. Joe showed his allegiance to the party by writing "Confessions of a Drone" in The Independent magazine, in which he denounced capitalism and described himself as one of the idle, young rich.

When Eugene V. Debs ran for president of the United States in 1908, Patterson became his national campaign manager. Ironically, Patterson's grandfather had so detested Debs that he ordered every mention of the socialist in the Tribune to be preceded by "Dictator" and every story's end to be followed by "Jail Debs the Traitor!"[4] Medill rescinded his directive after Joe's father threatened to resign as editor if the order was carried out.

Patterson waved the proletariat banner for several years. He lived on a farm in Libertyville, Illinois, and wrote novels, plays, and magazine articles, when he was not busy raising cattle and hogs. His novel, *A Little Brother of the Rich,* castigated women of his social class as excessive drinkers and vulgar exhibitionists and created a furor in Chicago. A play, *Dope,* maintained that narcotic addiction sprang from slum conditions. His most successful play, *The Fourth Estate,* written in collaboration with Harriet Ford, attacked corrupt politics and the venal press. *Rebellion,* both a novel and a play, followed, and it enraged most Roman Catholic clergymen because of its stand on divorce.

McCormick, an attorney, was handling legal business for the *Tribune* and also acting as its unsalaried treasurer when Patterson's father died in 1910. The general manager was James Keeley, who owned no stock in the company but supervised all departments of the paper.

McCormick persuaded his cousin to leave the farm and return to the *Tribune* as Sunday editor and to take charge of features, with himself directing the paper's business. Patterson bombarded Keeley with suggestions for features, and many were ignored. The cousins did not relish Keeley's management and assumed complete control of the paper in 1914, with the aid of stockholder proxies during a board of directors meeting. With his power gone, Keeley departed from the *Tribune.*

Patterson and McCormick did so well with the *Tribune* that Arthur Brisbane, a personal friend of the family, wrote Patterson's mother that they were doing the best newspaper work in the country. He also said Hearst would gladly pay them $50,000 a year and a percentage of all the profits above $500,000 a year.

Patterson traveled to Mexico in 1914 as a *Tribune* reporter during the U.S. occupation of Vera Cruz. He was also the paper's correspondent in Germany, France, and Belgium during the early months of World War I and sailed for home in September 1915 on a British ammunition carrier. While aboard, he concluded that America's best policy should be one of isolationism, an opinion that remained with him throughout his life.

Patterson feared, as had the younger Bennett and Hearst, that if the nation were ever invaded, it would be by the Japanese, who would try to surprise the United States and obtain the initial advantage. He wrote that descendants of the old samurai, a caste that believed the only honorable occupation for a gentleman was war, dominated Japan. Patterson added that the Japanese had engaged in five wars in the preceding twenty-five years, and all had been glorious and profitable: "Aside from the fact that they like fighting and dislike us, we are the next logical victim, being a near neighbor, unmilitary and rich—a wonderful nation to loot."[5]

Brisbane ridiculed Patterson's concern that Japan might one day invade the United States: "You will grow old and die without seeing any war. All the fight will be kicked out of the European nations by the time this war ends—they will have enough for fifty years to come. And Japan I think will not try to cross a trench seven thousand miles wide and wipe up this nation."[6]

Patterson returned to Mexico in 1916, this time as a soldier with the Illinois National Guard, and rose to sergeant. When America entered the war on the Continent the following year, Patterson went overseas as a lieutenant with the first Guard group to go to Europe, the 42nd (Rainbow) Division, and was promoted to captain. He fought in five major campaigns and was gassed at Montigny. His division commander, Brig. Gen. Douglas MacArthur, reportedly called him "the most brilliant natural-born soldier that ever served under me."[7] To his men, Captain Patterson was known as "Aunty Joe" because of his concern for their welfare.

While on military leave before the armistice, Patterson visited London and was impressed with Lord Northcliffe's *Daily Mirror,* a picture tabloid with a circulation of eight hundred thousand, more than that of any paper in America. Returning to the Continent, the captain and his cousin, now a colonel, discussed postwar plans for a New York City paper while on a French farmyard near Mareuil-en-Dole. Legend has it that the New York *Daily News* was conceived while the two men talked on a manure pile. Patterson vehemently denied the story, but McCormick enjoyed saying it was so.

Patterson returned to London the following year and spent the night at Lord Northcliffe's country home. The press baron told him a tabloid could succeed in a large American city if it were kept simple and bright to attract the masses. His advice impressed the Chicagoan, and he was determined to publish his own picture tabloid in Manhattan.

New York City's population in 1919 was more than five million, including many immigrants to whom a paper packed with photographs and news digests would have appeal. The size of the publication, furthermore, would prove handier than the standard-sized sheet for the subway rider.

No time was to be lost in the venture. Just off Park Row, at 55 Frankfort Street, Hearst had equipped a plant and was considering issuing his own tabloid. Others, too, had observed Northcliffe's success and thought of trying to duplicate it. McCormick and Patterson agreed that Patterson would run the tabloid since it was his brainchild, and that he would also continue as co-editor of the *Chicago Tribune.*

When Patterson's proposed paper was announced, others contemplating tabloids suspended their plans. The date was June 26, 1919, for the first issue of the *Illustrated Daily News*. Its offices were in the Mail Building, at 25 City Hall Place, in the shadow of Park Row. The tabloid would be printed on *Evening Mail* presses, with the rent $166.67 a month. Patterson, on the eve of the new paper's launching, was unaware that his would be the country's first successful twentieth-century tabloid and that one day it would possess the greatest circulation the country had known.

At this time, thirteen general dailies were published in Manhattan as the *News* prepared to roll for the first time. The *Times*, with a circulation of more than 367,000, led the six morning papers. The *World* and the *American* were not far behind, with the *Sun*, *Tribune*, and *Herald* trailing in that order. Among the seven afternoon publications was the *Journal* with a circulation of 685,428, almost double that of the *Evening World*, while the *Evening Sun*, *Globe and Commercial Advertiser*, *Telegram*, *Mail*, and *Post* lagged. In addition, three general papers were published in Brooklyn: *Standard Union*, *Eagle*, and *Times*.

The new daily was issued as a morning paper for two cents. It contained sixteen pages and was half the size of a standard newspaper. Patterson and McCormick were listed as editors and publishers, with the captain its president and the colonel first vice president and treasurer. On the eve of publication, advertising told of the new daily and broadly hinted at the type of paper it would be. An advertisement in the conservative *Times* stated, "See New York's Most Beautiful Girls Every Morning in the *Illustrated Daily News*."

The paper's first editorial produced no grandiose hopes for journalism:

> We shall give you every day the best and newest pictures of the interesting things that are happening in the world. . . .
> No story will be continued to another page—that is to save you trouble.
> . . . You can read it without eye strain.[8]

Newspaper Row's skeptics laughed at the first number, although it sold 150,000 copies. It was heavily devoted to pictures, and a photo of the Prince of Wales dominated the front page. Features were those of the *Chicago Tribune*, and dispatches came from United Press wires. To lure readers, a beauty contest, with a first prize of $10,000, was announced. Although $42,000 was spent advertising it, the contest was a failure. Circulation director Max Annenberg told general manager William Henry Field, "We're licked. We better pick up our marbles and go home."[9] But Patterson had no intention of doing so.

Editorial personnel at the *Times*'s office derided the new daily. Their managing editor, Carr Van Anda, a Patterson friend for years, felt differently.

"No, I think you are wrong," he told them. "This paper should reach a circulation of two million."[10]

On the second day of publication, the *News* headed its editorial column with a surprising acknowledgment: "So far our printing has been the worst in New York. Before we're through it will be the best. Watch us."

Just as he had done on the *Tribune,* absentee publisher Patterson busied himself with suggestions about how to improve the *News.* After Annenberg told of difficulties attending the tabloid, the publisher wrote Field:

> Get in a crowd picture every day if possible, either bathing beaches, Brooklyn Bridge, or something of the sort, kids in Central Park. Caption these pictures, "Were You There?" Say the first ten people who prove they were members of the crowd will receive $5.00 a piece at the Illustrated Daily News office. They must apply in person.
>
> Remember, lay emphasis on romantic happenings and print pictures of girls who are concerned in romances, preferably New York girls. Also, one or more pictures every day with reference to a crime committed the previous day in New York. Please remember particularly, make it snappy, make it local, make it news.[11]

Circulation declined sharply after the first few days. During one week in July sales averaged 10,596, the lowest the paper was ever to know, but improvement began in September. In early November Patterson wrote Mc-Cormick that the loss of the *News* until the first week of January would be about $350,000. He said its circulation was sixty thousand and predicted that within a year it would reach one hundred thousand. A sharp rise began late in November, when the paper launched a limerick contest. Four lines were published daily, and a prize of $100 was offered each day for the best fifth line supplied by a reader. The first limerick produced more than ten thousand entries. People at parties would show a copy of the *News* and spend the evening creating last lines. The contest ended more than three months later, boosting circulation to more than a million. But that impressive increase vanished swiftly with the conclusion of the contest.

Hearst did not enjoy having another paper in the city that wooed the semiliterate masses. Less than two weeks after the *News* began publishing, Brisbane told Patterson, whom he called an Illinois Don Quixote, that a tabloid would never succeed in New York because the city never wanted things by halves. As sales rose, Brisbane wired Patterson, asking if he would consider selling the *News* to him personally for $50,000. The Chicagoan immediately asked Field what was in the wind and was told that Hearst's top lieutenant said the tabloid really was for himself and not for his chief. Patterson, however, was suspicious and rejected the offer.

Readers discovered that the paper was not only easy to read but also contained almost as much prominent news, although in briefer form, as the standard journals. They also found that its editorials were written in language they could understand, and that they could read the paper on subway trains without jabbing the eyes of adjacent passengers.

Patterson called the *Illustrated Daily News* an "awkward" title. It was changed to *The New York Illustrated News,* and he termed that "rotten." While in New York in November he changed the named to *The News.* The legend, "New York's Picture Newspaper," was added to the title the following summer, and soon after the paper inherited its final name, *Daily News.*

There was nothing backward about the tabloid. It claimed the best movie page in town and boasted that its fiction, under such titles as "The Wise Virgin," was the best in America. Each day a scantily clad girl was featured among its photographs. Readers enjoyed the paper's special features, including "The Best Joke I Ever Heard," "A Friend in Need," "Most Embarrassing Moment," and "Bright Sayings of Children." Its most popular columnist was the *Chicago Tribune*'s Bert Leston Taylor, writing "A Line O' Type or Two" under the initials of B. L. T. Comic strips included *The Gumps, Gasoline Alley,* and *Harold Teen.* Most of these features also appeared in the *Tribune,* and Patterson either had suggested the idea or encouraged the originator.

Letters to the editor, published in the column "Voice of the People," were written in simple, unedited language that appealed to the paper's readers. Some of them gave advice that they thought might improve the tabloid.

By the time the *News* celebrated its first birthday in 1920, its average daily circulation had far exceeded Patterson's hopes. In October a tight schedule for news matter and advertising was adopted, causing sales to recede gradually. Patterson wrote Field that the tightness of the paper was a contributing factor, but it was valuable and would not be changed. Another reason, he added, was that the *News* had forgotten the origin of its success, the interest of young women. He said the paper was trying too hard to attract men with the sporting page, and the tabloid could not compete with other papers in sports or the stock market.

Patterson also blamed the decline of sales on the lack of novelty. He said the paper had become placid, looking the same as other dailies, and insisted that the publication have novelty in ideas and assignment. Although Patterson did not want the paper to be objectionable, he wanted more spice put in court cases, such as divorce trials. He also called for more pictures of girls in bathing suits and frequent photos of brides.

Circulation rose again, aided by a movie contest, a serial story read avidly in subway trains, and a "Politeness Contest." The *News* was on its way toward solid success by 1921, thriving on almost forty contests and funds in less than two years. It moved in April to its own plant at 23–25 Park Place under a twenty-one-year lease and installed new presses and typesetting machines.

The steady rise of the *News* dug into the *American*'s sales and disturbed Hearst. He imported a lottery feature being used in Chicago to help the *American* stem its growth. The tabloid retaliated with its own lottery, strewing coupons around the city, and holders of lucky numbers received cash gifts. The paper's first drawing was held in Battery Park. Patterson wrote Field that the drawings must be held in public, rain or shine: "The point is we have our drawing in public and the opposition does not."[12]

The *News* ran full-page advertisements about the contest in its pages, with the figure $600,000 bordering on all four sides. One ad announced its circulation had passed the half-million mark and added, "This is supposed to be a scheme for boosting circulation. We think it is punk. Mr. Hearst started it. He wants more readers for his three cent paper. If he can afford to get readers this way, so can we—only more so."[13]

The contest was costly, and circulation results were disappointing. Many readers angrily refused the paper because the dealers' supply of coupons had been exhausted and none were available. Clergymen and others condemned the lottery. Within two weeks, much to the relief of both sides, it was halted on a request from Postmaster General Will H. Hays.

Brisbane again asked Patterson if he and McCormick would sell their paper. He offered each a salary of at least $100,000 and a share in the profits after purchase. Patterson asked Brisbane if the offer had anything to do with Hearst's political ambitions. Brisbane replied that he had not the remotest idea of any politics in connection with the *News*. He said Hearst had ordered presses of the tabloid's type and that if the publisher started a new paper, he would have to work on it despite his reluctance. Patterson answered that he and his cousin would not sell the *News*. He also said that their friendship should not be interrupted if Brisbane operated a new tabloid in the city. "Business is business," he added.[14]

Despite their friendliness, a *News* editorial could not resist twitting Hearst's chief aide:

Arthur Brisbane says that "in the United States last year 1,238,000 *brand new* babies were born."

Startling statistics, but incomplete. Mr. Brisbane should tell a waiting world how many old, or slightly shopworn babies were born last year.[15]

For the first time in more than two decades, Hearst had met a formidable foe who could play his game, dollar for dollar. The *News* was here to stay; its sensationalism followed a pattern set by the elder Bennett and carried along by Pulitzer and Hearst. It established little that was new in journalism, differing from standard dailies mainly in size, emphasis upon pictures, and the brevity of news stories. Newspapermen scoffed at it, and many refused to work for what they considered "the gum chewer's sheetlet" and a paper "edited for morons." But the tabloid's popularity could not be disputed, and its left-ear box in the nameplate read, "The largest circulation in America."

Hearst owned twenty-three newspapers in the United States, as well as magazines, a music publishing firm, ranches, forests, mines, and real estate. He possessed a movie company with a star he had created, Marion Davies, and believed that films and the newly rising radio were cutting into the attention given by readers to newspapers. The tycoon told an interviewer that the power of the American press was declining because the reactionary interests and predatory corporations that owned or influenced many newspapers promoted their own interests rather than the public's welfare.

No matter how much Hearst bolstered his *American,* he realized that a standard-sized paper could not threaten the *News,* and he decided it was time to start his own tabloid. The first issue of the *Daily Mirror* came off the presses on June 24, 1924, five years after the debut of the *News.* It was printed on Frankfort Street, near the Brooklyn Bridge, where Hearst had considered issuing one years before. An editorial stated that the *Mirror's* program would be 90 percent entertainment and 10 percent information. Little attempt was made to be original, and its makeup and features closely followed those of the *News.*

The day after the *Mirror's* debut, the *News* ran an editorial, "BOW TO A TODDLING RIVAL":

THE NEWS was first in America to discover the "ol' swimmin' hole" of picture newspaperdom. It has been having a wonderful time for five years.

We are not selfish, however. . . .

No, as we splash gayly about, viewed by more than 800,000 admiring purchasers daily, we send back to Mr. Hearst, as he gingerly tests the temperature with a hesitant big toe, this exuberant yell: "Come on in! The water's fine!"[16]

An editorial on the *Mirror*'s third day was headlined "THANKS, MAJOR!" It said that Patterson and McCormick had "made a wonderful copy of Northcliffe's paper." (The *Mirror* did not mention why it called Patterson a major, a rank he did not obtain until two years later in the Field Artillery Reserve.) The editorial continued:

> We are sorry we haven't a picture of Colonel Bertie McCormick, to print beside that of his cousin and fellow officer Major Patterson. . . . The only consolation . . . is found in the fact that both are enormously rich, millions, millions and millions piled up. Also, both of these young gentlemen enjoy a good fight.
> AND THEY ARE GOING TO GET IT.[17]

Three months after the *Mirror* began publication, magazine publisher Bernarr Macfadden issued the city's third tabloid, *The New York Evening Graphic.* It was published in the old *Evening Mail* building, which had been the first home of the *News.* Macfadden, widely known as the Father of Physical Culture, thought nothing of walking thirty miles from his home in Nyack, New York, to Manhattan. He wanted his paper to possess the best qualities of two of his magazines, *True Story* and *Physical Culture,* and to promote his theories on remaining healthy.

With Emile Gauvreau, formerly of the Hartford *Courant,* as his managing editor, Macfadden was determined that his paper represent clean and constructive journalism. The first issue was published on September 15, 1924, and its lead editorial indicated that the *Graphic* did not intend to copy the *News* or *Mirror:*

> We intend to dramatize and sensationalize the news and some stories that are not new. . . .
>
> *We want to show our readers how to live 100 per cent.*
> *Don't be a dead one! Gird up your loins.*
> Make ready to fight for the thing that you want in life and if you read the GRAPHIC with sufficient regularity you can be assured of worthwhile assistance.

The paper announced an Apollo-Diana contest, with prizes totaling $10,000 for ideal marriages: "The *Graphic* today launches the first substantial attempt by any publication to improve the race by encouraging marriages of the physically fit."[18]

The *Graphic,* more than any other paper in journalism, was a forerunner of scandal sheets such as the *National Enquirer, Globe,* and *Star* sold in supermarkets. Macfadden's hope of a nonsensational paper was gone. On the second day of publication the *Graphic* ran a first-page, first-person headline:

"Poor Boy 19, Facing Noose, Cries
MUST I DIE WHEN RICH KILLERS GET LIFE"

Other headlines in those early editions read:

"THEY LIED ABOUT OUR LOVE
I DID NOT MARRY MY BROTHER!"

"Stick to Women They're Safer Than Horses"

"I Did Not Bury My Baby Alive"

One of the stories focused on surgery for the current heavyweight boxing champion. The headline, in odd makeup, read:

Jack Dempsey's Nose Does
Not Fit
His Face

W. Augustus Pratt, Famous
Facial Surgeon, Gives Jack
A Knock-Out Wallop
(Artistically Speaking) by
Pointing Out That With His
New Nose Jack, as a Sheik,
Is a Champion Pugilist[19]

Editor & Publisher wrote that "unique" *Graphic* photographs illustrating stories were evidently "the work of movie actors responding to some director who has a stock of properties in a studio."[20] Harry Grogin of the art department had perfected a technique that became known as the "composograph," in which the head of a prominent person was pasted upon the body of a model. Besides its emphasis on sex and sensationalism, the *Graphic* was noted for its "Daily Physical Culture Page," for which Macfadden wrote a column, "Keeping Fit," and other articles advising readers on how to eat and take care of themselves. A cartoon, *Lottie Pop*, showed an Amazonian prizefighting woman living up to Macfadden's principle. A comic strip dedicated to health was entitled *Ozzy and His Gym*.

On the staff was Walter Winchell, a former tap dancer and writer for a weekly, the *Vaudeville News*. He wrote a column called "Your Broadway and

Mine" and made gossip-writing an art by focusing upon illicit romances, expectant births, and information that no other columnist printed. He remained with the *Graphic* until 1929, when he went over to the *Mirror*. He was joined on that paper a few months later by Gauvreau, whom he despised.

When the *Graphic* printed an editorial blast against the *News*, Patterson wrote Field about what to do the next time there was an attack:

> You will, I think, find some pictures of Bernarr Macfadden dressed only in his epidermis and a pair of trunks, with his long hair, lifting weights. . . . [U]se this full length picture of him. Quote or paraphrase some of Macfadden's most violent words about idea thieves and point out that he came into New York with the third illustrated tabloid paper. The only original aspect of his paper was that he tried to launch it with a stock selling scheme which the law prevented.[21]

Tabloids spread from one coast to the other. Besides New York, they were published in Boston, where Hearst had the *Advertiser*, and Baltimore, Washington, Los Angeles, and San Francisco. An *Editor & Publisher* survey among newspaper editors in July showed that long train rides were not the dominant reason for their success but that the main attractions were pictures, condensation, and their ability to give all the news of the day.

During the first seven years of the *News*'s existence, Patterson was an absentee publisher, supervising the paper from his Chicago office. His days of socialism had long been buried, but his desire to help the masses remained. The masthead on the editorial page daily contained a six-point platform:

1—A Seat for Every Child in the Public Schools.
2—A 5-Cent Fare and Better Service.
3—Improved Traffic Conditions on the Streets.
4—A Bridge Across the Hudson to New Jersey.
5—Stricter Regulation of the Sale of Pistols.
6—Save the Parks for the People.

In an effort to retain the five-cent subway fare, he wrote a memo about New York's mayor as elections approached:

> Hylan hasn't been a very good mayor. Everyone knows he is a messenger boy for Hearst. But he has saved the five cent fare so far. . . . If there is a scheme to put over an increase in subway fare, the backers of this scheme may as well save themselves the trouble. The News will expose it, oppose it and help defeat it, even if it has to support Hylan to do it.[22]

Patterson had said he would move to New York when the circulation of the *News* reached a million. Early in 1926, as the paper galloped toward that mark, he prepared to leave for the East to administer the affairs of both the *News* and the cousins' weekly magazine, *Liberty.* McCormick took over the *Tribune,* and Patterson assumed full charge of the *News.*

The *News* became the first paper in the nation to pass the million mark on a regular basis in March 1926. Reuben Maury, a magazine writer, was appointed the paper's editorial writer. He had the ability to reflect Patterson's views as if they were the founder's. Not long after, Harvey Duell, managing editor of *Liberty,* was named city editor, and the tabloid's quality of writing and editing improved. To broaden the paper's coverage, Patterson obtained an Associated Press franchise by purchasing the *Commercial Bulletin,* a financial daily.

Patterson was content to work in unpressed trousers and a turtleneck sweater, a manner of attire he had adopted in Chicago, and signed interoffice memoranda "JMP." To learn the reading habits of the masses, he rode the subway train or stood upon its platform, looking over the shoulders of *News* customers to see the features they were perusing. He also watched people buying papers at newsstands. If the unsuspecting purchasers were well-dressed, an accompanying movie cameraman photographed them so that the films could convince prospective advertisers that his paper appealed to people with buying power.

Patterson sometimes went alone on walks or visited such places as Coney Island, where he mingled with the multitudes and listened to their opinions. The Bowery was one of his favorite haunts, and the wealthy publisher made friends among the derelicts and panhandled with the best of them. He could usually solicit the price of a night's lodging and a meal or two. To Bowery bums, he might be "Joe," but in the office he was "Mr. Patterson" to most of his staff. He often took his office boy to a baseball game or drank with the reporters, but if they showed too much familiarity, he quickly revealed a flaring temper. Frequently, Patterson covered stories with his hirelings, and when he had an idea that might make a good item, he sent them scurrying for information, regardless of expense.

Patterson's presence in New York came amid the roaring decade that followed World War I. It was the golden age of sports, with Jack Dempsey boxing, Babe Ruth swatting home runs, Bobby Jones ruling the golf world, and Bill Tilden and Helen Wills Moody dominating tennis. That, too, was an era of jazz and bootlegging arising from Prohibition, and Al Capone reigned as the lord of gangsters.

The fight for circulation among the tabloids unleashed the most frenzied sensationalism the city had observed since Hearst had challenged Pulitzer as Newspaper Row's overlord. Tabloids spun the wheels of ballyhoo, and standard-sized newspapers, striving to keep pace, sensationalized more than they had in years. The city's three tabloids claimed two of every five readers of dailies in Manhattan, but despite their assertion, most of the circulation gains were not made at the expense of the larger journals.

Nineteen-year-old Gertrude Ederle of New York swam the English Channel on August 6, 1926, in fourteen and a half hours, the first woman to do so. She was acclaimed in Europe and returned home a national heroine. Patterson had financed the venture as a stunt, and the *News* made the most of it. When the S.S. *Berengaria* sailed into New York waters three weeks later with Miss Ederle aboard, a *News* plane dropped floral pieces on the top deck. When the wonder swimmer set foot at the Battery, the paper gave her a red Buick roadster with a rumble seat in back, as she had requested.

Four years before, the Reverend Edward Wheeler Hall of the Church of St. John the Evangelist in New Brunswick, New Jersey, and a choir singer, Mrs. James Mills, had been found murdered near that city, but a grand jury failed to indict anyone. The case was reopened in 1926 when the *Mirror* claimed it had uncovered new evidence that promised a solution to the crime. Mrs. Hall and her two brothers were arrested, but they were acquitted after one of the most lurid trials in years. Author Silas Bent measured the amount of space given to the story and found that the *Times*, with 528,300 words, led both the *American* with its 347,000 and the *News* with 223,400.

The romantic exploits of the over-fifty real-estate operator Edward "Daddy" Browning, his fifteen-year-old wife, Frances, known as "Peaches," and her ever-present mother filled the front pages of tabloids on dull news days. The *Mirror* reveled in calling Browning "Bunny" and "Lovey-Dovey" and also disclosed that he was wooing young girls while separated from his wife. Browning's reaction was a $100,000 suit against the *Mirror*, which wrote, "It is the first time in his record that he has objected to the publicity in which he is used to wallowing."[23]

During the publicity given by the *Graphic* to the Brownings, a composograph represented the honeymoon bedroom scene as related by Peaches. Browning's face was pasted on the body of a reporter clad in pajamas, and he was seen shouting, "Woof, woof, I'm a goof." Peaches was pictured as a half-clad figure shrinking away from him. "When Peaches refused to parade nude!" screeched the *Graphic*.[24]

Police in towns and cities barred papers containing details of their matrimonial adventures. Edward Doherty of the *Mirror* was outspoken: "Newspaper men—including the present writer—have written columns about 'Bunny' and 'Peaches' and 'Mamma' in the firm belief that they were writing news. They are all saps, including this writer."[25]

The *Graphic* made the *News* and *Mirror* seem almost conservative by comparison, and a newspaperman tagged it the "Porno Graphic." The sheik of the movies, Rudolph Valentino, died that August 23, and frenzied women created disturbances outside the Frank E. Campbell undertaking parlor in the city. Months later, the *Graphic* ran a front-page composograph showing tenor Enrico Caruso and Valentino in the great beyond and dressed in togas, "watching a spirit audience from a lower plane about to greet a troup [*sic*] of spirit actors who play in a spirit world."[26]

The *Graphic*'s circulation soared, and that paper seesawed with the *Journal* for leadership among the afternoon papers. Gauvreau posted a memorandum on the bulletin board: "The circulation of the *Graphic* has reached the point where it is tearing the guts out of the presses. This has resulted from my policy of sensationalism. Any man who cannot be yellow has no place on the staff."[27]

The *Mirror* could not overcome its copycat label, and the *Graphic* held fast to its propensity for excessive sensationalism. Scandalous as the *News* was, its leadership in the tabloid field was unquestioned. Ruth Snyder, wife of a *Motor Boating* magazine art editor, and Judd Gray, a corset salesman, had been convicted of killing her husband with a sash weight in the Snyder home in Queens, New York. As time neared for the electrocutions of the couple at Sing Sing, Patterson told managing editor Frank J. Hause, "If this woman dies, I want a picture of her."[28] Photographers were barred from the prison's death chamber, but the *News* imported Tom Howard, a Washington photographer unknown to New York newspapermen, for the occasion. A specially devised camera was strapped to his ankle, and a long cable ran up his leg and through a hole in his trouser pocket to a shutter bulb in his hand.

A full-page photo of the murderess in the electric chair appeared in the paper in an extra edition on January 13, 1928, with just a single word on the front page: "DEAD!" A caption read that it was the first Sing Sing execution picture ever taken and the first of a woman's electrocution anywhere. It was reprinted the following day, and the paper called it "the most talked-of feat in the history of journalism." Not only did the photograph create a sensation, but the wickedness of tabloidism was assailed throughout the country.

The condemnation hurled at the *News* was forgotten in the praise bestowed upon Patterson's paper that fall, after it ran other exclusive photographs that Newspaper Row proudly showed the rest of the nation.

The British steamer *Vestris* foundered off the Virginia coast with a loss of 110 lives. Rescue ships brought survivors to New York, and *News* reporters and photographers scurried about, seeking pictures of the sinking vessel. Photographer Martin McEvilly gave crewmember Fred Hanson ten dollars for an undeveloped roll of film he had shot during the disaster. Because of the value of the photos, Hanson received another fifteen hundred dollars. One picture showed crew and passengers struggling to launch one of the last lifeboats as the steamship listed precariously to starboard shortly before the sinking. The photographs established the *News* as a tabloid capable of competing with standard-sized journals in the news-gathering field.

With its increased prosperity, the *News* outgrew its Park Place building, and a new one was planned. As it was being constructed at 220 East 42nd Street, Hearst selected property three blocks north, on East 45th Street, for his *Mirror*. While both buildings were rising, the stock market started tumbling on October 24, 1929, and the shadow of the Great Depression was cast.

The *Mirror*'s structure was completed first, but more impressive was the thirty-seven-story *News* edifice, into which the paper moved the following February. It was a monument to tabloidism, at a cost of almost $11 million. A seventeen-foot globe revolved in the lobby, with bronze compass points inlaid on the terrazzo floor. A marble façade over the main entrance of the building displayed workingmen and -women, with a legend, attributed to Abraham Lincoln, at the bottom of the carved panels: HE MADE SO MANY OF THEM. The uptown move of the two newspapers struck another blow to journalism on Park Row and the downtown area.

Patterson had always been concerned with the welfare of the common people, who had made possible his imposing building. As the Depression followed the stock market crash, the *News* was the first among the tabloids to realize that readers no longer viewed sauciness, titillation, and crime as their primary interests. "People," he said, "don't care so much now about playboys, Broadway, and divorces. They want to know how they're going to eat. From now on we'll pay more attention to the average man and his family."[29] Less space was devoted to gangsterism and love nests, and pictures of women became less suggestive. The world was changing, and so was the *News*.

As *Editor & Publisher* expressed it, Patterson was a genius.

15

The Passing of Park Row

DURING THE 1920s, when tabloids were on the rise, Hearst finally gave up hopes of becoming president. However, he could not escape controversy as he continued his efforts to embroil the United States in a war with Mexico.

Fireworks started in 1927, shortly after the *American* and *Evening Journal* moved from the Park Row area to 220 South Street, facing the East River. On November 14, after holding on to an explosive story for five months, he released it in the *American* under a front-page banner: "MEXICO PLOT AGAINST U.S." From then through early December, documents purportedly described a conspiracy between Mexico and Japan against the United States. Mexico was reported as sending a million dollars to foment an anti-U.S. revolution in Nicaragua, bribing American clergymen, and attempting to control members of the U.S. press.

The *American* ran a story reporting that President Plutarco Elias Calles had approved the payment of $1,215,000 to bribe four U.S. senators. Their names were not disclosed, but the Senate's reputation was at stake, and a five-member committee was appointed to investigate the authenticity of the documents. A hearing was held within a week, and an alleged letter from Calles to his half-brother, Arturo M. Elias, consul general in New York, named Senator William E. Borah of Idaho as receiving $500,000, Senators George W. Norris of Nebraska and Thomas J. Heflin of Alabama as each getting $350,000, and Robert M. La Follette Jr. as receiving $15,000.

The consul general took the stand and denied that the papers were authentic. Hearst also testified that day. He acknowledged that the disclosed situation had become "increasingly serious," but he was absolutely certain that none of the senators had ever received as much as a penny. He admitted that none had been given an opportunity to deny the charges before publication.

The committee learned that an unidentified American citizen living in Mexico had notified John Page, an International News Service correspondent stationed in Mexico City, about the documents. Page had hired an investigator, Miguel R. Avila, a Texan working below the border, to obtain them, and they were purchased for about $20,000. During the hearing, the papers were acknowledged to be forgeries, not only by the panel's handwriting experts but also by Hearst's own experts.

Norris, ill at home in Washington, denounced Hearst in an "open letter" to him that was read on the Senate floor. He described Hearst as the publisher of a chain of newspapers that constituted the "sewer system of American journalism." Norris asserted that analysis of Hearst's testimony before the panel "leads to the inevitable conclusion that you are not only unfair and dishonest, but that you are entirely without honor." The senator added that it was peculiar that Calles would spend money to bribe lawmakers whose views were the same as his: "You evidently believed that if a revolution could be started, it would mean financial benefit for your investments in Mexico."[1]

A signed Hearst editorial appeared in the *American* the next day. He expressed disappointment that Congress had manifested no interest in the disclosures about Mexico. These included Mexico's assistance to Nicaraguan revolutionaries despite U.S. support of the government, Mexico's intimate relations with Bolshevik Russia, and Mexico's revolutionary movements in other parts of the world, including China. In addition, there was Mexico's draft of a secret treaty with Japan to colonize in Mexico and Nicaragua so that the Japanese would be available in times of war. Hearst wrote that Congress paid attention only when the so-called senatorial letters were printed.

> It is true, as Mr. Norris said . . . that I have property valued at approximately four million dollars in Mexico, which I had possessed in peace and security through the friendship and favor of the Mexican Government.
>
> Certainly nobody but a perfect jackass—and Senator Norris is not that—at least not a perfect one—could imagine that my property holdings were benefited by losing the friendship and favor of the Mexican Government.[2]

Hearst added that he published the documents because he opposed any interests contrary to those of the U.S. government. Shortly after his editorial, he told his editors that he would no longer dispute his handwriting experts' opinion that all the documents were fraudulent, even though he believed the essential facts were not fabricated. The Senate committee later reported that there was no doubt all the papers were forgeries, but it took no action against Hearst. The case dealt him a humiliating blow, and if he had aimed at drawing the United States into a war with Mexico, he was again defeated.

The *World* continued its crusading at the advent of the twenties. Herbert Bayard Swope, winner of the first Pulitzer Prize for a reporter's work in 1917, became the paper's executive editor three years later. He instituted the "op ed" page, the literary page opposite the editorials, and here columns were printed at various times by Franklin Pierce Adams, Harry Hansen, Samuel Chotzinoff, Robert Littell, and Heywood Broun. With Frank Cobb, chief of the editorial page, the paper garnered a Pulitzer award for distinguished public service with a three-week exposure of the secrets of the Ku Klux Klan in 1921 and another for focusing the spotlight on the evils of Florida labor camps in 1923. Cobb died before that year ended, and the paper seemed unable to produce the dynamic editorials Joseph Pulitzer had admired, although scholarly Walter Lippmann was named chief of the editorial page.

As the decade reached the midway mark, the influence of the *Times* and the popularity of the *Daily News* undermined the strength of the *World* so much that it was forced to increase its daily price to three cents in 1925. A rise in the cost of white paper and ink was blamed, but more important was the decline in earnings. They had dwindled sharply from $500,000 in 1922, although the paper still showed a profit. The increase in price caused its circulation to decline, and by the beginning of 1927, the *World* was forced to return to two cents.

The *World* disheartened liberals that year when a rift arose between editor Ralph Pulitzer and Heywood Broun, who later helped organize the New York Newspaper Guild. Broun, in his column "It Seems to Me," dared express his feelings about the Sacco-Vanzetti case that was stirring the nation. Nicola Sacco, a shoe-factory employee, and Bartolomeo Vanzetti, a fish peddler, had been arrested on May 5, 1920, in connection with the murders of a paymaster and his guard in South Braintree, Massachusetts, less than a month before. That was a period of the "Red raids" launched by Attorney General A. Mitchell Palmer following the war, and citizens were fearful of foreign-born radicals. The suspects were charged with participating in the killings.

After a trial before Superior Court Judge Webster Thayer, they were convicted of murder in the first degree in 1921, but the case dragged on, and the more liberal press took up their cause not only in the United States but also in Europe and Central and South America. In 1926 Celestino F. Madeiros, a Portuguese man convicted of murder, confessed to taking part in the South Braintree killings. That should have cleared the pair, but his evidence was rejected. Seven years after the double murder, Thayer sentenced Sacco and Vanzetti to death in the electric chair during the week of July 10, 1927.

Governor Alvin T. Fuller and an advisory committee composed of President A. Lawrence Lowell of Harvard University, President Samuel Stratton of the Massachusetts Institute of Technology, and former Probate Judge Robert Grant investigated the case. Fuller granted a reprieve to Sacco and Vanzetti until early August, when it was announced that the execution would be held later that month. The governor said that the doomed pair had had a fair trial.

Broun was outraged by Fuller's announcement. He charged that the governor's only intention was to put a higher polish upon the proceedings:

> What more can these immigrants from Italy expect? It is not every prisoner who has a President of Harvard University throw on the switch for him. . . . If this is a lynching, at least the fish peddler and his friend the factory hand may take unction to their souls that they will die at the hands of men in dinner coats or academic gowns, according to the conventionalities required by the hour of execution.[3]

Broun continued his criticism the next day. He charged that the governor had apparently overlooked entirely the large amount of testimony from reliable witnesses: "From now on, I want to know, will the institution of learning in Cambridge, which once we called Harvard, be known as Hangman's House?"[4]

Lippmann disagreed with Broun. He wrote in an editorial that the committee's report showed "fairness, consideration, shrewdness and coolness," and he urged the governor to commute the sentences to life imprisonment.[5]

Pulitzer warned Broun not to write another inflammatory column that clashed with the editorial position. He did anyway, and it was killed. Pulitzer explained that the *World* exercised its right of final decision as to what would be published in its columns and omitted all articles by the writer when he continued to write on the Sacco-Vanzetti case.

Broun sent a letter to Pulitzer, together with another column in which he wrote:

> By now I am willing to admit that I am too violent, too ill-disciplined, too indiscreet to fit pleasantly into *The World*'s philosophy of journalism. And since I cannot hit it off with *The World* I would be wise to look for work more alluring. . . . In farewell to the paper, I can only say that in its relations to me it was fair, generous and gallant. But that doesn't go for the Sacco-Vanzetti case.

Pulitzer responded in the same issue that it was the function of a writer to write and the function of an editor to edit. "The World," he said, "still considers Mr. Broun a brilliant member of its staff, albeit taking a witch's

Sabbatical."[6] Less than a week later Sacco and Vanzetti died in the death chamber at Charlestown State Prison, as did Celestino Madeiros.

Broun became a staff member of *The Nation* shortly after that, writing a weekly column called "It Seems to Heywood Broun." He rejoined the *World* on January 2 while continuing with the magazine. The paper said nothing about Broun's appearing in both publications until May, when he wrote in *The Nation,*

> There ought to be a place in New York city for a liberal newspaper. . . . There will be no argument, I think, that the *World* comes closest to being an American *Manchester Guardian,* but it is at best on the outer rim of the target. . . .
>
> It does not seem to me that the paper possesses either courage or tenacity.[7]

That was more than Pulitzer could tolerate. He fired Broun, saying briefly that his disloyalty to the *World* made any further association impossible. Broun replied, " 'Disloyalty,' unexplained, might mean to the reader anything from robbing the till to sitting on Ralph Pulitzer's hat." He said that his disloyalty "consisted in thinking and in saying that the *World* was sometimes silent when there was need for clamor. I said that on occasion it lacked editorial courage."[8]

Broun joined the *Telegram*'s staff ten days after his ouster. He expressed himself in *The Nation* as happy, adding that he now had a spot where he could daily "lift up my voice without being bothered by the fear that perhaps I am not precisely in tune with the rest of the choir."[9]

The Nation conducted a symposium on how free a writer should be to criticize the paper that pays his salary. William Allen White wrote, "The editor still is boss, the employee still has his royal right to resign or be fired. . . . No cause is involved, no principle at stake." Waldo Cook, editor of the Springfield *Republican,* answered, "Mr. Broun is a journalistic prima donna. Prima donnas are privileged to be impudent to the stage manager and the director-general, are they not?" Theodore Dreiser, author of *An American Tragedy,* replied, "I have long observed that it is a rare American newspaper or magazine that offers any space to anyone who has a vital criticism of our American life to offer."[10]

A little more than five months after Broun's dismissal, the *World* lost its executive editor. Swope was preoccupied with other interests, including horse racing and the stock market. When he departed, he said, "I am a little tired of being a hired man. The *World*'s position is limited because of the will of its founder."[11] A codicil to the elder Pulitzer's will enjoined his sons and their descendants to preserve the *World* as a public institution.

It was obvious by 1930 that the *World* was not the paper of former years. Liberals had always turned to its editorial page as the morning publication in New York that championed the rights and liberties of the individual. The elder Pulitzer had wanted his heirs to appeal to the labor class and provide a strong editorial page. But despite Lippmann's brilliance, that page lacked the dynamism it had known under Cobb. The newspaper had also become a daily of selective news, and many fine stories were omitted. As the *Times* and *Herald Tribune* became larger in size, the *World* shrank.

When staff members complained to the morning edition's city editor, James Wyman Barrett, that certain stories had not been covered, he replied that there were not enough reporters because the *World* did not have sufficient money to hire them.

With the Depression in full force, reports spread along Newspaper Row that the *World* might be sold. Some years before, when *Fourth Estate* magazine had written that the Pulitzer sons might dispose of the property, Joseph Jr. and Ralph Pulitzer denounced such rumors as ridiculous because of their father's wish. To newspapermen, it seemed incredible that the *World* might collapse, but in February 1931 Pulitzer's three sons asked Surrogate James A. Foley to disregard the will.

Herbert Pulitzer, management head since Ralph's retirement the year before, cited three reasons for the morning and evening editions' losing their former prosperity. He blamed the crowded newspaper field in New York and said it was not economical for one company to publish a morning edition, a Sunday paper, and an evening paper. He also pointed to the "so-called high-class" newspapers such as the *Times* and *Herald Tribune* in the morning and the *Sun* in the evening as taking away circulation and more expensive advertising from the *World,* which always hewed to the middle ground. Proof was submitted that disclosed the three editions had sustained huge losses for five consecutive years, with the deficits in both 1929 and 1930 being more than a million dollars.

Pulitzer added that he had attempted to negotiate a sale with Adolph Ochs of the *Times,* Ogden Reid of the *Herald Tribune,* and Cyrus H. K. Curtis, owner of the *Evening Post,* but that the only responsive chord came from Roy Howard, chairman of the Scripps-Howard chain. He also said that the rapid growth of the tabloids had been a drain on the *World* papers, attracting the cheaper forms of advertising as well as some of the *World*'s readers who preferred a more sensational paper.

As Foley delayed a decision, employees of the *World* made a last-ditch effort to prevent the transfer of the property to Howard and attempted to purchase the papers themselves. Barrett became chairman of the World Employees' Cooperative Association, which sought to mutualize the newspapers. He announced that employees had made pledges of $600,000. Promises of aid from outside sources, including $100,000 from Lieutenant Governor Herbert H. Lehman, pushed the figure beyond the million-dollar mark.

Their efforts were fruitless. Unbeknownst to the employees, the Pulitzer brothers and Roy Howard had already signed a $5 million contract for the sale of the morning and evening *World*s and the Sunday edition. All that was needed now was Foley's approval. Also unaware of the contract were Paul Block, publisher of the Brooklyn *Standard-Union,* and Frank E. Gannett, owner of the *Brooklyn Daily Eagle.* Each offered to buy the *World* papers for $500,000 more than what Scripps-Howard had bid.

The surrogate refused to pass on the merits of rival offers, explaining that that was not his function. After considering whether he could release the Pulitzers from their father's injunction to perpetuate the *World,* Foley ruled that the papers could be sold. In emergencies, he wrote, "to protect the beneficiaries of a trust from serious loss . . . the law, in the case of necessity, reads into the will an implied power of sale."[12]

Ochs was in Honolulu when he heard that Foley had approved the sale. He called the disappearance of the *World* "one of the greatest calamities that has occurred in the history of American journalism." He added that the elder Pulitzer had accumulated a fortune of at least $25 million in the thirty years the *World* was under his control and management:

> Unfortunately, he did not show his wisdom and foresight in arranging for the continuance of the World after his death. He put the dead hand on it . . . and handicapped it in a manner so inconsistent with the whole course of his living conduct and ideas.
>
> His three sons . . . if left with a free hand, would doubtless have been able to continue the World with increasing strength and popularity.[13]

Ochs said he would have saved the *World* for the employees if he had been in New York. He disclosed that, four months before, the Pulitzers had offered him the morning and Sunday papers for $10 million but that there was no thought of selling the whole property.

Howard scoffed at the comment: "I'm afraid Mr. Ochs, as did several others, waited too long for *The World* to die and that they wanted it for nothing."[14] Of almost 2,900 *World* employees, fewer than 400 joined the *Telegram*'s force.

The *World* died on February 27, 1931, and former members of the morning editorial staff held a funeral service in Manhattan. In Hollywood, those who had worked for the Pulitzers in New York and remembered the papers' tradition of freedom, courage, and honor conducted an "End to the World" wake, complete with coffin.

The *World-Telegram* was published at its new plant on West Street, away from Park Row. The last of the general dailies had vanished from Newspaper Row. The city's only living newspaper Giants—Ochs, Hearst, and Patterson—were now in editorial headquarters elsewhere. Park Row would never again shape the thoughts of the city, the nation, and the world. Never again would so many American newspapers be concentrated in such a small, contiguous area.

Poet Percy Bysshe Shelley's "Ozymandias" forecast the fate of America's great newspaper street when he wrote:

> Look on my works, ye Mighty, and despair!
> Nothing beside remains. Round the decay
> Of that colossal wreck, boundless and bare
> The lone and level sands stretch far away.

EPILOGUE

After almost sixty years in journalism, Adolph Simon Ochs died in Chattanooga on April 8, 1935, following a cerebral hemorrhage at the age of seventy-seven. The *Times* remained in the family, and he was succeeded by Arthur Hays Sulzberger, who had married Ochs's only child, Iphigene. In 1991 Arthur Ochs Sulzberger Jr. was named publisher of the paper that had become one of the most prestigious in the world.

Joseph Patterson endorsed Franklin Delano Roosevelt for the presidency in 1932 and supported his program for improving the conditions of the "common man" during the Great Depression. He continued to back Roosevelt but, always the isolationist, turned against him when he feared that the president's foreign policy might lead the United States into a European war. After the Japanese bombed Pearl Harbor in 1941, Patterson appeared at the White House and offered to support the war effort. Roosevelt criticized him severely for his condemnation and rejected his services.

Patterson died on May 26, 1946, of cirrhosis of the liver at the age of sixty-seven. Fiercely independent and never the tool of any interest, the *News* stayed in the hands of the Tribune Company, the parent organization, for forty-five years after his death. But a 114-day strike, which began in December 1962 and affected all of the general dailies, became the city's longest walkout and damaged the paper's financial strength. It continued to boast the largest circulation in the country, however, until overtaken by a financial daily, the *Wall Street Journal*.

After sustaining a $114 million loss in 1991, the *News* became the property of British publisher Robert Maxwell. His reign lasted less than eight months, when he was found dead in the waters off the Canary Islands after having mysteriously disappeared from his yacht. The paper filed for bankruptcy and was purchased two years later by Mortimer B. Zuckerman, owner of *U.S. News and World Report* and *Atlantic Monthly*.

William Randolph Hearst was the last survivor of the Giants who had molded Park Row into America's most influential force. His papers helped clinch Roosevelt's presidential nomination in 1932. Before long, Hearst became disenchanted with the president's "New Deal" and bitterly referred to it as the "Raw Deal." His inconsistencies, however, did not extend to his extravagant spending.

As the Depression shrouded the nation in the thirties, his cash flow ebbed, and on the verge of bankruptcy, Hearst and his advisers reorganized his holdings. For the first time, control of his finances was taken out of his hands. Not only were a number of his papers sold, leased, or merged, but some magazines, radio stations, and art treasures were also disposed of. In New York the *American* and *Journal* were combined in 1937 as the *Journal-American.*

After fifty-six years of involvement in New York newspapers, the last four in failing health, Hearst died on August 14, 1951, at the age of eighty-eight. His five sons were active in running his remaining papers, which included the *Journal-American* and *Mirror.* The ailing tabloid shut down permanently in October 1963.

Automation and wages were two of the reasons for the long strike. Another was the movement of readers to the suburbs in the years following the war. The papers there appealed to them, and they did not miss the New York dailies. The stiffest competition in the suburbs came from Long Island's *Newsday,* a paper founded by Patterson's daughter, Alicia. In addition, radio and television attracted many of the city's readers and some of the advertising that had gone to New York papers.

The *Sun* was sold in January 1950 to Scripps-Howard's *World-Telegram.* The *Herald Tribune, Journal-American,* and *World-Telegram and Sun,* all losing millions, announced plans in 1966 to merge into a single new company, publishing the *Herald-Tribune* in the morning, *The World Journal* in the afternoon, and the *World Journal Tribune* on Sunday. A strike over the issue of severance pay for almost three thousand employees prevented the printing on April 25, the day before publication. But this time, unlike the blackout of 1962–63, other papers continued to publish. Agreements were worked out with all the unions, and the first edition of the *World Journal Tribune* was published on September 12. The new paper, after losing more than $5 million, ended publication less than eight months later.

Disappearance of the *World Journal Tribune* left New York with only two morning dailies, the *Times* and *News,* and one afternoon publication, the *Post.* Australian and British press tycoon Rupert Murdoch purchased the *Post* in late 1976 from liberal-minded Dorothy Schiff and turned it into a sensational newspaper. Murdoch lost millions of dollars before selling the daily to a New York real-estate developer, Peter Kalikow, and then repurchased it five years later.

From time to time general tabloids continued to rise in New York, but none was sensational or financially successful. *PM,* the city's first new journal in sixteen years, was launched in 1940 and accepted no advertising for six of its eight years before it succumbed. It was followed by *The Star* and *The Daily Compass,* both of which had short existences. In the nineties *New York Newsday* became the last major daily to be launched in the city, but it was unable to show a profit and shut down its presses within a few years.

Only the *Times* remains to recall the days when Park Row and its Giants reigned supreme in the newspaper world.

Most of *When Giant*
pers. Whenever th'
the paper itself.
The contribu
this history. Tl
the United State
Frederic Hudso
was founded. He re.
dominance.

James Parton, in *The Life of i.*
provided invaluable information on the *i.*
of Greeley but also on Horatio David Sheppai.
wrote *Memoirs of James Gordon Bennett and His Time.*,
the senior Bennett, much to the editor's displeasure.

George Britt's biography of Frank A. Munsey, *Forty Years—i.*
lions, is a definite "must" in a discussion of the great newspaper wreci.
The life of Joseph Patterson can best be seen in his own works and files and
in Jack Anderson's three-part series that appeared in the *New Yorker* magazine on August 6, 13, and 20, 1938.

1. *Sun,* Sept. 3, 1833.
2. Ibid., Mar. 31, 18
3. Ibid., June 30, 1
4. *New York Tran*
5. *Sun,* Aug. 28
6. Ibid., Sept
7. Ibid., an
8. *New Y*
9. Ibid
10. *Ste*

INTRODUCTION

The account contained in the introduction is taken especially from the following sources: Edward Ellis, *Epic of New York City* (New York: Coward-
McCann, 1966); Moses King, ed., *King's Handbook of New York City* (Boston: Moses King, 1892); Benson J. Lossing, *History of New York City,* vol.
1 (New York: Perine Engraving, 1884); John Mabry Matthews, *Recollections*
of Persons and Events (New York: Sheldon, 1865); Frank Moss, *The American*
Metropolis, 3 vols. (New York: Peter F. Collier, 1897); Isaac N. P. Stokes,
comp., *The Iconography of Manhattan Island, 1498–1909,* vol. 6 (New York:
Robert H. Dodd, 1915–28); William L. Stone, *History of New York City*
from the Discovery to the Present Day (New York: Virtue & Yorston, 1872);
"Manna-hatin": The Story of New York (New York: The Manhattan Company, 1929).

CHAPTER 1

4.

35.

cript, Sept. 5, 1834.

, 1835.

1, 1835.

versary issue, Sept. 3, 1883.

rk Herald, Sept. 3, 1835.

, Sept. 5, 1835.

dman and Woodberry, *Works of Edgar Allan Poe,* 144–45.

CHAPTER 2

1. *Herald,* May 6, 1835.
2. Ibid., Mar. 23, 1837.
3. *Sun,* Oct. 9, 1835.
4. *Herald,* Oct. 10, 1835.
5. Ibid., Oct. 15, 1835.
6. Ibid., Dec. 17, 1835.
7. Ibid., Dec. 29, 1835.
8. Ibid., Jan. 1, 1836.
9. Ibid., Jan. 4, 1836.
10. Ibid., Jan. 20, 1836.
11. Ibid., Jan. 19, 1836.
12. Ibid., Jan. 21, 1836.
13. *Sun,* Jan. 21, 1836.
14. Anonymous, *Life & Writings of James Gordon Bennett,* 13.
15. *Herald,* Apr. 11, 1836.
16. Ibid., Apr. 12, 1836.
17. Ibid., Apr. 13, 1836.
18. Ibid., Apr. 14, 1836.
19. Ibid., Apr. 16, 1836.
20. *Sun,* Apr. 16, 1836.
21. Ibid., Apr. 18, 1836.
22. *Herald,* Apr. 21, 1836.
23. Ibid., May 10, 1836.
24. Ibid., May 11, 1836.
25. Ibid., July 16, 1836.
26. Ibid., July 20, 1836.

27. Ibid., Aug. 18, 1836.

28. Ibid., Feb. 28, 1837.

29. Ibid., June 9, 1836.

30. Hudson, *Journalism in the United States,* 443.

31. *Herald,* Mar. 14, 1836.

32. Ibid., Mar. 7, 1837.

33. Ibid., Aug. 28, 1837.

34. Ibid., Nov. 4, 1837.

35. Ibid., Apr. 25, 1838.

36. Ibid., Oct. 15, 1838.

37. Ibid., May 6, 1840. Bennett referred to Charles King, later president of Columbia College.

38. Ibid., May 1, 1839.

39. Ibid., Dec. 25, 1839.

40. Ibid., Apr. 26, 1838.

41. Ibid., Nov. 10, 1837.

42. Ibid., Mar. 16, 1836.

43. Ibid., Jan. 10, 1837.

44. Ibid., Apr. 27, 1839.

45. Ibid., Dec. 31, 1839.

46. Anonymous, *Life & Writings,* 25.

47. *Herald,* Feb. 2, 1837.

48. Ibid., Dec. 7, 1837.

49. Ibid., Oct. 29, 1839.

50. Ibid., June 7, 1836.

51. Ibid., Nov. 2, 1837.

52. Hoover, *Park Benjamin,* 105–6.

53. *Evening Star,* June 1, 1840.

54. *Courier and Enquirer,* June 3, 1840.

55. *Herald,* May 30, 1840.

56. Ibid., June 2, 1840.

57. Ibid., June 30, 1840.

58. Ibid., June 1, 1840.

CHAPTER 3

1. Griswold, *Passages from the Correspondence,* 92–93; letter dated July 10, 1841.

2. *Tribune,* Apr. 10, 1841.

3. Ibid., July 21, 1841.

4. *Herald,* Sept. 2, 1842.

5. *Tribune,* Nov. 20, 1841.

6. Greeley, *Recollections of a Busy Life,* 264.

7. *Tribune,* Feb. 13, 1845.

8. Ibid., May 13, 1846.

9. Ibid., Dec. 9 and 11, 1848.

10. *Herald,* July 31, 1849.

11. *Tribune,* Aug. 1, 1849.

12. *Herald,* Aug. 2, 1849.

13. Slater, *Correspondence of Emerson and Carlyle,* 499.

14. *Courier and Enquirer,* Jan. 27, 1844.

15. *Tribune,* Jan. 12, 1850. Greeley has been reported as directing his ire at William Cullen Bryant. But Charles Anderson Dana, who was working for Greeley at the time, wrote in the *Sun* on Sept. 4, 1869, that John Bigelow, co-editor and co-owner with Bryant of the New York *Evening Post,* had been the target.

CHAPTER 4

1. Greeley, *Recollections of a Busy Life,* 139.

2. *Times,* Sept. 18, 1851.

3. Hudson, *Journalism in the United States,* 622.

4. *Herald,* Jan. 6, 1852.

5. *Times,* July 15, 1852.

6. *Herald,* July 22, 1852.

7. Ibid., Nov. 8, 1852.

8. *Times,* Sept. 22, 1852.

9. Ibid., June 19, 1852

10. *Tribune,* Nov. 8, 1852.

11. *Times,* Nov. 10, 1852.

12. Letter from Greeley dated Aug. 16, 1853, to St. John, quoted in Hudson, *Journalism in the United States,* 625–26.

13. *Times,* Oct. 13, 1854.

14. *Herald,* Mar. 7, 1857.

15. *Times* and *Herald,* Aug. 17, 1858.

16. *Times,* July 16, 1859.

17. *Herald,* Aug. 4, 1861.

CHAPTER 5

1. *Herald,* Oct. 19, 1859.

2. Ibid., Nov. 7, 1860.

3. Ibid., Mar. 29, 1861.

4. Ibid., Jan. 6, 1861.

5. *Tribune,* Nov. 29, 1860.

6. Ibid., Feb. 18, 1861.

7. *Herald,* Apr. 6, 1861

8. Ibid., Apr. 9, 1861.

9. *Times,* Apr. 12, 1861.

10. Ibid., Apr. 15, 1861.

11. *Tribune* from June 26 through July 4, 1861.

12. Ibid., July 25, 1861.

13. Greeley's letter to Lincoln, dated July 29, 1861. Original in Robert Todd Lincoln Collection, Library of Congress, 10921.

14. Correspondence between Simon Cameron and Raymond, dated Dec. 11 and 13, 1861. Original letters at New York Public Library.

15. *Times,* Dec. 11, 1861.

16. *Evening Post,* July 16, 1862.

17. *Tribune,* Aug. 25, 1862.

18. Ibid., Sept. 23, 1862.

19. *Times,* July 15, 1863.

20. Smith, *Sunshine and Shadow in New York,* 522–23.

21. Nevins, *Evening Post,* 160.

22. Richardson, *Secret Service,* 508–9; *Tribune,* Jan. 14, 1865.

23. Wing, "When Lincoln Kissed Me," 9.

CHAPTER 6

1. *Times,* Aug. 17, 1866.

2. L. J. Jennings, *Galaxy* (Apr. 1870): 468.

3. *Tribune,* June 19, 1869.

4. "George Jones," 142.

5. *Evening Post,* June 3, 1872.

6. *World,* June 3, 1872.

7. Truman, "Anecdotes of Andrew Johnson," 438–39.

8. A letter to the author from Otto A. Epp, editor and publisher of the *Greeley County Republican,* Tribune, Kansas, Apr. 28, 1947.

9. Greeley Papers, Library of Congress, letter dated Nov. 4, 1872.

10. *Tribune,* Nov. 7, 1872.

CHAPTER 7

1. *Sun,* Dec. 6, 1872.

2. Ibid., Jan. 27, 1868.

3. Ibid., anniversary issue, Sept. 3, 1883.

4. O'Brien, *Story of the Sun,* 266–67. O'Brien says that Cummings used to tell that story.

5. *Sun,* Sept. 20, 1869.

6. Ibid., Jan. 6, 1871.

7. Ibid., Apr. 16, 1870.

8. Ibid., Mar. 14, 1871.

9. *Times,* Sept. 20, 1870.

10. Ibid., Feb. 2, 1871.

11. *Harper's Weekly,* Feb. 22, 1890, 142.

12. *Sun,* Apr. 13, 1878.

13. *Times,* June 29, 1872.

14. Seitz, *The James Gordon Bennetts,* 220.

15. Stanley, *How I Found Livingstone,* xviii.

16. *Sun,* Aug. 28, 1872.

17. Ibid., July 15–Nov. 6, 1872.

18. Ibid., Apr. 24, 1875.

19. Ibid., Jan. 3, 1871.

20. Irwin, "New York Sun," 301–10.

21. Swinton, "New York Daily Papers," 239.

22. Irwin, "New York Sun," 310.

23. Ibid.

24. *Sun,* July 6, 1875.

25. Swinton, "New York Daily Papers," 239.

26. *Sun,* Oct. 13 and Nov. 2, 1878.

27. Ibid., Oct. 18, 1880.

CHAPTER 8

1. Field, *Little Book of Western Verse,* 96–103.

2. *World,* Oct. 30, 1911.

3. Ibid., May 11, 1883.

4. Ibid., May 13, 1883.

5. Ibid.

6. Ibid., twentieth anniversary issue, May 10, 1903.

7. Ibid., May 16, 1883.

8. Ibid., May 23, 1883.

9. *Sun,* May 15, 1883.

10. *World,* May 16, 1883.

11. Ibid., Sept. 26, 1883.

12. *Sun,* Oct. 24, 1884.

13. *World,* Oct. 30, 1884.

14. Ibid., twentieth anniversary issue, May 10, 1903.

15. Ibid., Mar. 16, 1885.

16. Ibid., Mar. 20, 1885.

17. *Sun,* Nov. 5–8, 1887.

18. *World,* Nov. 3–8, 1887.

19. *Sun,* Nov. 9, 1887.

20. *World,* Nov. 10, 1887.

21. Cochrane, *Nellie Bly's Book,* 6.

22. Meloney, "Joseph Pulitzer," 114.

23. *World,* Oct. 11, 1889.

24. *Herald,* Oct. 17, 1890.

25. Seitz, *Joseph Pulitzer,* 182.

26. Ibid., 33.

27. Creelman, "Joseph Pulitzer," 246.

28. *World,* Dec. 18, 1895.

29. *Sun,* Dec. 21, 1895.

30. *World,* Dec. 21, 1895.

31. Ibid., Jan. 3, 1896.

CHAPTER 9

1. Steffens, "Hearst," 10.

2. A letter from William Randolph Hearst to *Time,* Jan. 11, 1932, displaying his irritation at reports he had been expelled from Harvard and stating that he had been rusticated in 1886. He also blamed an excess of political enthusiasm.

3. Irwin, "American Newspapers," 17.

4. Older, *William Randolph Hearst,* 137.

5. Winkler, *W. R. Hearst,* 106–7.

6. Barrett, *Joseph Pulitzer,* 173.

7. Seitz, *Joseph Pulitzer,* 214.

8. Ibid., 215.

9. *Journal,* Oct. 17, 1896.

10. Ibid., Dec. 13, 1896.

11. Ibid., Jan. 30, 1897.

12. *World,* Mar. 20, 1897.

13. Ibid., Mar. 28, 1897.

14. *Sun,* Mar. 26, 1897.

15. *Journal,* Mar. 29, 1897.

16. *Journal and Advertiser,* Apr. 2, 1897.

17. *Sun,* Mar. 22, 1897.

18. Fenton, *Dana of the Sun*, 273.
19. *World*, Feb. 8, 1897.
20. Allen, *Frederic Remington*, 11.
21. *Journal*, Aug. 19, 1897.
22. Winkler, *W. R. Hearst*, 148.
23. *Journal*, Oct. 11, 1897.
24. *Times*, Oct. 12, 1897.
25. *Journal*, Feb. 9, 1898.
26. Ibid., Feb. 10, 1898.
27. Ibid., Feb. 17, 1898.
28. *Evening Journal*, Feb. 17, 1898.
29. *Journal*, Feb. 18, 1898.
30. Ibid., Feb. 22, 1898.
31. Ibid., Feb. 25, 1898.
32. *World*, Feb. 19–24, 1898.
33. *Evening Post*, Feb. 24, 1898.
34. *Journal*, Mar. 3, 1898.
35. Ibid., Mar. 15, 1898.
36. Rickover, *How the Battleship Maine Was Destroyed*, 95. Rickover, head of the Navy's nuclear-propulsion program, wrote that the 1898 naval investigation, in blaming the loss of the ship on the Spaniards, "appears to have been guided less by technical consideration and more by the awareness that war was not inevitable."
37. *Journal*, Apr. 6, 1898.
38. Ibid., Apr. 12, 1898.
39. *World*, Apr. 10, 1898.
40. *Evening Post*, Mar. 28, 1898.
41. *Journal*, Mar. 19, 1898.
42. *World*, Mar. 20, 1898.
43. Creelman, *On the Great Highway*, 190.
44. Ibid., 211–12.
45. *World*, June 8, 1898.
46. *Evening Post*, Mar. 17, 1898.
47. "New Political Force," 336.

CHAPTER 10

1. *World*, Jan. 1, 1901.
2. Ibid.
3. *The Journalist*, Nov. 4, 1905, 37.
4. Ochs manuscript, May 17, 1895, *Times* archives.
5. *Times*, Apr. 9, 1935.

6. Davis, *History of The New York Times,* 203.

7. *Times,* Aug. 19, 1896.

8. Ibid., Oct. 25, 1896.

9. Ibid., Oct. 10, 1898.

CHAPTER 11

1. *Journal,* Feb. 4, 1900.

2. Ibid., Apr. 10, 1901.

3. Ibid., June 1, 1901.

4. *Press,* Sept. 7, 1901.

5. *Journal,* Sept. 22, 1901.

6. *Sun,* Sept. 17 and 20, 1901.

7. *Times,* Dec. 4, 1901.

8. "Over the Coffee and the Cigars," 269.

9. *Times,* Apr. 9, 1904.

10. *American,* Oct. 16, 1905.

11. Ibid., Nov. 8, 1905.

12. *Journal,* Nov. 8, 1905.

13. Ibid., Nov. 10, 1905.

14. *World,* Apr. 28, 1906.

15. O'Connor, *The Scandalous Mr. Bennett,* 268. According to the *Herald,* May 15, 1918, a syndicate asked Bennett if he would sell the paper.

16. *Herald,* May 27, June 3, July 15, 1906.

17. Redding, "Bennett of the Herald," 855.

18. *Times,* Sept. 18, 1906.

19. *American,* Nov. 1, 1908.

20. Lundberg, *Imperial Hearst,* 120.

21. *Journal,* Dec. 13, 1907.

22. *World,* Dec. 16, 1908.

23. Ibid., Jan. 4, 1911.

24. *Journal,* Oct. 30, 1911.

CHAPTER 12

1. "Wants to Be Yellow," 5.

2. *Evening Journal,* July 27, 1910.

3. *Times,* Oct. 19, 1907.

4. *American,* Apr. 7, 1912.

5. *Times,* Apr. 8, 1912.

6. *Globe and Commercial Advertiser,* Apr. 16, 1912.

7. *Times,* Mar. 16, 1915.

8. *American,* May 8, 1915.

9. Ibid., June 6, 1915.

10. Wheeler, "At the Front," 340–42.

11. *American,* Oct. 11, 1916.

12. Ibid., Apr. 11, 1917.

13. Ibid., Apr. 18, 1917.

14. *Tribune,* June 2, 1918.

15. *Sun,* May 11, 1918.

16. *Times,* Sept. 16, 1918.

17. *Herald,* Sept. 17, 1918.

18. Cobb, *Exit Laughing,* 119.

19. Chapin, *Charles Chapin's Story,* 190.

CHAPTER 13

1. Steffens, *Autobiography,* 393.

2. Britt, *Forty Years,* 85.

3. *Editor & Publisher,* Dec. 26, 1925, 8.

4. *Sun,* Dec. 22, 1925.

5. *Herald,* Jan. 17, 1920.

6. Fowler, *Skyline,* 179.

7. *Times,* Aug. 5, 1922.

8. Wardman, "Fight of the New York Herald," 3–9.

9. *News,* Aug. 23, 1922.

10. *Herald,* Aug. 28, 1922.

11. *American,* May 29, 1923.

12. Britt, *Forty Years,* 250.

13. Walker, *City Editor,* 83.

14. *Herald Tribune,* Aug. 16, 1924.

15. Ibid., Aug. 18, 1924.

16. *Editor & Publisher,* Jan. 2, 1926, 41.

17. *Times,* Dec. 31, 1925.

18. Emporia (Kansas) *Gazette,* Dec. 23, 1925.

CHAPTER 14

1. *Times,* Oct. 19, 1919.

2. *World,* Oct. 30, 1919.

3. Tebbel, *Life and Good Times,* 243.

4. JMP papers, Box 4, Folder 17. Letter from Burton Rascoe to Patterson's daughter Alicia, dated June 23, 1949.

5. Patterson, *Note Book of a Neutral,* 90–92.

6. JMP papers, Series 1, Box 1, Folder 8. Letter dated Jan. 19, 1916.

7. *News,* May 27, 1946.

8. Ibid., June 26, 1919.

9. Ibid., June 22, 1969.

10. Walker, *City Editor,* 66.

11. JMP papers, Series 1, Box 17, Folder 1, Letter dated July 8, 1919.

12. Ibid., Box 4, Folder 8.

13. *News,* Dec. 3, 1921.

14. JMP papers, Series 1, Box 6, Folder 8. Letter dated May 15, 1922.

15. *News,* June 19, 1924.

16. Ibid., June 25, 1924.

17. *Mirror,* June 26, 1924.

18. *Graphic,* Sept. 15, 1924.

19. Ibid., Sept. 16, 20, and 27, 1924.

20. *Editor & Publisher,* Sept. 20, 1924, 5.

21. JMP papers, Series 1, Box 17, Folder 3.

22. Ibid., Subseries 3, Box 17, Folder 3.

23. *Mirror,* Oct. 9, 1926.

24. *Graphic,* Jan. 26, 1927.

25. *Mirror,* Oct. 7, 1926.

26. *Graphic,* Mar. 17, 1927.

27. Walker, *City Editor,* 72.

28. *Editor & Publisher,* June 24, 1939, 46.

29. *News,* June 25, 1957.

Chapter 15

1. *Times,* Dec. 20, 1927.

2. *American,* Dec. 21, 1927.

3. *World,* Aug. 5, 1927.

4. Ibid., Aug. 6, 1927

5. Ibid., Aug. 8, 1927.

6. Ibid., Aug. 17, 1927.

7. Broun, "It Seems to Heywood Broun," May 9, 1928, 532.

8. Ibid., May 16, 1928, 553, 557.

9. Ibid., May 23, 1928, 576.

10. "The Rights of a Columnist," 607–8.
11. Kahn, *The World of Swope,* 309.
12. *Times,* Feb. 27, 1931.
13. *Editor & Publisher The Fourth Estate,* Mar. 21, 1931, 5–6.
14. *Times,* Mar. 21, 1931.

BIBLIOGRAPHY

BOOKS ON JOURNALISM

Abbot, Willis J. *Watching the World Go By*. London: John Lane The Bodley Head, 1933.

Allen, Douglas. *Frederick Remington and the Spanish-American War*. New York: Crown Publishers, 1971.

Andrews, Cutler J. *The North Reports the War*. Pittsburgh: University of Pittsburgh Press, 1955.

Anonymous, *Life & Writings of James Gordon Bennett, Editor of the New York Herald*. New York: n.p., 1844.

Armstrong, William M. *E. L. Godkin: A Biography*. Albany, N.Y.: New York State University Press, 1978.

Baehr, Harry W. Jr. *The New York Tribune since the Civil War*. New York: Dodd, Mead, 1936.

Barrett, James W. *The End of the World: A Post-Mortem*. New York: Harper and Brothers Publishers, 1931.

————. *The World, The Flesh and Messrs. Pulitzer*. New York: Vanguard Press, 1931.

————. *Joseph Pulitzer and His World*. New York: Vanguard Press, 1941.

Bent, Silas. *Ballyhoo: The Voice of the Press*. New York: Boni and Liveright, 1927.

Benton, Joel, ed. *Greeley on Lincoln, with Mr. Greeley's Letters to Charles A. Dana and a Lady Friend*. New York: Baker and Taylor, 1893.

Berger, Meyer. *The Story of The New York Times: 1851–1951*. New York: Simon and Schuster, 1951.

Bessie, Simon Michael. *Jazz Journalism, The Story of the Tabloid Newspapers*. New York: Russell and Russell, 1969.

Bigelow, John. *Retrospections of an Active Life, 1867–1871*. Vol. 4. Garden City, N.Y.: Doubleday, Page, 1913.

Bleyer, Willard Grosvenor. *Main Currents in the History of American Journalism*. Boston: Houghton Mifflin, 1927.

Bond, F. Fraser. *Mr. Miller of "The Times": The Story of an Editor*. New York: Charles Scribner's Sons, 1931.

Boylan, James, ed. *The World and the 20's*. New York: Dial Press, 1973.

Britt, George. *Forty Years—Forty Millions: The Career of Frank A. Munsey*. New York: Farrar and Rinehart, 1935.

————, ed., for The Silurians. *Shoeleather and Printer's Ink: 1924–1974*. New York: Quadrangle/The New York Times Book Co., 1974.

Brown, Charles H. *William Cullen Bryant*. New York: Charles Scribner's Sons, 1971.

Brown, Francis. *Raymond of the Times*. New York: W. W. Norton, 1951.

Browne, Junius Henri. *The Great Metropolis: A Mirror of New York*. Hartford: American Publishing, 1869.

Bullard, Frederick Lauriston. *Famous War Correspondents*. Boston: Little, Brown, 1914.

Carlson, Oliver. *Brisbane: A Candid Biography*. New York: Stackpole Sons, 1937.

————. *The Man Who Made News: James Gordon Bennett*. New York: Duell, Sloan and Pearce, 1942.

Carlson, Oliver, and Ernest Sutherland Bates. *Hearst, Lord of San Simeon*. New York: Viking Press, 1936.

Chambers, Julius. *News Hunting on Three Continents*. New York: M. Kennerly, 1921.

Chapin, Charles. *Charles Chapin's Story: Written in Sing Sing Prison*. New York: G. P. Putnam's Sons, 1920.

Chapman, John. *Tell It to Sweeney: The Informal History of the New York Daily News*. Garden City, N.Y.: Doubleday, 1961.

Churchill, Allen. *Park Row*. New York: Rinehart, 1958.

Clarke, Donald Henderson. *Man of the World: Recollections of an Irreverent Reporter*. New York: Vanguard Press, 1950.

Clarke, Joseph I. C. *My Life and Memories*. New York: Dodd, Mead, 1925.

Cobb, Irvin S. *Exit Laughing*. Indianapolis: Bobbs-Merrill, 1941.

Cochrane, Elizabeth. *Nellie Bly's Book: Around the World in Seventy-Two Days*. New York: Pictorial Weeklies, 1890.

Coggeshall, W. T. *The Newspaper Record*. Philadelphia: Lay and Brother, 1856.

Cohen, Daniel. *Henry Stanley and the Quest for the Source of the Nile*. New York: M. Evans, 1985.

Cohen, Lester. *The New York Graphic: The World's Zaniest Newspaper*. Philadelphia: Chilton Books, 1964.

Cornell, William M. *The Life and Public Career of Hon. Horace Greeley.* Boston: D. Lothrop, 1882.

Cortissoz, Royal. *Life of Whitelaw Reid.* Vols. 1 and 2. New York: Charles Scribner's Son, 1921.

Cox, Joseph A. *The Recluse of Herald Square: The Mystery of Ida E. Wood.* New York: Macmillan, 1964.

Creelman, James. *On the Great Highway: The Wanderings and Adventures of a Special Correspondent.* Boston: Lothrop Publishing, 1901.

Crockett, Albert Stevens. *When James Gordon Bennett Was Caliph of Bagdad.* New York: Funk and Wagnalls, 1926.

Crouthamel, James L. *Bennett's New York Herald and the Rise of the Popular Press.* Syracuse: Syracuse University Press, 1989.

————. *James Watson Webb: A Biography.* Middletown, Conn.: Wesleyan University Press, 1969.

Crozier, Emmet. *Yankee Reporters: 1861–65.* New York: Oxford University Press, 1956.

Dana, Charles A. *The Art of Newspaper Making, Three Lectures.* New York: D. Appleton, 1895.

Davis, Elmer. *History of the New York Times: 1851–1921.* New York: The New York Times, 1921.

Decker, Karl. *The Story of Evangelina Cisneros.* New York: Continental Publishing, 1897.

Dicken-Garcia, Hazel. *Journalistic Standards in Nineteenth-Century America.* Madison: University of Wisconsin Press, 1989.

Downey, Fairfax. *Richard Harding Davis: His Day.* New York: Charles Scribner's Sons, 1933.

Duncan, Bingham, *Whitelaw Reid: Journalist, Politician, Diplomat.* Athens, Ga.: University of Georgia Press, 1975.

Dryfoos, Susan W. *Iphigene, Memoirs of Iphigene Ochs Sulzberger of the New York Times Family, as told to her granddaughter Susan W. Dryfoos.* New York: Dodd, Mead, 1981.

Eggleston, George Cary. *Recollections of a Varied Life.* New York: Henry Holt, 1910.

Emery, Edwin. *The Press and America: An Interpretative History of Journalism.* 2d ed. Englewood Cliffs, N.J.: Prentice-Hall, 1962.

Fahrney, Ralph Ray. *Horace Greeley and the Tribune in the Civil War.* Cedar Rapids: Torch Press, 1936.

Fenton, Alfred H. *Dana of the Sun.* New York: Farrar and Rinehart, 1941.

Fine, Barnett. *A Giant of the Press.* New York: Editor and Publisher, 1933.

Fowler, Gene. *Skyline: A Reporter's Reminiscence of the 1920s*. New York: Viking Press, 1961.

Gauvreau, Emile. *My Last Million Readers*. New York: E. P. Dutton, 1941.

Gies, Joseph. *The Colonel of Chicago*. New York: E. P. Dutton, 1979.

Goldberg, Isaac. *Major Noah: American-Jewish Pioneer*. Philadelphia: Jewish Publication Society of America, 1938.

Gramling, Oliver. *AP: The Story of News*. New York: Farrar and Rinehart, 1940.

Grattan, C. Hartley. *Bitter Bierce: A Mystery of American Letters*. Garden City, N.Y.: Doubleday, Doran, 1929.

Greeley, Horace. *Recollections of a Busy Life*. New York: J. B. Ford, 1868.

Hale, William Harlan. *Horace Greeley: Voice of the People*. New York: Harper and Brothers, 1950.

Hearst, William Randolph Jr., with Jack Casserly. *The Hearsts: Father and Son*. Niwot, Colo.: Roberts Rinehart Publishers, 1991.

Hoe, Robert. *A Short History of the Printing Press*. New York: printed and published for Robert Hoe, 1902.

Hohenberg, John. *Foreign Correspondence: The Great Reporters and Their Times*. New York: Columbia University Press, 1964.

―――. *The News Media: A Journalist Looks at His Profession*. New York: Holt, Rinehart and Winston, 1968.

―――, ed. *The Pulitzer Prize Story*. New York: Columbia University Press, 1959.

Hoover, Merle M. *Park Benjamin, Poet & Editor*. New York: Columbia University Press, 1948.

Horn, Maurice, ed. *World Encyclopedia of Comics*. New York: Chelsea House Publishers, 1976.

Hudson, Frederic. *Journalism in the United States, from 1690 to 1872*. New York: Harper and Brothers, 1873.

Hughes, Helen McGill. *News and the Human Interest Story*. Chicago: University of Chicago Press, 1940.

Ingersoll, Lurton D. *The Life of Horace Greeley*. New York: Beekman Publishers, 1974.

Ireland, Alleyne. *An Adventure with a Genius: Recollections of Joseph Pulitzer*. New York: E. P. Dutton, 1920.

Irwin, Will. *The American Newspaper*. Ames, Iowa: Iowa State University Press, 1969.

―――. *The Making of a Reporter*. New York: G. P. Putnam's Sons, 1942.

————. *Propaganda and the News*. New York: Whittlesey House, McGraw Hill, 1936.

Johnson, Gerald W. *An Honorable Titan: A Biographical Study of Adolph S. Ochs*. New York: Harper and Brothers, 1946.

Jones, Robert W. *Journalism in the United States*. New York: E. P. Dutton, 1947.

Kahn, E. J. Jr. *The World of Swope*. New York: Simon and Schuster, 1965.

King, Homer W. *Pulitzer's Prize Editor: A Biography of John A. Cockerill, 1845–1896*. Durham, N.C.: Duke University Press, 1965.

Klein, Henry H. *My Last Fifty Years: An Autobiographical History of "Inside New York."* New York: Isaac Goldman, 1935.

Kluger, Richard. *The Paper: The Life and Death of the New York Herald Tribune*. New York: Alfred A. Knopf, 1986.

Knightley, Philip. *The First Casualty*. New York: Harcourt Brace Jovanovich, 1975.

Kramer, Dale. *Heywood Broun: A Biographical Portrait*. New York: A. A. Wyn, 1949.

Laney, Al. *Paris Herald: The Incredible Newspaper*. New York: D. Appleton-Century, 1947.

Lee, Alfred McClung. *The Daily Newspaper in America*. New York: Macmillan, 1947.

Lee, James Melvin. *History of American Journalism*. Garden City, N.Y.: Garden City Publishing, 1923.

Linn, James Weber. *James Keeley, Newspaperman*. Indianapolis: Bobbs-Merrill, 1937.

Linn, William Alexander. *Horace Greeley: Founder and Editor of The New York Tribune*. New York: D. Appleton, 1903.

Leonard, Thomas C. *The Power of the Press: The Birth of American Political Reporting*. New York: Oxford University Press, 1986.

Lundberg, Ferdinand. *Imperial Hearst, A Social Biography*. New York: Equinox Cooperative Press, 1936.

MacDougall, Curtis D. *Hoaxes*. New York: Dover Publications, 1940.

McGivena, Leo E., et al. *The News: The First Fifty Years of New York's Picture Newspaper*. New York: News Syndicate, 1969.

McJimsey, George T. *Genteel Partisan: Manton Marble: 1834–1917*. Ames, Iowa: Iowa State University Press, 1971.

McRae, Milton A. *Forty Years in Newspaperdom: The Autobiography of a Newspaper Man*. New York: Brentano's Publishers, 1924.

Mallen, Frank, *Sauce for the Gander*. White Plains, N.Y.: Baldwin Books, 1954.

Martin, Ralph G. *Cissy*. New York: Simon and Schuster, 1979.

Mathews, Joseph J. *George W. Smalley*. Chapel Hill: University of North Carolina Press, 1973.

Maurice, Arthur Bartlett. *New York in Fiction*. New York: Dodd, Mead, 1891.

Maverick, Augustus. *Henry J. Raymond and the New York Press for Thirty Years*. Hartford, Conn: A. S. Hale, 1870.

Mayes, Martin. *The Development of the Press in the United States*. Columbia, Mo.: Missourian Press, 1935.

Miller, Webb. *I Found No Peace: The Journal of a Foreign Correspondent*. New York: Simon and Schuster, 1936.

Milton, Joyce. *The Yellow Kids: Foreign Correspondents in the Heyday of Yellow Journalism*. New York: Harper and Row, 1989.

Mitchell, Edward P. *Memoirs of an Editor: Fifty Years of American Journalism*. New York: Charles Scribner's Sons, 1924.

Moore, John W., comp. *Moore's Historical, Biographical, and Miscellaneous Gatherings Relative to Printers, Printing, Publishing, and Editing from 1420 to 1886*. Concord, N.H.: Republican Press Association, 1886; reprinted Detroit: Gale Research Company, 1968.

Morgan, Gwen, and Arthur Veysey. *Poor Little Rich Boy (and how he made good)*. Carpentersville, Ill.: Crossroads Communications, 1985.

Mott, Frank Luther. *A History of American Magazines: 1885–1905*. Vol. 4. Cambridge, Mass.: Belknap Press of Harvard University Press, 1957.

————. *American Journalism: A History of Newspapers in the United States through 250 Years, 1690 to 1940*. New York: Macmillan, 1942.

Munsey, Frank E. *Founding of the Munsey Publishing House*. New York: December, 1907.

Murray, George. *The Madhouse on Madison Street*. Chicago: Follett Publishing, 1965.

Nevins, Allan. *The Evening Post: A Century of Journalism*. New York: Boni and Liveright, 1922.

O'Brien, Frank M. *The Story of the Sun*. New York: George H. Doran, 1918; 2nd ed. New York: D. Appleton, 1928; reprinted New York: Greenwood Press, 1968.

O'Connor, Richard. *Heywood Broun: A Biography*. New York: G. P. Putnam's Sons, 1975.

————. *The Scandalous Mr. Bennett*. Garden City, N.Y.: Doubleday, 1962.

Ogden, Rollo, ed. *Life and Letters of Edwin Lawrence Godkin.* 2 vols. New York: Macmillan, 1907.

Older, Mrs. Fremont. *William Randolph Hearst: American.* New York: D. Appleton-Century, 1936.

Paine, Albert Bigelow. *Th. Nast, His Period and His Pictures.* Princeton, N.J.: Pyne Press, facsimile of the Macmillan 1904 edition.

Parton, James. *Famous Americans of Recent Times.* Boston: Ticknow and Fields, 1867.

————. *The Life of Horace Greeley: Editor of the New York Tribune.* New York: Mason Brothers, 1855.

Patterson, Joseph Medill. *The Note Book of a Neutral.* New York: Duffield, 1916.

Perkins, A. J. G., and Theresa Wolfson. *Frances Wright: Free Enquirer: The Study of an Experiment.* New York: Harper and Brothers, 1939.

Pray, Isaac C. *Memoirs of James Gordon Bennett and His Times.* New York: Stringer and Townsend, 1855.

Rascoe, Burton. *We Were Interrupted.* Garden City, N.Y.: Doubleday, 1947.

————. *Before I Forget.* New York: Literary Guild of America, 1937.

Rhea, George Bronson. *Facts and Fakes about Cuba.* New York: George Munro's Sons, 1897.

Rhodes, James Ford. *Historical Essays.* New York: Macmillan, 1909.

Richardson, Albert D. *The Secret Service, the Field, the Dungeon, and the Escape.* Hartford: American Publishing, 1865.

Rogers, Jason. *Newspaper Building: Application of Efficiency to Editing, to Mechanical Production, to Circulation and Advertising.* New York: Harper and Brothers, 1918.

Rosebault, Charles J. *When Dana Was the Sun: A Story of Personal Journalism.* Westport, Conn.: Greenwood Press, 1970.

Rosewater, Victor. *History of Cooperative News-Gathering in the United States.* New York: D. Appleton, 1930.

Russell, Charles Edward. *These Shifting Scenes.* New York: Hodder and Stoughton, 1914.

Salisbury, Harrison E. *Without Fear or Favor: The New York Times and Its Times.* New York: Times Books, 1980.

Schiller, Dan. *Objectivity and the News.* Philadelphia: University of Pennsylvania Press, 1981.

Schudson, Michael. *Discovering the News: A Social History of American Newspapers.* New York: Basic Books, 1978.

Seitz, Don C. *Horace Greeley: Founder of the New York Tribune*. Indianapolis: Bobbs-Merrill, 1926.

———. *Joseph Pulitzer, His Life & Letters*. New York: Simon and Schuster, 1924.

———. *The James Gordon Bennetts: Father and Son*. Indianapolis: Bobbs-Merrill, 1928.

Seldes, George. *Freedom of the Press*. Indianapolis: Bobbs-Merrill, 1935.

———. *Lords of the Press*. New York: Julian Messner, 1938.

Stanley, Henry Morton. *How I Found Livingstone*. New York: Arno Press, 1970 [reprint of Charles Scribner's Sons 1913 edition].

Starr, Louis M. *Bohemian Brigade: Civil War Newsmen in Action*. New York: Alfred A. Knopf, 1954.

Steel, Ronald. *Walter Lippmann and the American Century*. New York: Vintage Books, 1981.

Steffens, Lincoln. *The Autobiography of Lincoln Steffens*. New York: Harcourt, Brace and World, 1958.

Stevens, John D. *Sensationalism and the New York Press*. New York: Columbia University Press, 1991.

Stoddard, Henry Luther. *Horace Greeley: Printer, Editor, Crusader*. New York: G. P. Putnam's Sons, 1946.

Stone, Candace. *Dana and the Sun*. New York: Dodd, Mead, 1938.

Swanberg, W. A. *Citizen Hearst: A Biography of William Randolph Hearst*. New York: Charles Scribner's Sons, 1961.

———. *Pulitzer*. New York: Charles Scribner's Sons, 1967.

Talese, Gay. *The Kingdom and the Power*. Garden City, N.Y.: Anchor Press/Doubleday, 1978.

Tarbell, Ida. *A Reporter for Lincoln: Story of Henry E. Wing, Soldier and Newspaperman*. New York: Macmillan, 1927.

Taylor, S. J. *Stalin's Apologist: Walter Duranty, the New York Times's Man in Moscow*. New York: Oxford University Press, 1990.

Tebbel, John. *An American Dynasty: The Story of the McCormicks, Medills, Pattersons*. Garden City, N.Y.: Doubleday, 1947.

———. *The Life and Good Times of William Randolph Hearst*. New York: E. P. Dutton, 1952.

Tebbel, John, and Sarah Miles. *The Press and the Presidency, From George Washington to Ronald Reagan*. New York: Oxford University Press, 1985.

Thirteen correspondents of *The New York Times*. *We Saw It Happen: The*

News Behind the News That's Fit to Print. Edited by Hanson W. Baldwin and Shepard Stone. New York: Simon and Schuster, 1938.

Trietsch, James M. *The Printer and the Prince: A Study of the Influence of Horace Greeley upon Abraham Lincoln As Candidate and President.* New York: Exposition Press, 1955.

Van Deusen, Glyndon G. *Horace Greeley: Nineteenth Century Crusader.* New York: Hill and Wang, 1953.

Villard, Henry. *Memoirs of Henry Villard, Journalist & Financier.* 2 vols. Boston: Houghton, Mifflin, 1904.

Villard, Oswald Garrison. *Some Newspapers and Newspaper-Men.* New York: Alfred A. Knopf, 1923.

———. *The Disappearing Daily: Chapters in American Newspaper Evolution.* New York: Alfred A. Knopf, 1944.

———. *The Press Today.* New York: The Nation, 1930.

Waldrop, Frank C. *McCormick of Chicago: An Unconventional Portrait of a Controversial Figure.* Englewood Cliffs, N.J.: Prentice-Hall, 1966.

Walker, Stanley. *City Editor.* New York: Frederick A. Stokes, 1934.

Wendt, Lloyd. *Chicago Tribune: The Rise of a Great American Newspaper.* Chicago: Rand McNally, 1979.

Weiner, Ed. *Let's Go to Press: A Biography of Walter Winchell.* New York: G. P. Putnam's Sons, 1955.

Weisberger, Bernard A. *Reporters for the Union.* Boston: Little, Brown, 1953.

Wilmer, Lambert A. *Our Press Gang; or, a Complete Exposition of the Corruptions and Crimes of American Newspapers.* Philadelphia: J. T. Lloyd, 1859.

Wilson, James Harrison. *The Life of Charles A. Dana.* New York: Harper and Brothers, 1907.

Winchell, Walter. *Winchell Exclusive.* Englewood Cliffs, N.J.: Prentice-Hall, 1975.

Winkler, John K. *W. R. Hearst: An American Phenomenon.* New York: Simon and Schuster, 1928.

———. *William Randolph Hearst: A New Appraisal.* New York: Hastings House, 1955.

Wood, Clement. *Bernarr Macfadden: A Study in Success.* New York: Lewis Copeland, 1929.

Young, May D. Russell, ed. *Men and Memories: Personal Reminiscences by John Russell Young.* New York: F. Tennyson Neely, 1901.

Zabriskie, Francis Nicoll. *Horace Greeley, The Editor.* New York: Funk and Wagnalls, 1890.

GENERAL WORKS

Abbot, Lymon. *Henry Ward Beecher*. New York: Chelsea House, 1980.

Allen, Frederick Lewis. *Only Yesterday*. New York: Bantam Books, 1959.

Asbury, Herbert. *All Around the Town*. New York: Alfred A. Knopf, 1934.

————. *The Gangs of New York: An Informal History of the Underworld*. New York: Alfred A. Knopf, 1927.

Bailey, Ronald H. *The Civil War: Forward to Richmond*. Alexandria, Va.: Time-Life Books, 1983.

Barnum, P. T. *Struggles and Triumphs; or, Fifty Years' Recollections*. Buffalo: Courier, 1884.

Bassett, Margaret. *Profiles and Portraits of American Presidents*. Rev. ed. New York: David McKay, 1976.

Beale, Howard K. *The Critical Year: A Study of Andrew Johnson and Reconstruction*. New York: Harcourt, Brace, 1930.

Bernstein, Iver. *The New York City Draft Riots: Their Significance for American Society and Politics in the Age of the Civil War*. New York: Oxford University Press, 1990.

Bird, Caroline. *The Invisible Scar*. New York: Pocket Books, 1967.

Bowen, Croswell. *The Elegant Oakey*. New York: Oxford University Press, 1956.

Boyer, O. Richard. *The Legend of John Brown*. New York: Alfred A. Knopf, 1973.

Branch, E. Douglas. *The Sentimental Years 1836–1860*. New York: D. Appleton-Century, 1934.

Bullough, William A. *The Blind Boss and His City—Christopher Augustine Buckley and Nineteenth Century San Francisco*. Berkeley: University of California Press, 1979.

Callow, Alexander B. Jr. *The Tweed Ring*. New York: Oxford University Press, 1965.

Catton, Bruce. *The Coming Fury: The Centennial History of the Civil War*. Vol. 1. Garden City, N.Y.: Doubleday, 1961.

Clapp, Margaret. *Forgotten First Citizen: John Bigelow*. Boston: Little, Brown, 1947.

Cleaves, Freeman. *Old Tippecanoe, William Henry Harrison and His Times*. Port Washington, N.Y.: Kennikat Press, 1969.

Collier, Peter, and David Horowitz. *The Rockefellers: An American Dynasty*. New York: Holt, Rinehart and Winston, 1976.

Commager, Henry Steele, ed. *Documents of American History*. Vol. 1. New York: Appleton-Century Crofts, 1968.

Cook, Adrian. *The Armies of the Streets: The New York City Draft Riots of 1863*. Lexington: University Press of Kentucky, 1974.

Deak, Istvan. *The Lawful Revolution: Louis Kossuth and the Hungarians: 1848–1849*. New York: Columbia University Press, 1979.

Depew, Chauncey M. *My Memories of Eighty Years*. New York: Charles Scribner's Sons, 1924.

Dulles, Foster Rhea. *Labor in America: A History*. New York: Thomas Y. Crowell, 1964.

Dunlap, Orrin E. Jr. *Marconi: The Man and His Wireless*. New York: Macmillan, 1938.

Dunshee, Kenneth Holcomb. *As You Pass By*. New York: Hastings House, 1952.

Ellis, Edward. *Epic of New York City*. New York: Coward-McCann, 1966.

Field, Eugene. *A Little Book of Western Verse*. New York: Charles Scribner's Sons, 1895.

Flugel, Felix, and Harold Underwood Faulkner, eds. *Readings in the Economic and Social History of the United States*. New York: Harper and Brothers, 1939.

Flynn, Edward J. *You're the Boss*. New York: Viking Press, 1947.

Gilder, Rodman. *The Battery*. Boston: Houghton Mifflin, 1936.

Goebel, Dorothy Burne. *William Henry Harrison: A Political Biography*. Indianapolis: Historical Bureau of the Indiana Library and Historical Department, 1926.

Grinnell, Josiah Bushnell. *Men and Events of Forty Years*. Boston: D. Lothrop, 1891.

Griswold, Rufus Wilmot. *Passages from the Correspondence and Other Papers of Rufus W. Griswold*. Cambridge, Mass: W. M. Griswold, 1898.

Hale, Edward Everett Jr. *William H. Seward*. Philadelphia: George W. Jacobs, 1910.

Harris, Charles Townsend. *Memories of Manhattan in the Sixties and Seventies*. New York: Derrydale Press, 1928.

Headley, Joel Tyler. *The Great Riots of New York: 1712 to 1873*. New York: E. B. Treat, 1873.

Hemstreet, Charles. *The Story of Manhattan*. New York: C. Scribner's Sons, 1907.

Hershkowitz, Leo. *Tweed's New York: Another Look*. Garden City, N.Y.: Anchor Press/Doubleday, 1978.

Hofstadter, Richard, William Miller, and Daniel Aaron. *The United States: The History of a Republic.* Englewood Cliffs, N.J.: Prentice-Hall, 1960.

Hone, Philip. *The Diary of Philip Hone: 1828–1851.* Vol. 2. New York: Dodd, Mead, 1889.

Howe, Wirt. *New York at the Turn of the Century, 1899–1916.* Toronto: privately printed, 1946.

Johnson, William W. *The Old West: The Forty-Niners.* New York: Time, 1974.

Jones, John B. *A Rebel War Clerk's Diary.* Edited by Earl S. Miers. New York: A. S. Barnes, 1961.

Jordan, Robert P. *The Civil War.* Washington, D.C.: National Geographic Society, 1969.

King, Moses, ed. *King's Handbook of New York City.* Boston: Moses King, 1892.

Knickerbocker, Jacob. *Then and Now.* Boston: B. Humphries, 1939.

Leech, Margaret. *In the Days of McKinley.* New York: Harper and Brothers, 1959.

Leopold, Richard W. *Robert Dale Owen: A Biography.* New York: Octagon Books, 1969.

Longstreet, Stephen. *City on Two Rivers: Profiles of New York—Yesterday and Today.* New York: Hawthorn Books, 1975.

Lossing, Benson J. *History of New York City.* Vol. 1. New York: Perine Engraving, 1884.

Lothrop, Thornton K. *William Seward.* New York: Chelsea House, 1983; reprint of Houghton Mifflin, 1899.

Lowell, D. O. S. *A Munsey-Hopkins Genealogy, Being the Ancestry of Andrew Chauncey Munsey and Mary Jane Merritt Hopkins, the Parents of Frank A. Munsey, His Brothers and Sisters.* Boston: privately printed, 1920.

Lundberg, Ferdinand. *America's 60 Families.* New York: Citadel Press, 1946.

Lynch, Denis Tilden. *"Boss" Tweed: The Story of a Grim Generation.* New York: Blue Ribbon Books, 1927.

Lyon, Peter, *Success Story: The Life & Times of S. S. McClure.* New York: Charles Scribner's Sons, 1963.

McCabe, James D. Jr. *Lights and Shadows of New York Life; or, the Sights and Sensations of the Great City.* New York: Farrar, Straus and Giroux, 1970.

McCague, James. *The Second Rebellion: The Story of the New York City Draft Riots of 1863.* New York: Dial Press, 1968.

McCullough, David. *The Great Bridge.* New York: Simon and Schuster, 1972.

McSpadden, J. Walker. *How They Sent the News*. New York: Dodd, Mead, 1936.

"Manna-hatin": The Story of New York. New York: Manhattan, 1929.

Matthews, John Mabry. *Recollections of Persons and Events*. New York: Sheldon, 1865.

Morgan, H. Wayne. *America's Road to Empire: The War with Spain and Overseas Expansion*. New York: John Wiley and Sons, 1965.

Morison, Samuel Eliot, and Henry Steele Commager. *The Growth of the American Republic*. Rev. ed. Vol. 2. New York: Oxford University Press, 1937.

Moskowitz, Henry. *Alfred E. Smith: An American Career*. New York: Thomas Seltzer, 1924.

Moss, Frank. *The American Metropolis*. 3 Vols. New York: Peter F. Collier, 1897.

Myers, Gustavus. *The History of Tammany Hall*. New York: Dover Publications, 1971.

Nevins, Allan. *Ordeal of the Union*. Vol. 2. New York: Charles Scribner's Sons, 1947.

Oates, Stephen B. *To Purge This Land with Blood: A Biography of John Brown*. New York: Harper and Row, 1970.

Osgood, Rev. Samuel. *New York in the Nineteenth Century*. New York: John F. Trow, 1866.

Parrington, Vernon Louis. *Main Currents in American Thought*. New York: Harcourt, Brace, 1958.

Parry, Albert. *Garrets and Pretenders: A History of Bohemianism in America*. New York: Dover Publications, 1960.

Pringle, Henry F. *Theodore Roosevelt: A Biography*. New York: Harcourt Brace, 1930.

Riesenberg, Felix, and Alexander Alland. *Portrait of New York*. New York: Macmillan, 1939.

Roberts, Ellis H. *New York: The Planting and the Growth of the Empire State*. Boston: Houghton, Mifflin, 1890.

Robertson, Constance (Noyes). *The Unterrified*. New York: H. Holt, 1946.

Rosenwaike, Ira. *Population History of New York City*. Syracuse: Syracuse University Press, 1972.

Sandburg, Carl. *Abraham Lincoln: The War Years*. Vol. 1. New York: Harcourt, Brace, 1939.

Slater, Joseph, ed. *The Correspondence of Emerson and Carlyle*. New York: Columbia University Press, 1964.

Smith, Matthew Hale. *Sunshine and Shadow in New York*. Hartford: J. B. Burr, 1869.

Spann, Edward K. *The New Metropolis: New York City, 1840–1857*. New York: Columbia University Press, 1981.

Spargo, John. *Karl Marx: His Life and Work*. New York: B. W. Huebsch, 1910.

Spencer, Donald S. *Louis Kossuth and Young America: A Study of Sectionalism and Foreign Policy: 1848–1852*. Columbia, Mo.: University of Missouri Press, 1977.

Stedman, Edmund C., and George E. Woodberry. *The Works of Edgar Allan Poe*. Vol. 8. Chicago: Stone and Kimball, 1895.

Still, Bayrd. *Mirror for Gotham: New York As Seen by Contemporaries from Dutch Days to the Present*. New York: New York University Press, 1956; reprinted: New York: Fordham University Press, 1995.

Stoddard, Henry L. *As I Knew Them: Presidents and Politics from Grant to Coolidge*. New York: Harper and Brothers, 1927.

Stokes, Isaac N. P. *New York Past and Present: Its History and Landmarks, 1524–1939*. Richmond: Plantin Press, 1939.

———, comp. *The Iconography of Manhattan Island, 1498–1909*. Vol. 6. New York: Robert H. Dodd, 1915–28.

Stone, William L. *History of New York City from the Discovery to the Present Day*. New York: Virtue and Yorston, 1872.

Swift, Lindsay. *Brook Farm, Its Members, Scholars, and Visitors*. New York: Corinth Books, 1961.

Todd, Charles B. *A Brief History of the City of New York*. New York: American Book, 1899.

Van Deusen, Glyndon G. *Thurlow Weed: Wizard of the Lobby*. Boston: Little, Brown, 1947.

Waterman, William Randall. *Frances Wright*. New York: Columbia University, 1924.

Werstein, Irving. *The Draft Riots, July 1863*. New York: Julian Messner, 1971.

Wilson, Rufus Rockwell. *New York: Old and New*. Philadelphia: J. B. Lippincott, 1902.

Woodward, C. Vann. *Mary Chesnut's Civil War*. New Haven: Yale University Press, 1981.

WPA Guide to New York City. Rev. ed. New York: Pantheon Book, 1982.

Magazines, Articles, and Pamphlets

"Address Delivered by Mr. Munsey." *Munsey's Magazine* 28, no. 5 (Feb. 1903): 662–66.

Alexander, Jack. "Vox Populi." *The New Yorker* 14, no. 25 (Aug. 6, 1938): 16–21; 14, no. 26 (Aug. 13, 1938): 19–24; 14, no. 27 (Aug. 20, 1938): 19–23.

"A 'Man on Horseback' in American Journalism." *Current Opinion* 75 (Aug. 1923): 158–60.

An Insider. "New York Editors and Daily Papers." *The Chautauquan* 27, no. 1 (Apr. 1898): 56–64.

An advertisement in *Newspaperdom* 27, no. 18 (Jan. 14, 1915): 2.

An advertisement in *The Fourth Estate* 4, no. 95 (Dec. 19, 1895): 30.

"Arthur Brisbane." *The Journalist* 31, no. 24 (Oct. 4, 1902): 278; 38, no. 3 (4 Nov. 4, 1905): 37.

"Associates Reveal Incidents of Munsey's Life." *Editor & Publisher* 58, no. 32 (Jan. 2, 1926): 6, 41.

Brisbane, Arthur. "Joseph Pulitzer." *Cosmopolitan* 33, no. 1 (May 1902): 51–54.

———. "William Randolph Hearst." *Cosmopolitan* 33, no. 1 (May 1902): 48–50.

Broun, Heywood. "It Seems to Heywood Broun." *The Nation* 126, no. 3267 (Feb. 15, 1928): 179; 126, no. 3279 (May 9, 1928): 532; 126, no. 3280 (May 16, 1928): 557; 126, no. 3283 (June 6, 1928): 631.

Bryan, Clark W. *The Progress of American Journalism*. Holyoke, Mass.: C. W. Bryan, 1885.

"Bulldog's Tail." *Time* 6, no. 20 (Nov. 16, 1925): 27–28.

"Charles A. Dana." *The Critic* 28, no. 818 (Oct. 23, 1897): 237.

"Charles A. Dana." *Harper's Weekly* 13, no. 674 (Nov. 27, 1869): 753.

"Complete Inside Story of Huge New York Herald-Tribune Amalgamation." *Editor & Publisher* 56, no. 43 (Mar. 22, 1924): 3–6, 25.

Cosgrave, John O'Hara. "How 'Dead Hand' Killed Pulitzer Dailies." *Editor & Publisher The Fourth Estate* 63, no. 42 (Mar. 7, 1931): 5, 52, 54.

Creelman, James. "James Gordon Bennett." *Cosmopolitan* 33, no. 1 (May 1902): 44–47.

———. "Joseph Pulitzer—Master Journalist." *Pearson's Magazine* 21 (Mar. 1909): 246.

————. "The Dramatic Intensity of Joseph Pulitzer." *Current Literature* 46, no. 4 (Apr. 1909): 382–85.

Cummings, Amos. "The Attack on the Tribune Office." *The Journalist* 2, no. 29 (Oct. 10, 1885): 1.

"Death Suddenly Summons Frank Munsey at Height of Power and Success." *Editor & Publisher* 58, no. 31 (Dec. 26, 1925): 3–4.

"Did Mayor Gaynor Speak the Truth?" *Editor & Publisher* 11, no. 5 (July 29, 1911): 14.

"Drastic, But Deserved." *Editor & Publisher* 57, no. 14 (Aug. 30, 1924): 20.

Dyer, Oliver. *The New York Sun, Its Rise, Progress, Character and Condition.* New York, 1870.

"Editorial Chair of the Tribune." *Putnam's Magazine* 1, no. 5 (May 1868): 638–39.

"Fabulous Rise of N.Y. Daily News Due to Capt. Patterson's Genius." *Editor & Publisher* 72, no. 25 (June 24, 1939): 46.

"Farewell Dinner to the Old Sun Building." n.p. (July 11, 1915).

"Fate or Folly." *The Fourth Estate* 4, no. 83 (Sept. 26, 1895): 5.

Forman, Allan. "The New Crop." *The Journalist* 37, no. 2 (Apr. 29, 1905): 20.

"Frank A. Munsey Now Globe Owner" *Editor & Publisher* 56, no. 1 (June 2, 1923): 7.

"George Jones, of the 'New York Times.'" *Harper's Weekly* 34, no. 1731 (Feb. 22, 1890): 142.

Gleason, Arthur H. "Mr. Hearst's Forgeries." *Collier's Weekly* 50, no. 3 (Oct. 5, 1912): 10–11, 37–38.

Hager, J. Henry. "Personal Reminiscences of Horace Greeley." *The Bookman* 13, no. 2 (Apr. 1901): 126–31.

Halstead, Murat. "Greeley, Breakfasts with Horace." *Cosmopolitan* 36, no. 6 (Apr. 1904): 698–702.

Hamshar, Walter. "Gambling Ship off Long Island Was Prohibition Sensation." *Silurian News* 30, no. 1 (May 1976): 1, 4.

Hapgood, Hutchins, and Arthur Bartlett Maurice. "The Great Newspapers of the United States: The New York Morning Newspapers." *The Bookman* 14, no. 6 (Feb. 1902): 567–84.

"Hard but Fair Fight for World Readers." *Editor & Publisher The Fourth Estate* 63, no. 43 (Mar. 14, 1931): 7.

Hazeltine, Mayo W. "Charles Anderson Dana." *The North American Review* 186, no. 618 (July 5, 1907): 505–14.

"Heywood Broun." *The Nation* 126, no. 3280 (May 16, 1928): 553.

"Horace Greeley." *Harper's Weekly* 15, no. 768 (Sept. 16, 1871): 876–78.

"In Interview Hearst Speaks Plainly of Policies of His Organization." *Editor & Publisher* 57, no. 3 (June 14, 1924): 3–4.

Irwin, Will. "The American Newspapers: The Fourth Current." Part 3. *Collier's Weekly* 46, no. 22 (Feb. 18, 1911): 14–17, 24, 27.

———. "The American Newspapers: The Unhealthy Alliance." Part 10. *Collier's Weekly* 47, no. 11 (June 3, 1911): 17–18, 28–29, 31.

———. "The New York Sun." *The American Magazine* 67, no. 3 (Jan. 1909): 301–10.

"James Gordon Bennett." *Gleason's Pictorial Drawing Room Companion* 7, no. 24 (Dec. 16, 1854): 384.

"James Gordon Bennett's Scintillations." *The Galaxy* 14, no. 2 (Aug. 1872): 258–63.

Jennings, L. J. "Mr. Raymond and Journalism." *The Galaxy* 9, no. 4 (Apr. 1870): 466–74.

Leary, John L. Jr. "Last Night Scene in N.Y. World Office." *Editor & Publisher The Fourth Estate* 63, no. 42 (Mar. 7, 1931): 7.

Levermore, Charles H. "The Rise of Metropolitan Journalism, 1800–1840." *The American Historical Review* 6, no. 3 (Apr. 1901): 446–65.

Life 68, no. 1771 (Oct. 5, 1919): 584.

"Life-Story of Charles M. Palmer, the Well-Known Publisher and Newspaper Broker." *Newspaperdom* 27, no. 18 (Jan. 14, 1915): 7.

Lippmann, Walter, and Charles Merz. "A Test of the News." *The New Republic* 23, no. 296 (Aug. 4, 1920, Supplement): 1.

Lord, Chester S. "Reminiscences of Charles A. Dana and the Old New York Sun." *Saturday Evening Post* 194, no. 5 (July 30, 1921): 8–9, 52, 55.

"Macfadden Paper Clean Constructive Journalism." *Editor & Publisher* 57, no. 14 (Aug. 30, 1924): 5.

Maloney, Thomas A. "The Bennett Home for Journalists; Story of a Shattered Dream." *New York University News Workshop* (Mar. 1951): 5–6.

"Manton Marble." *Harper's Weekly* 14, no. 684 (Feb. 5, 1870): 81–82.

"Medill Patterson, Socialist." *Editor & Publisher* 5, no. 38 (Mar. 10, 1906): 2.

Meloney, William Brown. "Joseph Pulitzer, The Blind Editor." *The American Magazine* 69, no. 1 (Nov. 1909): 113–25.

Mix, James B. *The Biter Bit; or the Robert Macaire of Journalism*. Washington, D.C.: 1870.

Morris, Franklin. "Charles A. Dana." *The Chautauquan* 21, no. 3 (June 1895): 325–29.

"Much For Little." *The Fourth Estate* 4, no. 80 (Sept. 5, 1895): 1.

Nevins, Allan. "Frank A. Munsey: The Last Phase." *McNaught's Monthly* 5, no. 3 (Mar. 1926): 67–70.

"New Tabloids in New York and Montreal." *Editor & Publisher* 57, no.17 (Sept. 20, 1924): 5, 23.

"N.Y. News, Now 15, Holds Grip on Masses." *Editor & Publisher* 67, no. 7 (June 30, 1934): 5–6, 39.

"Ochs, Amazed by World Sale, Declares Staff Could Have Made Papers Pay." *Editor & Publisher The Fourth Estate* 63, no. 44 (Mar. 21, 1931): 5–6.

Old-Time Editors and Reporters of the Tribune. *Fun from Under the Old Hat.* New York: Fay and Cox, 1872.

O'Loughlin, Edward T. *Hearst and His Enemies.* New York: Edward T. O'Loughlin, 1919; reprinted New York: Arno Press, 1970.

"Over the Coffee and the Cigars." *The Journalist* 31, no. 23 (Sept. 27, 1902): 269.

Patterson, Joseph M. "Confessions of a Drone." *The Independent* 61, no. 3013 (Aug. 30, 1906): 493–95.

"Pulitzer History an Epic of Journalism." *Editor & Publisher The Fourth Estate* 63, no. 41 (Feb. 28, 1931): 13, 50–51, 64.

Redding, Leo L. "Bennett of the Herald." *Everybody's Magazine* 30, no. 6 (June 1914): 846–58.

Rickover, Hyman G. *How the Battleship Maine Was Destroyed.* Washington, D.C.: U.S. Government Printing Office, 1976.

Roche, John F. "Roy Howard Reveals Inside Details of Negotiations for N.Y. World." *Editor & Publisher The Fourth Estate* 63, no. 42 (Mar. 7, 1931): 6.

———. "Telegram Takes 400 of 'World' Staff." *Editor & Publisher The Fourth Estate* 63, no. 42 (Mar. 7, 1931): 9–10.

"Roster of Famous N.Y. World Men Reads Like Newspaper 'Who's Who.'" *Editor & Publisher The Fourth Estate* 63, no. 41 (Feb. 28, 1931): 65–66.

"Roy W. Howard's Career." *Scripps-Howard News* 19 (Dec. 1964, Special Edition): 3, 5, 7, 9–11.

"Scripps-Howard Buys The New York Telegram." *Scripps-Howard News* 1, no. 4 (Mar. 1927): 1.

"Scripps-Howard Buys the 'World.' " *Editor & Publisher The Fourth Estate* 63, no. 41 (Feb. 28, 1931): 5–10.

Seitz, Don C. "Our Last American Duel." *McNaught's Monthly* 4, no. 1 (July 1925): 8–9.

Sherover, Max. *Fakes in American Journalism*. Brooklyn: Free Press League, 1916.

"600 Employees of Globe Disbursed." *Editor & Publisher* 56, no. 2 (June 7, 1923): 13–14.

Steffens, Lincoln. "Hearst, the Man of Mystery." *The American Magazine* 63, no. 1 (Nov. 1906): 3–22.

"Success Vindicated E. W. Scripps' Ideals." *Editor & Publisher The Fourth Estate* 63, no. 41 (Feb. 28, 1931): 14, 66.

Swerling, Jo. "The Picture Papers Win." *The Nation* 121, no. 3146 (Oct. 21, 1925): 455–57.

Swinton, John. "Memoranda As to the Late Charles A. Dana." *The Chautauquan* 26, no. 6 (Mar. 1898): 610–13.

———. "The New York Daily Papers and Their Editors." *The Independent* 52, no. 2669 (Jan. 25, 1900): 237–40.

"The Comic Life of Horace Greeley." *Wild Oats*. 113 Fulton Street, N.Y. 1872.

"The Late James Gordon Bennett." *Harper's Weekly* 16, no. 808 (June 22, 1872): 481–82.

"The Menace of Munsey." *Harper's Weekly* 56, no. 2911 (Oct. 1912): 4.

The Nation 126, no. 3281 (May 23, 1928): 576.

"The New Political Force." *The Nation* 66, no. 1714 (May 5, 1898): 336–37.

The New York Tribune: A Sketch of Its History. New York: n.p., Oct. 1883.

"The Rights of a Columnist: A Symposium on the Case of Heywood Broun versus the New York World." *The Nation* 126, no. 3282 (May 30, 1928): 607–9.

"The Sun and the Globe Are Consolidated." *The Fourth Estate* 30, no. 1527 (June 2, 1923): 4.

Three Lookers On in Venice. "The War of the Giants Against James Gordon Bennett." n.p., no. 1 (1840).

Truman, Maj. Benjamin C. "Anecdotes of Andrew Johnson." *The Century Magazine* 85, no. 3 (Jan. 1919): 435–40.

Turner, Hy, and Bob Lipsyte. "The Brief, Bogus Life of the Great Sin Ship." *True* 46, no. 343 (Dec. 1965): 66, 94.

"Wants to Be Yellow." *Editor & Publisher* 11, no. 24 (Dec. 9, 1911): 5.

Wardman, Ervin. "The Fight of the New York Herald against the $5,000,000 Bonus Raid." *Militant American Journalism.* New York: n.p., 1922.

"What a Newspaper Should Be." *Putnam's Magazine* 1, no. 3 (Mar. 1868): 328–38.

"What Is the Lure of the Tabloid Press." *Editor & Publisher* 57, no. 9 (July 26, 1924): 7, 34.

Wheeler, H. D. "At the Front with Willie Hearst." *Harper's Weekly* 61, no. 3068 (Oct. 9, 1915): 340–42.

"William Randolph Hearst." *The Journalist* 31, no. 25 (Oct. 11, 1902): 287–88.

Williams, Maj. George F. "Three Great Editors." *The Inland Printer* 26, no. 2 (Nov. 1900): 249–53; 26, no. 3 (Dec. 1900): 434–36.

Wing, Henry E. "When Lincoln Kissed Me: A Story of the Wilderness Campaign." *The Christian Advocate* 88, no. 1 (Jan. 2, 1913): 9–12.

"World Employees Pledged $600,000 toward Purchase Price." *Editor & Publisher The Fourth Estate* 63, no. 41 (Feb. 28, 1931): 11.

"World's Greatest Marine Disaster." *Editor & Publisher* 11, no. 44 (Apr. 27, 1912): 18.

"World's Unjust Fate." *Editor & Publisher The Fourth Estate* 63, no. 41 (Feb. 28, 1931): 38.

"Yacht-Race Bulletins." *Newspaperdom* 4, no. 5 (Sept. 12, 1895).

"Yankee Lad's Grim Climb up Golden Ladder." *Editor & Publisher* 8, no. 31 (Dec. 26, 1925): 7–8.

NEWSPAPERS

New York Newspapers

American
Courier and Enquirer
Daily News
Evening Journal
Evening Post
Evening Signal
Evening Star
Evening Sun
Evening World

Free Inquirer
Globe
Globe and Commercial Advertiser
Graphic
Herald
Herald Tribune
Journal
Journal-American
Journal and Advertiser
Journal of Commerce
Log-Cabin
Mail
Mirror
Press
Sun
Sun and Globe
Telegram
Telegram & Evening Mail
Times
Transcript
Tribune
World

Other Newspapers

Albany *Evening Journal*
Emporia (Kansas) *Gazette*
San Francisco *Examiner*

Special Editions of Newspapers

St. Louis *Post-Dispatch*, One Hundredth Anniversary of Joseph Pulitzer (6 Apr. 1947).
Sun, Anniversary Issue (3 Sept. 1883).
The World, 20th Anniversary Issue (10 May 1903).
The World and Its New Home, special edition of *The World* issued on opening of Pulitzer Building (10 Oct. 1890).
San Francisco *Examiner*, Chicago World's Fair Special Issue (4 June 1893).
Daily News Souvenir Edition 47, no. 44.

Special Collections

Greeley Papers. Library of Congress. Letter dated Nov. 4, 1872.
Joseph Medill Patterson papers. Donnelley Library, Lake Forest College, Illinois.
Ochs Manuscript. May 17, 1895. *Times* Archives.

Unpublished Letters

Correspondence between Simon Cameron and Henry Jarvis Raymond, dated Dec. 11 and 13, 1861; original letters at New York Public Library.
Horace Greeley's letter to Lincoln, dated July 29, 1861; original letter in Robert Todd Lincoln Collection, Library of Congress, 10921.
Letter to the author from Otto A. Epp, editor and publisher of the *Greeley County Republican,* Kansas, dated Apr. 28, 1947.

Dictionaries and Directories

Abrams, Alan E., ed. *Journalist Biographies Master Index*. Detroit: Gale Research Company, 1979.
Allen Johnson, ed. "Bennett, James Gordon." *Dictionary of American Biography*. Vol. 1. New York: Charles Scribner's Sons, 1957.
Ashley, Perry J., ed. "American Newspaper Journalists, 1690–1872." *Dictionary of Literary Biography*. Vol. 43. Detroit: Gale Research Company, 1978.
N. W. Ayer and Son's American Newspaper Annual and Directory.

INDEX